SCOTTISH STEAM: A CELEBRATION

Keith Langston

PEN & SWORD
TRANSPORT

First published in Great Britain in 2014 by
Pen & Sword Transport
An imprint of
Pen & Sword Books Ltd
47 Church Street
Barnsley
South Yorkshire
S70 2AS

ISBN 978 1 84563 163 5

A CIP catalogue record for this book is available from the British Library.

Typeset in 11pt Minion by Mac Style, Driffield, East Yorkshire
Printed and bound in India by Replika Press Pvt Ltd

Pen & Sword Books Ltd incorporates the imprints of Pen & Sword Archaeology, Atlas, Aviation, Battleground, Discovery, Family History, History, Maritime, Military, Naval, Politics, Railways, Select, Transport, True Crime, and Fiction, Frontline Books, Leo Cooper, Praetorian Press, Seaforth Publishing and Wharncliffe.

For a complete list of Pen & Sword titles please contact
PEN & SWORD BOOKS LIMITED
47 Church Street, Barnsley, South Yorkshire, S70 2AS, England
E-mail: enquiries@pen-and-sword.co.uk
Website: www.pen-and-sword.co.uk

CONTENTS

ACKNOWLEDGEMENTS

This is a Perceptive Images 2014 © publication exclusively for Pen & Sword Books Ltd.

Additional editorial material was supplied by David Anderson, whose encouragement and railway knowledge was invaluable.

The author would like to thank all the skilled railway photographers who have allowed their images to be used, and they include David Anderson, Michael Bentley, Fred Kerr, Dugald Cameron OBE, Bill Rhind Brown and Edward Talbot, and also archivists and image collection owners John Chalcroft (of Rail Photoprints) and Mike Morant.

This book is dedicated to the memory of accomplished steam era photographers Hugh Ballantyne and Brian Robbins, who both sadly passed away during 2013. As testament to their undoubted skills several examples of both photographer's work are included.

Keith Langston, September 2013

Chapter 1

INTRODUCTION

Scotland occupies approximately a third of the land area of Britain of which a huge percentage is upland in nature, and decidedly rural. The railway age was responsible for greatly improving transport links, not just throughout the country but with its immediate neighbour England.

Communities in the more remote mainland parts of the Highlands were, after the coming of steam railways, able to travel at will to the countries urban conurbations, and beyond. No more did they need to risk life and limb crossing bleak and often inhospitable terrain on foot or horseback. Furthermore, the railway metals became the arteries which brought the life blood of commerce to the whole of the country.

Scotland's engineering prowess is unquestionably world famous. Nations marvelled at the vessels once built by the honest sweat and toil of Scottish artisans. By tradition Glaswegian workers built magnificent ships and fitted them with precision built engines, which allowed them to ply the oceans of the world. The ships were powered at first by steam and then by internal combustion. Unfortunately the once vibrant shipyards of the Clyde are now in decline.

This 2009 image of a preserved Stanier 'Black Five' storming along the Highland Line serves to illustrate the rugged beauty of the upland terrain through which that railway passes. *David Gibson*

Ex-North British Railway (NBR) Cowlairs built 'K' class (LNER D34) St Margaret's allocated 'Glen' 4-4-0 BR No 62484 GLEN LYON is seen at Longniddry with a Dunbar–Edinburgh Waverley service in May 1950. ***Rail Photoprints Collection***

The story of Scotland's pioneer railway builders is a fascinating one in its own right, but what of the steam locomotives which hauled those trains? Early Scottish locomotive builders responded to a need for powered traction to help exploit efficiently, and distribute economically, the products of the coal, mineral and steel industries.

Fortunately, for the world in general and Great Britain in particular, those early steam locomotive builders developed their skills to such an extent over the decades that Scotland became a major centre for the manufacture of steam railway locomotives. Interestingly one Glasgow based locomotive builder was also a licensed manufacturer of the WWI 'Sopworth Pup' bi-planes and furthermore that self same company supplied the engines for the ill fated airship 'R101'. Another is said to have built in the region of 4,500 steam locomotives before becoming part of a record breaking 'combine' in 1903.

Exports of locomotives through such ports as Glasgow and Leith created enormous wealth for the country and their manufacture provided thousands of Scottish workers with jobs, over many years. The export story of the famous North British Locomotive Company (NBL) is well known, and something of which Scotland can be rightly proud. Even in modern times Glasgow built locomotives are still at work in various corners of the world!

Scottish builders also supplied large numbers of what became known as the 'Kilmarnock' type industrial locomotives and over 100 Andrew Barclay Sons & Co built engines survive in the 21st century, still working on the preserved railways of the UK, perchance the famous 'Caledonia Works' makers plate is as recognisable today as it was during the peak of the firm's locomotive building activities.

In order to keep what is a very complex and wide ranging subject within a manageable time scale this book mainly focuses on the Scottish built standard gauge locomotives which came into the ownership of British Railways on 1 January

Working hard climbing away from the main line, ex-North British Railway (NBR) Reid designed 'J35/4' class 3F 0-6-0 No 64489 (NBR No 202, LNER Nos 4489 and 9202) was pictured whilst heading a special train along the Haddington Branch Line in June 1960. The Haddington Branch Line in East Lothian was a 4.8 mile (7.7 km) branch line extending from the East Coast Main Line at Longniddry and terminating at Haddington. The line was in mixed traffic use from June 1846 until December 1949 and thereafter mainly used as a freight only branch until it's closure in March 1968.

1948. In order to complement that account details of important earlier locomotive types and the railways which operated them are also included.

Steam haulage over the Anglo–Scottish east and west coast routes always attracted the attention of steam railway photographers, and this celebration recognises that fact. For those 'of an age' this publication provides nostalgic memories, and for those born later perchance a timely reminder of Scotland's fantastic steam railway history.

An impressive statistic worthy of note is that the newly created British Railways took into stock just over 20,000 working steam locomotives in 1948 and of those almost 4,500 (a fifth of the total) were built in Scotland!

Gresley's experimental 'W1' LNER No 10000 was known as the 'Hush Hush' due to the secrecy which surrounded its creation. The 4-6-4 was completed at Doncaster Works in 1929 and the locomotive's high pressure boiler was designed and built for the LNER in Glasgow by shipbuilders and boiler makers Yarrow & Company. The locomotive had a corridor tender and accordingly ran non-stop London-Edinburgh services during 1930. The 'Hush Hush' is pictured new out of the works in 1929.

In the year 2013 a group of preservationists announced their intention build a new Gresley 'P2' 2-8-2 locomotive. 'P2' No 2002 EARL MARISCHAL is pictured being turned circa 1935, the location is Aberdeen Ferryhill depot. The P2s were fitted with tablet exchange apparatus for use on the single line section between Usan and Montrose South, that included the single track viaduct over the Montrose Esk Basin. The tablet exchanger operated through an elliptical hole cut in the cab end of the left hand tender side sheet. Locos Nos 2001 and 2002 were fitted with the tablet exchange apparatus before they entered regular service. The other P2s were fitted when new. *Both superb images are a part of the Rail Photoprints Collection*

Part I

THE LOCOMOTIVE BUILDERS

Perhaps the most famous locomotive ever built in Glasgow. Neilson & Co built the Dugald Drummond designed 4-2-2 Caledonian Railway (CR) No 123 in 1886. The locomotive, which was exhibited at the Edinburgh Exhibition in 1886, became the last 'Single Wheeler' to run on a British railway, being finally withdrawn for preservation in 1965. The engine is seen heading east along the side of the River Tay, near Kinfauns (between Perth and Dundee) with a special train comprising of two restored CR coaches in the summer of 1958. *David Anderson*

Chapter 2

NEILSON & COMPANY – NEILSON, REID & CO LTD

Also Kerr, Mitchell & Neilson – Kerr, Neilson & Company

The steam engineers Neilson & Company was initially formed in 1836/37 at McAlpine Street, Glasgow by William Neilson and James Mitchell. Mainly financed by James Beaumont Neilson the company began by producing stationary and marine engines.

In 1837 the firm moved to new premises in Hyde Park Street, Glasgow and shortly afterwards Walter Montgomerie Neilson, the son of the financier joined the firm in order to complete an apprenticeship in steam engineering. Associates/employees at that time included two engineers who would later become famous in their own rights namely Patrick Stirling and Henry Dübs.

At that time a new partnership was formed between James B. Neilson, James Mitchell and Stewart Kerr. The partnership, known and operating as, Kerr, Mitchell & Neilson at Hyde Park Foundry was dissolved in 1840 and James B. Neilson and Stewart Kerr formed Kerr, Neilson & Company which also operated from a works on Hyde Park Street. That company of engineers, boiler makers, iron boat builders, smiths and founders operated at a loss and in 1843 the partnership was dissolved reportedly leaving James B. Neilson to pay its debts.

Walter M. Neilson wanted to develop a steam locomotive building business in order to supply Scottish railways with Scottish built engines. By 1843 locomotive construction had got under way and the company built an initial batch of 0-4-0 configured locomotives. James Mitchell returned to the firm in order to look after the financial side of the enterprise and once more the partnership became known as Neilson & Mitchell.

The partnership of Walter Neilson and James Mitchell, engineers and founders, of Hyde Park, Finnieston and City Road, London was dissolved in 1847, the business then passed into the control of Walter M. Neilson and thereafter it operated under the name of Neilson and Co. In addition to locomotive construction the firm also manufactured the stationary engines which were used on the Cowlairs Incline, then operated by the Edinburgh & Glasgow Railway.

The firm ceased manufacturing stationary and marine engines in 1855 in order to concentrate solely on steam locomotive building. The company had developed several designs of locomotive and was known to have supplied four coupled tank engines together with 2-4-0 and 0-4-2 tender engines to amongst others the Edinburgh & Carlisle Railway and the Caledonian Railway, they also exported some to India.

Engineer James Reid had been employed as works manager by Neilson & Co but in 1858 he was replaced in that post by Henry Dübs who was at the time judged to have far more experience of locomotive design and construction. As a part of his joining package Henry Dübs was given a partnership in the firm, as for James Reid he moved to Manchester in order to take up a post with Sharp, Stewart & Company. However, the move south of the border did not herald an end to Reid's career with Neilson & Co; more simply the prelude to a six year break.

The order book was full circa 1861 and the work load had increased to such an extent that new workshops were needed. Accordingly the company moved from Hyde Park Street to the Springburn area of Glasgow and the new premises there were also named Hyde Park Works. Although the firm had concentrated on railway locomotive manufacture since 1855 other products were occasionally built, for example in 1862 Walter M. Neilson exhibited a radial steam hammer at the 1862 London Exhibition, albeit under his own name.

Neilson & Co works plate dating from 1897. *Keith Langston*

In 1864 it was all change again at Neilson & Co as Henry Dübs decided to seek pastures new and left to set up his own business based at a Polmadie, Glasgow premises to be known as Queen's Park Works. When doing so he reportedly took several key members of Neilson's staff with him. That change no doubt precipitated the move back to Scotland of James Reid (from Sharp, Stewart & Company) who was also made a partner in the firm, presumably Reid was then sufficiently experienced in locomotive design and construction!

In addition to locomotive building the firm built two Woolf Compound Beam Engines for the Leicester Waterworks (Cropston pumping station). Throughout the 1870s a large number of 0-4-4T locomotives were built for the London, Chatham & Dover Railway, the Midland Railway and the Great Eastern Railway. Other types of engines were built for both the home and export market including a batch of 50 0-4-4T engines for India, and in fact in 1872 the firm also built its first eight coupled locomotives which were also exported to the Indian sub-continent. Change again in 1876 when James Reid, the locomotive engineer and designer who Neilson once sacked became the firm's sole proprietor!

The first locomotives of a 2-6-0 configuration (Mogul) ever to run on British rails were designed by William Adams for the Great Eastern Railway; they were built by Neilson & Co in 1879. The year of 1884 was another one of change, in that the firm's founder Walter M. Neilson left the company and set up the Clyde Locomotive Works thus leaving the proprietor Reid in overall charge.

In 1886 the company built the locomotive which is arguably their most famous, the 4-2-2 'Single Wheeler' No 123 for the Caledonian Railway (CR), which was the inspiration of the celebrated locomotive engineer Dugald Drummond. The loco was sent to the 1896 Edinburgh Exhibition where it was awarded a Gold Medal. During the locomotive trials from London to Scotland on the 8th of August, 1888, No 123 ran between Carlisle and Edinburgh, a distance of 100 miles in 102 minutes, almost 'even timing'.

The company continued to produce locomotives for home and abroad and in 1898 its name was changed to Neilson, Reid & Company Ltd. By 1900 the by then established and worldwide known company had produced an estimated 5,394 steam locomotives including industrial types. At that time they employed in the region of 3,500 workers who were capable of producing 300 locomotives per year.

By 1903 intense competition from American locomotive builders meant that the smaller companies were unable to compete in the rapidly growing world market. There was a recognised need for amalgamation in order to succeed in the competitive market place. Neilson, Reid & Co Ltd joined 'The Combine' and with two other established locomotive builders formed the North British Locomotive Co Ltd.

Neilson & Co built preserved Ex-CR 4-2-2 No 123 is seen at Haymarket in June 1963, prior to working a special trip over minor lines in the area. The elegant 'Single Wheeler' is perhaps the most well known Neilson locomotive. *David Anderson*

Neilson & Co built locomotive classes included in British Railway listings

LSWR 'A12' 0-4-2 1MT, also known as '04'

William Adams designed the 'A12' class 0-4-2 locomotives for the London & South Western Railway (LSWR) and they were introduced into traffic between 1887 and 1895. In Scotland the Glasgow & South Western Railway operated tender type engines in the 0-4-2 configuration whilst south of the border the largest user of the type was the LSWR. The 'A12' engines were known as Adams 'Jubilee' class as the first batch appeared in the Golden Jubilee of Queen Victoria's reign. Originally 90 of the class were built, 50 at the railway's Nine Elms Works and 40 by Neilson & Co Ltd.

The Neilson built batch carried the LSWR numbers 607–646. They were used extensively on all parts of that railway's network and were reputed to have a good turn of speed. The railway began withdrawing the class in 1928 and only 4 examples (all Neilson built) survived nationalisation (1948) they were allocated the BR numbers 30618, 30627, 30629 and 30636, they were the last locomotives with the 0-4-2 wheel arrangement to run on BR metals. However, BR withdrew the locomotives without ever re-numbering them and they were cut up in 1948/49.

Another Neilson engine, SR No 612 was withdrawn in 1946 and it became a departmental locomotive at Eastleigh Works renumbered DS319. It was used to supply steam when Bulleid Pacific boilers were being tested after welding repairs. That loco was finally withdrawn for scrap in 1951.

A handsome looking Adams designed 'A12' (04) class 0-4-2 No 632 built by Neilson & Co in 1893 for the LSWR, seen at Waterloo station, circa 1926. *Rail Photoprints Collection*

LSWR '0395' 0-6-0 1F

This William Adams designed class was introduced by the LSWR between 1881 and 1886 and there were originally 70 engines in the class, all of which were built by Neilson & Co Ltd. The class evolved into four variants and also included one batch of engines to which the SR attached larger 6-wheel tenders.

In 1916 a batch of 50 '0395' class engines were sold to the government and sent to work in the Middle East during the First World War, specifically in Palestine and Mesopotamia. The locomotives were never returned to the UK and several were lost at sea when the steamship *Arabic* was torpedoed.

The class were included in an LSWR mixed number system with a none consecutive sequence, and the NR examples were Nos 029, 69, 101, 154–155, 163, 167, 397, 400, 433, 436, 439–442, 496, 506 and 509.

Two more of the class were withdrawn by the SR leaving a total of 18 Neilson built engines to come into BR stock, those locomotives were numbered in the series 30564–30581. Withdrawals commenced in 1950 and none of the class survived beyond the end of 1959.

Driving wheel diameter 5' 1", 2-cylinder engine (inside)

Neilson & Co built LSWR '0395' class 0-6-0 BR No 30566 seen in Eastleigh shed yard, April 1956. This loco was delivered in December 1885 as LSWR No 101 (later re-numbered 0101and then 3101) withdrawn by BR in February 1959. *Hugh Ballantyne/ Rail Photoprints Collection*

Neilson built Adams LSWR '0395' class 0-6-0 BR No 30565 in the first form of BR branding is seen at Eastleigh in July 1953, some five months after the engine had officially been withdrawn by BR. This loco was delivered in November 1885 as LSWR No 69. *Mike Morant Collection*

Neilson & Co built Adams LSWR '0395' class 0-6-0 BR No 30577 is seen at Waterloo station in charge of a Railway Correspondence & Travel Society (RCTS) special train in November 1952. The occasion was a Bisley Tramway & North West Surrey Rail Tour in conjunction with 'M7' class 0-4-4T No 30027. The Neilson loco hauled the first and last legs of the trip Waterloo – Brookwood – Waterloo, the outward leg via Wimbledon and the inward leg via Twickenham. No 30577 was delivered to the LSWR in May 1883 as No 441 and withdrawn by BR in February 1956. ***Mike Morant Collection***

LSWR '0415' 4-4-2T 1P (Adams Radial*)

This class of 71 engines, specifically intended for passenger work, were designed for the LSWR by William Adams and built between 1882 and 1885, 28 locomotives were built by Robert Stephenson & Co, 12 by Beyer, Peacock & Co Ltd and 31 were built north of the border. Neilson & Co produced a batch of 11 in 1885 with Dübs & Co building a further 20 of the class. The Neilson & Co built examples carried LSWR numbers 479–489, after grouping the SR added an '0' prefix to the numbers.

The SR began withdrawing the class in 1916 as suburban route electrification became operational and by 1928 only two remained in SR ownership and they were used for working the Lyme Regis Branch. In 1917 Neilson engine No 0488 was sold out of service to the Ministry of Munitions and two years later was bought by the private East Kent Railway becoming their loco No 5. In 1946 the SR bought back the EKR Radial Tank renumbered it 3488 and added it to the Lyme Regis Branch loco pool. In 1948 BR took into stock those 3 remaining 4-4-2T locomotives allocating them the numbers 30582 (Robert Stephenson & Co loco) 30583 (Neilson & Co loco) and 30584 (Dübs & Co loco). They were withdrawn in July 1961 with No 30583 being selected for preservation and bought by the Bluebell Railway.

See also LSWR '0415' 4-4-2T 1P (Adams Radial) locomotives built by Dübs & Co.

Driving wheel diameter 5' 7", 2-cylinder engine (outside)

Preserved LSWR '0415' class 4-4-2T 1P is seen at the loco's Bluebell Railway home base as No 488 (became BR 30583). ***Mike Stokes Collection***

* A radial axle is an axle on a railway locomotive or carriage which has been designed to move laterally when entering a curve in order to reduce wear of both the wheel flanges and rails.

SECR '1302' 0-4-0CT 0F

In 1881 Neilson & Co built a crane tank specifically to work at Folkestone harbour to the design of James Stirling for the London, Chatham & Dover Railway. In 1905 it was transferred to the Ashford Locomotive Works of the South Eastern Railway Company and in 1925 the crane tank moved again in order to work at Lancing Carriage Works and was then numbered 2348. In 1938 the loco was fitted with an enclosed cab and re-numbered as 1302 moving to milk dock shunting duty at Stewarts Lane depot, with the crane jib out of use. The engine came into BR stock and was allocated the SR number 31302 and withdrawn by BR Southern Region in July 1949.

Driving wheel diameter 3' 3", 2-cylinder engine (inside)

Neilson & Co built SECR '1302' 0-4-0CT 0F in Southern Railway (SR) livery, the location is in all probability Stewarts Lane depot (BR 73A) circa 1939, note the enclosed cab. *Mike Morant Collection*

LBSCR 'D1' 0-4-2T 1P ('D1M')

The London Brighton & South Coast Railway (LBSCR) William Stroudley designed 0-4-2T 'D1' class was considered to be one of that railway's finest design and in total 125 of the engines were built between 1873 and 1887. Brighton Works constructed 90 of the class and Neilson & Co Ltd built a further 35. Some of the class originally carried the names of LBSCR locations. They were intended for passenger and general use on the railway's London suburban and branch line routes. The locomotives of this class designated 'D1M' were motor fitted for 'push-pull' working.

Over time scrapping had continued with the result that only 10 engines became BR stock but were however, withdrawn almost immediately. Of those 6 were Neilson & Co built, and their allocated BR numbers were 32234, 32235, 32239, 32252, 32253 and 32259 (for LBSCR numbers discount the 32 prefix). During part of the Second World War period three of these engines worked away from their home shed having been sent to Scotland, No (3)2605 to Ayr, No (3)2699 to Wick and No (3)2358 to Inverness, all three were Brighton built engines.

Driving wheel diameter 5' 6", 2-cylinder engine (inside)

Neilson & Co built LBSCR 'D1' class 0-4-2T SR No 2253 (LBSCR No 253) delivered in March 1882 was allocated the BR No 32253 but was scrapped in September 1949 without ever carrying that number, the loco is seen at Brighton depot (BR 75A). This member of the class was one of several which were converted for fire fighting during the Second World War. Those engines had a steam pump fitted over the rear buffer beam and that equipment was capable of throwing four powerful jets of water. In keeping with other members of the class No 2253 was motor fitted for 'push pull' working and as such was designated 'D1/M'. *Mike Morant Collection*

MR Johnson/Fowler 4-4-0 '2P'

The Midland Railway (MR) first introduced this Samuel Waite Johnson designed 4-4-0 class of 2-cylinder (inside) locomotives between 1882 and 1901. In total some 265 of the class were built for the MR and additionally 40 for the Midland & Great Northern Railway (M&GNR). Over the years a great deal of modification and re-building took place to the instructions of MR engineers Richard Deeley and Henry Fowler. Notable modifications included differing driving wheel diameters, Stephenson slide valves (in place of Stephenson piston valves), superheating, Belpaire fireboxes and extended smokeboxes.

Derby Works built the majority of the class with other locomotives being supplied by contractors Sharp, Stewart & Co Ltd, Beyer, Peacock & Co Ltd and Neilson & Co who delivered to the MR a batch of 10 locomotives in May and June 1901 (LMS Nos 553–562 – BR Nos 40553–40562). In 1948 BR took into stock 160 of the class allocating to them numbers in the series 40332–40562, which included all 10 of the Neilson built engines Nos 40553–40562 (for earlier numbers discount the 40 prefix). However, 3 of the Neilson built engines never carried their allocated BR numbers, they were locomotives Nos 40554, 40555 40561 which were scrapped 1949/50.

The last of the Neilson engines to remain in service was No 40557, which was withdrawn in March 1961.

See also 'MR Johnson/Fowler 4-4-0' 2P locomotives built by Sharp, Stewart & Co.

Driving wheel diameter 7' 0½", 2-cylinder engine (inside)

Neilson & Co built locomotive classes which came into British Railways ownership

Class	Wheel arrangement	Designer	Customer/ Number to BR	Build dates	BR number series*
'A12'	0-4-2	Adams	LSWR 4 locomotives	1892/93	30618, 30627 30629, 30636
'0395'	0-6-0	Adams	LSWR 18 locomotives	1881/85	30564–30581
'0415'	4-4-2T	Adams	LSWR 1 loco	1885	30583
'1302'(Crane tank)	0-4-0CT	Stirling	SECR 1 loco	1881	31302
'D1' ('D1/M')	0-4-2T	Stroudley	LBSCR 6 locomotives	1881/82	32234–32235 32239 32252–32253 32259
'MR 2P'	4-4-0	Johnson/ Fowler	MR 10 locomotives	1901	40553–40562

* The BR numbers are given for identification in BR listings and do not take into account missing numbers due to scrapping, or locomotives of the same class built by other companies, but do include locomotives with allocated numbers not carried.

MR Johnson '3F', 5' 3" 0-6-0

This class of Samuel Waite Johnson designed locomotives was introduced by the Midland Railway (MR) between 1875 and 1902, some of which were rebuilds of the earlier MR '43137' class and also the former MR 2F '58188' class. Selected locomotives were given Belpaire fireboxes and Deeley style cabs by Fowler from 1903 onwards. They were built by Derby Works and contractors Kitson & Co, Dübs & Co, Sharp, Stewart & Co, Neilson, Reid & Co and Neilson & Co. BR took into stock 324 of these 0-6-0 locomotives of which 98 were Neilson built, in the BR number series 43200, 43203, 43205–43210, 43212–43257, 43260–43299, 43474–43544 (for LMS numbers discount the 4 prefix).

Six of the Neilson built members of the class were supplied to the Somerset & Dorset Joint Railway (S&DJR), and they were Nos 43216, 43218, 43228, 43248 and 43260 (SDJR Nos 72–76).

None of the class survived in service beyond 1964 and the last Neilson built example was No 43521 which was withdrawn by BR in July 1963.

See also 'MR Johnson 3F' 0-6-0 3F locomotives built by Dübs & Co, Sharp, Stewart & Co, Neilson, Reid & Co.

Driving wheel diameter 5' 3", 2-cylinder engine (inside)

Neilson & Co built 'MR Johnson 3F' 0-6-0 3F No 43218 is seen at Evercreech Junction on the former Somerset & Dorset Joint Railway (S&DJR) in September 1959. This locomotive was delivered to the S&DJR in September 1902 and withdrawn by BR in May 1960. *Hugh Ballantyne/Rail Photoprints Collection*

Neilson & Co built 'MR Johnson 3F' 0-6-0 3F No 43248 is seen at Highbridge station S&JDR in March 1955. This locomotive was delivered to the S&DJR in September 1902 and withdrawn by BR in August 1958. *Hugh Ballantyne/Rail Photoprints Collection*

CR '294', 'Jumbo' 0-6-0 2F

Designed by Dugald Drummond this class of 0-6-0 locomotives became known as the Caledonian Railway (CR) 'Standard Goods' class nicknamed 'Jumbo' and they were introduced between 1883 and 1897. They were the forerunner of Drummond's '700' class of 0-6-0 engines introduced by the London & South Western Railway (LSWR) in 1897.

A total of 244 engines of the class were built under Drummond, John Lambie and John F. McIntosh in the aforementioned period making them the most numerous Caledonian Railway class. In addition to St Rollox Works they were built by contractor Neilson & Co. British Railways (BR) took into stock 238 of the class in allocating them numbers in the series 57230–57473 and of that total 35 were Neilson built, Nos 57230–57236 (CR 259, 260, 261–264, 335, 337) 57241–57249 (CR 298, 365, 367, 374, 403, 517, 548, 1924), 57252–57271 (CR 518–526, 681, 683–689, 1517, 1680, 1910) all built during Drummond's reign at the Caledonian Railway (1882–1890). A batch of 25 engines saw First World War service with the ROD the Neilson & Co built examples being BR numbers 57249, and 57268–57270.

Amendments to the design of various locomotives included the fitting of condensing equipment for working on the Glasgow underground, stovepipe style chimneys, Westinghouse brake equipment and also some of the engines were later rebuilt with LMS boilers.

Lambie built engines were BR numbers 57352–57392, McIntosh built engines were BR numbers 57387, 57388, 57473–57493 and Drummond built engines were BR numbers 57230–57351, and 57357.

None of the class survived in service beyond 1963 and the last Neilson built 'Jumbo' class locomotives in service for BR were Nos 57261 and 57270, both being withdrawn by BR in November 1963. Surprisingly no member of this large class survived into preservation.

See also CR '294', 'Jumbo' 0-6-0 2F locomotives built at St Rollox Works.

Driving wheel diameter 5' 0", 2-cylinder engine (inside)

Neilson & Co built CR '294 Jumbo' class 0-6-0 BR No 57243 is seen at Perth shed (63A) in near ex-works condition in March 1956. This 'Drummond' engine was delivered in December 1883 and withdrawn by BR in June 1959. Note the stovepipe chimney which was a BR addition. *David Anderson*

Neilson & Co built CR '294 Jumbo' class 0-6-0 BR No 57265 is seen in more or less original condition at Grangemouth shed (65F) in April 1956. This locomotive was delivered in April 1884 and withdrawn by BR in August 1962. *David Anderson*

Neilson & Co built 'Jumbo' BR No 57270, which at the time was allocated to Motherwell Shed (66B), passing its home depot tender first with a short 'up' Class J freight in March 1963. Locomotive No.57270 was one of 25 class members temporarily transferred to the ROD during the First World War. The loco was delivered in March 1884 and withdrawn by BR in November 1963. *J & J Collection-Sid Rickard/Rail Photoprints Collection*

MR '1252' 5' 7" 1P

Neilson & Co built a batch of 30 Johnson designed 0-4-4T locomotives for the Midland Railway (MR). This class was the original batch of engines built with 5' 7" diameter driving wheels which carried the MR numbers 1236–1265. Many of these engines were later rebuilt by the LMS with Belpaire boilers. Of the original build only 9 locomotives came into BR stock in the number series 58030–58038, but of those only 3 engines Nos 58033, 58036 and 58038 ever carried their allocated numbers. All of the class were scrapped before the end of 1954 with loco No 58038 being the last to be withdrawn in May 1954.

Driving wheel diameter 5' 7", 2-cylinder engine (inside)

MR '1P' 5' 4" 0-4-4T

This class was made up of locomotives from the MR second and third batches of this locomotive type which were originally numbered 1266–1430. Of the original total of 165 engines built by Derby Works, Dübs & Co and Neilson & Co, only 56 came into BR stock in the number series 58039–58091, and of those several never carried their BR allocated numbers. The Neilson & Co built examples, which were amongst a batch of variants fitted with condensing apparatus for working through the Metropolitan tunnels on the London suburban services; they were allocated BR numbers 58068–58072 (LMS 1371, 1373, 1375, 1377, 1379). All of the Neilson built 0-4-4T engines were delivered to the MR during the summer of 1893. None of the class survived in service beyond 1960 and the last to remain in BR service was No 58072 withdrawn in October 1956.

See also MR '1P' 5' 4" 0-4-4T locomotives built by Dübs & Co.

Driving wheel diameter 5' 4", 2-cylinder engine (inside)

Neilson & Co built 0-4-4T BR No 58072 is seen at Bath Green Park depot (71G) in May 1955. This loco was delivered to the MR in September 1893 and withdrawn by BR in October 1956. Note the condensing apparatus. *Hugh Ballantyne/Rail Photoprints Collection*

MR '2F' 4' 11" 0-6-0

This class of Johnson designed locomotives were a development of the MR designer's 'Class 2' engines which dated from 1875. They were the forerunners of several classes of 0-6-0 inside framed engines. The 4' 11" '2F' 0-6-0 were introduced between 1875 and 1902 and were built by Derby Works and the contractors Dübs & Co, Kitson & Co, Beyer, Peacock & Co and Neilson & Co. BR took into stock 96 of the class allocating to them numbers in the series 58114–58187 and 58229–58248 amongst those the Neilson built examples were numbered 58164–58187 and they were all delivered during 1876 (earlier numbers 2990, 2992–3018).

The Neilson built batch of engines were originally constructed using slightly smaller diameter cylinders and only 4 '10" diameter driving wheels, later rebuilt to 4' 11" diameter. None of the class survived in service beyond 1964 and the last Neilson built engine to remain in BR service was No 58182 which was withdrawn in January 1964 and was at that time the oldest locomotive running on BR.

See also MR '2F' 4' 11" 0-6-0 locomotives built by Dübs & Co.

Driving wheel diameter 4' 11" (4' 10" originally), 2-cylinder engine (inside)

Neilson & Co built MR '2F' 4' 11" 0-6-0 BR No 58168 is seen at Westhouses (18B) in March 1951. This engine was delivered in 1876 and withdrawn by BR in July 1960. Although re-numbered in the BR series note that the loco still carries LMS lettering on the tender. *Rail Photoprints Collection*

Neilson & Co built MR '2F' 4' 11" 0-6-0 BR No 58174 is seen at Monument Lane depot (3E) in July 1961. This locomotive was delivered to the Midland Railway (MR) in December 1876 and withdrawn by BR in December 1961. *Mike Morant Collection*

MR '2F' 5' 3" 0-6-0

This class of Johnson designed 0-6-0 locomotives for the Midland Railway was introduced between 1878 and 1902 and they were a 5' 3" diameter driving wheel version of the aforementioned 58114–58248 series of engines. They were built at Derby Works and additionally by the contractors Robert Stephenson & Co, Beyer, Peacock & Co, Sharp, Stewart & Co, Kitson & Co, Vulcan Foundry, Neilson, Reid & Co, Dübs & Co, and Neilson & Co. During the period of the Second World War 40 engines of this class were loaned to the Great Western Railway (GWR).

BR took into stock 109 of the class allocating to them numbers in the series 58188–58228 and 58249–58310. None of the class survived in service beyond 1962.

The Neilson built examples were numbered 58251–58254 (earlier numbers 3229, 3262, 3264, 3270) and 58267–58286 (earlier numbers 3473, 3477, 3479, 3485, 3473, 3492/93, 3503, 3508, 3511/12, 3516/17, 3525/26, 3533, 3536/37, 3539, 3543) and the last of those in BR service were Nos 58271 and 58305, both of which were withdrawn in June 1961. It should be noted that 6 of the Neilson & Co built engines never carried their allocated BR numbers being scrapped in 1948/49 they were Nos 58253, 58270, 58275, 58282, 58284 and LMS No 3473.

See also MR '2F' 5' 3" 0-6-0 locomotives built by Sharp, Stewart & Co, Dübs & Co and Neilson, Reid & Co.

Driving wheel diameter 5' 3", 2-cylinder engine (inside)

Neilson & Co built MR '2F' 5' 3" 0-6-0 BR No 58271 seen outside Nottingham (16A) depot, in May 1954. This loco was delivered in 1896 and withdrawn by BR in June 1961. *Hugh Ballantyne/Rail Photoprints Collection*

CR 'Single' 4-2-2 1P

Of the many fine locomotives built by Neilson & Co the famous Drummond designed Caledonian Railway 4-2-2 'Single' No 123 is perhaps the most widely known example, Neilson Works No 3553. The un-named locomotive was a one-off which was built in 1886 and placed on show at the Edinburgh Exhibition of that year. Following the exhibition the engine was acquired by the Caledonian Railway, no doubt because that railway's then Chief Mechanical Engineer Dugald Drummond had been heavily involved with its design.

No 123 was the only 'Single Wheeler' to ever work regularly on a Scottish Railway and the engine put in many years of useful service hauling main line trains, including taking part in the 1888 'Race to Scotland' between the East and West coast routes.

Immediately following the period of the First World War the locomotive's only regular work was hauling the Directors' Saloon. In 1914 the locomotive was placed on the Caledonian Railway duplicate list and re-numbered 1123.

Following grouping (1923) the engine was acquired by the LMS and the 4-2-2 was then allocated the number 14010 and the power classification 1P. In 1930 the LMS returned the engine to regular rostered work, which mainly consisted of hauling light passenger trains between Perth and Dundee. Accordingly the Neilson & Co built 'Single Wheeler' certainly became the last express type 4-2-2 to work in ordinary traffic in the British Isles, and probably in the world!

In 1935 the LMS retired the engine with a view to preservation and accordingly the famous engine was repainted in CR blue livery and displayed at St Rollox Works.

Returned to regular service by the LMS 4-2-2 No 14010 (CR123) is seen in 1932 whilst waiting to depart from Perth station with a train for Dundee, the fully operational Neilson built loco was then 42-years-old. ***Mike Morant Collection***

In 1953 the famous 'Single Wheeler' toured the UK with an exhibition train. CR locomotive No 123 is seen on September 1st of that year during a visit to Edinburgh Waverley station. ***David Anderson***

In 1953 the then non-serviceable engine was moved south in order to take part in an exhibition entitled 'Royal Journey', which was held at Battersea Wharf as part of the 'Festival of Britain' celebrations. A fitting choice as during its long working life No 123 had participated on Royal Train duty on several occasions. Later the 'Royal Journey' train, formed of No 123 and suitable vintage coaches, visited several locations throughout the UK.

The locations visited for 3 to 6 day long displays between 17 July and 12 November 1953 were, Birmingham, Llandudno, Chester, Morecambe, Edinburgh, Dundee, Glasgow, Leeds, Sheffield, Nottingham, Plymouth, Bristol and Cardiff. This writer has fond memories of unexpectedly coming across the engine and coaches at Llandudno station, on the occasion of a family trip to the seaside in July 1953.

In 1958 No 123 was put through the works receiving a complete overhaul to operating condition. The venerable engine then embarked on a second operating career hauling enthusiast specials and in the course of which visiting several UK wide railway locations which included the Bluebell Railway in Sussex. Finally the locomotive was withdrawn from service in 1965 and placed on display in the Glasgow Transport Museum, (the Riverside Museum – Scotland).

Driving wheel diameter 7', 2-cylinder engine (inside)

Ex-CR 'Single Wheeler' No 123 is seen in the company of preserved ex-North British Railway (NBR) 'Glen' class 4-4-0 No 256 GLEN DOUGLAS, seen at Oban station with the SLS 'Caley 123 to Oban' on 12 May 1962. The tour originated from Glasgow Central and travelled via Craigendoran Junction and Crianlarich West Junction to Oban and returned via Callander, Dunblane and Stirling to Glasgow Buchanan Street. *Mike Morant Collection*

During a 1964 visit to the lines serving Edinburgh 4-2-2 No 123 'lodged' and was serviced at Haymarket depot (64B), the loco is seen at the east end of that important steam era motive power depot. The 'Single Wheeler' is in the company of 'A2' 4-6-2 No 60534 IRISH ELEGANCE (then a 64B Haymarket allocated engine) and 'V2' 2-6-2 No 60801 (then a 52D Tweedmouth allocated engine). *David Anderson*

No 123 makes a delightful sight when seen after Easter snow at Killin Junction station in 1963. The occasion was a part of the SLS – 'Scottish Rambler No.2' (Joint Easter Rail Tour). CR No 123 was one of 14 rostered locomotives, NBR No 256 GLEN DOUGLAS, HR No 103, GNoSR No 49 GORDON HIGLANDER, and BR Nos 45588 KASHMIR, 46474, 57375, 60041 SALMON TROUT, 61324, 64603, 64618, 65323, 80023 and 80093. Loco No 123 hauled the Glasgow Central - Killin - Glasgow Central legs on the first day and also the Stranraer Town – Glasgow St Enoch leg on the fourth day double heading with GNoSR No 49. *Rail Photoprints Collection*

Ex-CR 'Single Wheeler' No 123 is seen at Glasgow Central station in 1965 whilst working a leg of the SLS – 'Scottish Rambler No.4' Easter Railtour, the tour marked the engine's last main line outing prior to being placed on static display. ***Dugald Cameron***

Preserved Neilson & Co built CR 'Single Wheeler' No 123 is seen coupled to ex-LSWR 'T9' class 4-4-0 No 120 (BR No 30120) prior to working a mainline 'Bluebell Special' from London Victoria station to the Bluebell Railway in 1963. Note the white painted coal in the tender of the 4-2-2, recognising a tradition afforded to some 'Royal Trains' of the period. *Mike Morant Collection*

Neilson & Co built locomotive classes which came into British Railways ownership.

Class	Wheel arrangement	Designer	Customer/ Number to BR	Build dates	BR number series*
'MR 3F' 5' 3"	0-6-0	Johnson	MR/SDJR 98 locomotives	1888/91	43200/3–43205/10 43212–43299 43474–43544
'294' Jumbo	0-6-0	Drummond	CR 35 locomotives	1883 1883 1884	57230–57236 57241–57249 57252–57270
'1252' 5' 7"	0-4-4T	Johnson	MR 9 locomotives	1875/76	58030–58038
'1P' 5' 4"	0-4-4T	Johnson	MR 5 locomotives	1893	58068–58072
'2F' 4' 11"	0-6-0	Johnson	MR 25 locomotives	1876	58164–58187
'2F' 5' 3"	0-6-0	Johnson	MR 24 locomotives	1890 1894/97	58251–58254 58267–58286
'Single' 7' 0"	4-2-2	Neilson & Co/ D Drummond	CR 1 loco	1886	123 (LMS 14010)

*The BR numbers are given for identification in BR listings and do not take into account missing numbers due to scrapping, or locomotives of the same class built by other companies, but do include locomotives with allocated numbers not carried.

GNoSR 'S' and 'T' class 4-4-0 2P – 'D41'

These were the only locomotives built (from 1860 onwards) by the Great North of Scotland Railway (GNoSR), and they were of the 4-4-0 wheel arrangement. The 'S' and 'T' classes of engines were designed by James Johnson and were later designated 'D41' by the LNER.

The class was introduced between 1893 and 1898 and originally 32 engines were built by the contractors Neilson, Reid & Co and Neilson & Co.

In 1948 BR took into stock a total of 22 'D41' 4-4-0s and they were allocated numbers in the BR series 62225–62256. Of those 14 engines were Neilson built and they were allocated the numbers 62225–62243 (earlier LNER Nos 6878–6899 for GNoSR numbers were applicable discount the 68 prefix). However, No 62235 was withdrawn in 1948 without ever carrying its BR number. None of the class survived in service beyond 1953 and the last of the Neilson built locomotive to remain in service was No 62225 which was withdrawn in February 1953.

See also GNoSR 'S & T' 4-4-0 2P – D41 locomotives built by Neilson, Reid & Co.

Driving wheel diameter 6'1", 2-cylinder engine (inside)

Neilson & Co built 'D41' 4-4-0 BR No 62231 is seen at Keith depot (61C) in 1951, the loco is in the company of 'D40' class No 62264 which was a Neilson Reid built engine. No 62231 was delivered to the GNoSR in February 1896 and withdrawn by BR in October 1952. *Rail Photoprints Collection*

NBR 'C' 0-6-0 2F – 'J36'

Designed for the North British Railway by Matthew Holmes the 'C' class 0-6-0 locomotives were the most numerous on the NBR, the original build total being 168 engines, the class was designated 'J36' by the LNER. The locomotives were built at Cowlairs Works and by the contractors Sharp, Stewart & Co and Neilson & Co. BR took into stock 123 'J36' class engines allocating to them numbers in the series 65210–65346.

Of that BR total only 9 locomotives were Neilson built and they carried the Nos 65237–65245 (NBR Nos 663–670, 673, 675, 677).

The class achieved a modicum of fame when a batch of 25 engines was selected to be sent overseas during the 1917–1918 period of the First World War. On their return to the UK those locos were given the names of famous military leaders and locations associated with the war. The names were painted on the centre driving wheel splasher, but at the time of nationalisation and for periods in BR ownership the locomotives often ran un-named.

None of the class remained in service beyond the end of 1967 and the last engine in BR service was No 65346 (a Cowlairs built example). However, the Neilson & Co built 'J36' class engine No 65243 MAUDE (delivered December 1891 and withdrawn in July 1966) was saved for preservation.

See also NBR 'C' 0-6-0 2F – 'J36' locomotives built at Cowlairs Works and also by Sharp, Stewart & Co.

Driving wheel diameter 5', 2-cylinder engine (inside)

Neilson & Co built 'J36'class 0-6-0 BR No 65243 MAUDE is seen between duties circa 1965. The locomotive which was previously NBR No 673, LNER Nos 9673 and 5243 was named in honour of the British Army First World War commander General Sir Frederick Francis Maude VC (awarded during the Crimean War). ***Mike Morant Collection***

Neilson & Co built 'J36'class 0-6-0 BR No 65243 MAUDE is seen trundling along the Aberdeen and Dundee Tay Bridge to Edinburgh main line near Dalmeny Junction with a sizable mixed freight train, in June 1957. ***David Anderson***

Preserved 'J36'class 0-6-0 BR No 65243 MAUDE spent some time at the National Railway Museum, York and the engine is seen on the turntable in the main hall during 2012. ***Keith Langston***

'J36'class 0-6-0 BR No 65241 is seen in pristine condition at Haymarket shed (64B) in March 1956, after a recent visit to Cowlairs Works. Delivered in November 1891 this 'J36' was withdrawn by BR in October 1962, in its 71st birthday year! The Neilson & Co built engine was previously NBR No 669, LNER Nos 9669 and 5241. ***David Anderson***

MS&LR 'F1' 2-4-2T 1P – (GCR 'Class 3')

A total of 39 Thomas Parker designed 2-4-2T engines were built between 1889 and 1892 for the Manchester, Sheffield & Lincolnshire Railway (MS&LR), which were built at Gorton Works and by the contractor Neilson & Co. The MS&LR changed its name to the Great Central Railway (GCR) in 1897, and these passenger tank locomotives were designated that railways 'Class 3'. Withdrawal of the class commenced in 1930. In 1948 3 of the locomotives came into BR stock and they were allocated numbers 67097–67100 but were scrapped in 1949 without ever carrying those numbers. Two of the engines were Gorton Works built examples and the third No 67100 was delivered by Neilsons in March 1891(previous LNER No 5598).

Driving wheel diameter 5' 7", 2-cylinder engine (inside)

NBR 'G' 0-4-0ST 0F - 'Y9'

This class of Matthew Holmes designed saddle tanks were introduced by the North British Railway (NBR) between 1882 and 1899 and designated 'G' class engines (LNER 'Y9'). The type were commonly referred to as 'Pugs' and 38 were built, they were intended for use at dockyards and other railway installations with tightly curved sections of track. The Caledonian Railway (CR) also built a class of 'Pugs' which became LMS '0F' '56010' class.

The NBR engines could be easily distinguished by virtue of their stovepipe chimneys. The diminutive engines were built with open backed cabs and no coal bunkers, it was therefore common practice to permanently couple them to small 4-wheeled wooden tenders converted from redundant wagons in order to add coal carrying capacity.

BR took into stock 33 of the engines allocating to them numbers in the series 68092–68124 of those 31 were built at Cowlairs Works but 2 engines BR Nos 68092 and 68093 (earlier numbers 10101 and 10102) were Neilson & Co built, the last of the pair in service being No 68093 withdrawn by BR in May 1955.

See also NBR 'G' 0-4-0ST 0F ('Y9' class Pug) locomotives built at Cowlairs Works.

Driving wheel diameter 3' 8", 2-cylinder engine (outside)

GNR 'J13' 0-6-0ST 3F – 'J52'

Great Northern Railway CMEs Patrick Stirling and Henry Alfred Ivatt both adopted the 0-6-0 saddle tank design as their standard GNR shunting engine. Between 1868 and 1909 a total of 264 of the 0-6-0ST engines designated 'J13' class were built. The engines attributed to Stirling were built with domeless boilers whilst those originated by Ivatt were built with domed boilers. Under the GNR/LNER rebuilding of both types under Gresley took place between 1922 and 1932.

The Stirling engines were designated 'J52/1' class by the LNER whilst the Ivatt locomotives were designated 'J52/2' class. The majority of these saddle tanks were originated from Doncaster Works but the contractors Robert Stephenson & Co Ltd, Sharp, Stewart & Co and Neilson & Co also participated in the build. BR took into stock 132 of the engines allocating to them numbers in the series 68757–68889 (LNER 8757–8889) of those Nos 68783–68802 (earlier numbers 8783–8802) were Neilson built between July 1896 and August 1897, all being 'J52/1 variants. None of the class survived beyond the end of 1961 and the last NBL built 'J52/1' in service with BR was No 68800, which was withdrawn in July 1958.

See also GNR 'J13' 0-6-0ST 3F (LNER 'J52') locomotives built by Sharp, Stewart & Co.

Driving wheel diameter 4' 8", 2-cylinder engine (inside)

MS&LR (GCR) '9A' 0-6-2T 2MT – 'N4'

A total of 55 Thomas Parker designed 0-6-2T engines were built between 1889 and 1892 for the Manchester, Sheffield & Lincolnshire Railway (MS&LR), they were built at Gorton Works and by the contractor Neilson & Co. The MS&LR changed its name to the Great Central Railway (GCR) in 1897, and these mixed traffic tank locomotives were designated as that railways '9A' class.

Neilson & Co built MS&LR (GCR) '9A' class 0-6-2T 2MT – (LNER 'N4'class) BR No 69231 is seen whilst shunting outside Sheffield Victoria station in 1953. This loco was delivered in November 1890 and withdrawn by BR in October 1954. *David Anderson*

Originally built with round topped boilers all of the class were later rebuilt with Belpaire boilers, they were also fitted with 'flower pot' chimneys during the LNER Gresley era. The GCR '9A' class engines were designated 'N4' class by the LNER and the class variants were 'N4/2' original engines introduced in 1889, 'N4/4' were developed from the former variant and fitted with enlarged coal bunkers. Variants 'N4/1' and 'N4/3' were locomotives of the other variants prior to being fitted with shortened chimneys by the LNER.

BR took into stock 22 of the class allocating to them numbers in the series 69225–69247, and of those Nos 69227–69241 as 'N4/2' variants (GCR Nos 605/606, 611, 614, 620, 622/623, 625, 628/29, 632, 635/36/37) and 69242–69247 as 'N2/4' variants (GCR No 713, 716, 718, 720/21, 724) were Neilson built. Scrapping of the class started in 1948 with several engines never carrying their allocated BR numbers, and none survived in traffic beyond the end of December 1954 with Nos 69228, 69230 and 69232 being the last.

Driving wheel diameter 5' 1", 2-cylinder engine (inside)

Neilson & Co built locomotive classes which came into British Railways ownership

Class	Wheel arrangement	Designer	Customer/Number to BR	Build dates	BR number series*
'S' and 'T' class 'D41'	4-4-0	Johnson	GNoSR 14 locomotives	1893 1893/96 1895	62225 62227–62235 62238–62243
'J36'	0-6-0	Holmes	NBR 9 locomotives	1891	65237–65245
'F1'	2-4-2T	Parker	MS&LR/GCR 1 loco	1891	67100
'Y9'	0-4-0ST	Holmes	NBR 2 locomotives	1882	68092–68093
'J52'	0-6-0ST	Stirling/Ivatt	GNR 20 locomotives	1896/97	68783–68802
'N4'	0-6-2T	Parker	MS&LR/GCR 20 locomotives	1890/92	69227–69247

* The BR numbers are given for identification in BR listings and do not take into account missing numbers due to scrapping, or locomotives of the same class built by other companies, but do include locomotives with allocated numbers not carried.

Neilson, Reid & Co, Glasgow

SECR 'B' 4-4-0 1P – 'B1'

The South Eastern & Chatham Railway introduced the James Stirling designed 'B' class 4-4-0 locomotives between 1898 and 1899. Originally the railway built 29 of the type at both Ashford Works and by contractors Neilson, Reid & Co. The class was later designated 'B1' and 27 examples were re-built by Wainwright, firstly with domed boilers and later with extended smokeboxes. BR took into stock 16 of the class allocating to them numbers in the series 31013–31459, and of those 14 were Neilson, Reid & Co built BR Nos in the series 31440–31459 (SECR Nos 440, 443–446, 449–455, 457, 459). However, scrapping started in 1948 with only one locomotive (BR No 31446–SECR No 446) withdrawn July 1949) surviving long enough to carry its allocated BR number.

Driving wheel diameter 7', 2-cylinder engine (inside)

SECR 'C' 0-6-0 3F (re-classified 2F in 1953)

The South Eastern & Chatham Railway introduced a Harry Wainwright designed 0-6-0 freight/mixed traffic engine which was designated that railway's 'C' class, between 1900 and 1908. A total of 109 0-6-0 'C' class engines were built at Ashford Works, Longhedge Works and by the contractors Sharp, Stewart & Co, and Neilson, Reid & Co. BR took into stock 106 of the class allocating to them numbers in the series 31004–31725, and of those locomotives Nos 31681–31695 (SECR Nos 593–695) were Neilson, Reid & Co built between May and July 1900.

Apart from 2 engines which were transferred to the service stock pool none of the class remained in traffic with BR after 1963, the last Neilson, Reid & Co built example being No 31690 withdrawn in June 1962. Another Neilson, Reid built example was converted into a saddle tank engine in 1917. See SECR 'S' class.

See also SECR 'C' 0-6-0 3F locomotives built by Sharp, Stewart & Co.

Driving wheel diameter 5' 2", 2-cylinder engine (inside)

Neilson, Reid & Co built Wainwright 'C' class 0-6-0 BR No 31688 is seen at Ashford depot (then 73F) in March 1959. This loco was delivered in July 1900 as SECR No 688 and withdrawn by BR in February 1960. ***Hugh Ballantyne/Rail Photoprints Collection***

SECR 'S' 0-6-0ST 2F

This was the only 'S' class locomotive built (originally loco circa 1900) and it was in fact built by converting a Wainwright 'C' class 0-6-0 tender engine into a saddle tank, in 1917. It was almost exclusively used for shunting work at Bricklayers Arms motive power depot (73B from 1948) and was originally numbered 685 and 1685. The 'S' class engine came into BR stock and was allocated No 31685 which it never actually carried. After a short period of allocation to Dover (74C) the engine was withdrawn in October 1951.

Driving wheel diameter 5' 2", 2-cylinder engine (inside)

The only Wainwright 'S' class locomotive SR No 1685 is seen on shed at Ashford (74A) early in the BR era. ***Mike Morant Collection***

Neilson, Reid & Co built CR '812' class 0-6-0 3F loco BR No 57571, is seen near Kentallen with a Ballachulish - Oban freight on a very grey day in August 1960. This loco was delivered in December 1899 becoming CR No 833, and withdrawn by BR in April 1962. ***Rail Photoprints Collection***

CR '812' 0-6-0 3F

The Caledonian Railway (CR) introduced this John Farquharson McIntosh designed class of 0-6-0 freight locomotives between 1899 and 1900. The 79 engines were built at St Rollox Works and by contractors Sharp, Stewart & Co, Dübs & Co. and Neilson, Reid & Co and they were an enlarged version of the CR 'Jumbo' class engines. As originally built they were fitted with 'Dunalastair I' type boilers and 'Dunalastair II' type cabs, most of the engines were later re-built with LMS boilers.

BR took into stock 76 of these engines and allocated to them numbers in the series 57550–57628.

The class was originally referred to as Mixed Traffic engines however, only 17 locomotives were fitted with Westinghouse brakes and 5 with vacuum for passenger train working. Of the BR total 19 were Neilson, Reid & Co built locomotives numbered 57568–57586 which were delivered between December 1899 and May 1900 as CR Nos 830–848 (LMS Nos 17568–17586). None of the class remained in traffic after 1963 and the last surviving Neilson, Reid & Co engines were Nos 57568 and 57581, which were both withdrawn by BR in November 1963.

See also CR '812' 0-6-0 3F locomotives built at St Rollox Works, Sharp, Stewart & Co and Dübs & Co.

Driving wheel diameter 5' 0", 2-cylinder engine (inside)

GNoSR Pickersgill 'V' 4-4-0 2P – 'D40' (BR reclassified as 1P in 1953)

Between 1899 and 1921 the Great North of Scotland Railway (GNoSR) introduced a Pickersgill designed class of 2-cylinder 4-4-0 locomotive which were designated 'V' class (BR number series 62260–62262, 62264–62265, 62267–62273). The locomotives were built at Inverurie Works and by Neilson, Reid & Co Ltd. The original order for the 1899 Neilson, Reid batch was for 10 engines, but due to the GNoSR experiencing financial difficulties at that time the contractor instead sold 5 engines to the South Eastern & Chatham Railway (SECR). Those engines remained at work on the Southern Railway (SR) until being withdrawn between 1925 and 1927.

The GNoSR eventually acquired 21 locomotives of the class which later passed into LNER ownership, who designated the class 'D40'. The LNER scrapped 3 of the class circa 1947 and accordingly BR took into stock 18 'D40' engines, of which 4 were Neilson Reid built (BR numbers 62260–62264 and GNoSR Nos 25, 26, 113, 114). Names were carried by 7 of the class and they were the only Scottish engines to carry cast brass nameplates.

None of the class remained in traffic beyond the end of 1958 and the last Neilson, Reid & Co built example to be withdrawn was No 62264 delivered in October 1899 and withdrawn by BR in March 1957.

See also GNoSR Pickersgill 'V' 4-4-0 2P – 'D40', built by the NBL and at Inverurie Works.

Driving wheel diameter 6' 1", 2-cylinder engine (inside)

Neilson, Reid & Co built GNoSR Pickersgill 'V' 4-4-0 2P – 'D40' BR No 62264 is seen at Elgin in March 1956. This loco was delivered to the GNoSR as No 915 in October 1899, and withdrawn by BR in March 1957 one year after this picture was taken. *Rail Photoprints Collection*

'MR Johnson 3F' 0-6-0

This class of Samuel Waite Johnson designed locomotives were introduced by the Midland Railway (MR) between 1875 and 1902. Some of which were rebuilds of the earlier MR '43137' class and also the former MR 2F '58188' class, selected locomotives were given Belpaire fireboxes and Deeley style cabs by Fowler from 1903 onwards. They were built by Derby Works and contractors Kitson & Co, Dübs & Co, Sharp Stewart & Co, Neilson & Co and Neilson, Reid & Co. BR took into stock 324 of these 0-6-0 locomotives of which 16 were Neilson Reid built, in the BR number series 43600–43629. None of the class survived in service beyond 1964 and the last Neilson Reid built example was No 43620 which was withdrawn by BR in February 1964.

See also 'MR Johnson 3F' 0-6-0 3F locomotives built by Dübs & Co, Sharp, Stewart & Co, Neilson & Co.

Driving wheel diameter 5' 3", 2-cylinder engine (inside)

GCR '9J' 0-6-0 3F – 'J11'

Between 1901 and 1910 the Great Central Railway (GCR) introduced a class of 0-6-0 freight locomotives designed by John G. Robinson, and in total 174 locomotives were built. The engines were built at Gorton Works and by the contractors Beyer, Peacock & Co Ltd, Vulcan Foundry Ltd, Yorkshire Engine Company and Neilson, Reid & Co.

Considered by many to be very handsome locomotives the engines earned the nick name 'Pom-Poms' because of their mellow exhaust beats. In LNER ownership the engines were designated 'J11' class and many admirers considered that the addition of 'flower pot' type chimneys during re-builds (ordered by Gresley) greatly disfigured the 'J11' engines.

Despite the earlier creation of 4 variants, which variously included lower boiler mountings, higher boiler mountings, superheating and varying tender capacities BR later combined them simply as 'J11' class engines.

A batch of 31 engines (including 6 Neilson, Reid built examples) were rebuilt with long travel piston valves and higher pitched boilers between 1942 and 1954 ('J11/3').

At around that time there was a proposal that the aforementioned variant could form a standard 0-6-0 class on BR and plans to build a large number of new engines were made, but later abandoned.

A total of 174 'J11' engines came into BR stock and they were allocated numbers in the series 64280–64453, 49 of those locomotives were Neilson Reid built between September 1901 and November 1902 (BR Nos 64280–64328, LNER Nos 4280–4328 and 5973–6051). None of the class survived in traffic beyond the end of 1962 and the last Neilson, Reid & Co built engines in traffic were Nos 64314 and 64324, both withdrawn by BR in September 1962.

Driving wheel diameter 5' 2", 2-cylinder engine (inside)

NBR 'D' 0-6-0T – 'J83'

The North British Railway (NBR) introduced a class of 40 Mathew Holmes designed 0-6-0T engines between 1900 and 1901. The locomotives were designated NBR 'D' class which was later changed to 'J83' class by the LNER. The engines were originally intended for shunting and freight transfer duties on the NBR and they were the most powerful 0-6-0T engines to be used on that railway. They were built by Sharp Stewart & Co (20 engines) and Neilson, Reid & Co (20 engines). Only one engine was scrapped prior to 1948 and therefore BR took into stock 39 engines allocating to them numbers in the series 68442–68481 (LNER Nos 8442–8481 9795–9814). The Neilson, Reid & Co built engines were numbered 68442–68461.

Neilson, Reid & Co built NBR 'D' 0-6-0T ('J83') BR No 68454 is seen at South Leith, east of Edinburgh in April 1956. This locomotive was delivered in April 1901 as NBR No 807 and withdrawn by BR in February 1962. *David Anderson*

Neilson, Reid & Co built NBR 'D' 0-6-0T ('J83') BR No 68457 is seen whilst performing ash removal duties at Edinburgh Haymarket shed (64B) in May 1955 and was at that time one of five of the depot allocation of the class. This locomotive was delivered in April 1901 as NBR No 810 and withdrawn by BR in March 1960. ***David Anderson***

Under LNER/BR a number of these engines were fitted with Westinghouse brakes and thereafter were often used for station pilot duties at both Glasgow Queen Street and Edinburgh Waverley stations, with the Edinburgh based engines repainted in light green livery by the LNER in 1947.

None of the class survived in traffic beyond 1962 and the last serving Neilson, Reid & Co engines were Nos 68445, 68448 and 68453, which were all withdrawn by BR in October 1962.

See also NBR 'D' 0-6-0T ('J83') locomotives built by Sharp, Stewart & Co.

Driving wheel diameter 4' 6", 2-cylinder engine (inside)

Neilson Reid & Co built locomotive classes which came into British Railways ownership

'B5'	4-6-0	Robinson	GCR 2 locomotives	1902	61680–61681
'D41'	4-4-0	Johnson	GNoSR 8 locomotives	1897/88	62246–62249 62251–62252 62255–62256
'D40'	4-4-0	Pickersgill	GNoSR 4 locomotives	1899	62260–62264
'MR 3F'	0-6-0	Johnson	MR/SDJR 47 locomotives	1899 1901/02	43600–43629 43710–43763
'J11'	0-6-0	Robinson	GCR 49 locomotives	1901/02	64280–64328
'J83'	0-6-0T	Holmes	NBR 20 locomotives		68442–68461

*The BR numbers are given for identification in BR listings and do not take into account missing numbers due to scrapping, or locomotives of the same class built by other companies, but do include locomotives with allocated numbers not carried.

Railway Company abbreviations used in this chapter.

CR – Caledonian Railway, **GNoSR** – Great North of Scotland Railway, **GNR** – Great Northern Railway, **MSLR** – Manchester, Sheffield & Lincolnshire Railway, **MR** – Midland Railway, **LSWR** – London & South Western Railway, **NBR** – North British Railway, **LBSCR** – London, Brighton & South Coast Railway, **SECR** – South Eastern & Chatham Railway, **S&DJR** – Somerset & Dorset Joint Railway.

Neilson, Reid & Co Ltd carried on the Neilson & Co tradition of building industrial locomotives and two standard gauge examples are shown here. Above is Bass Brewery 0-4-0ST No 10 (Neilson Reid works number 5567 of 1899) on the works at Burton- on -Trent with the Brewery Railway's saloon coach, seen during 1959. Below is Bass Brewery 0-4-0ST No 9 (Neilson, Reid works number 5907 of 1901) the loco is seen outside the brewery engine shed during 1960. *Both images Rail Photoprints Collection*

Neilson & Co built 0-4-0ST, an outside cylinder industrial saddle tank engine seen as Bass No 7 on the site of the former Bass Brewery at Burton on Trent, in 1960. *Rail Photoprints Collection*

Chapter 3

ANDREW BARCLAY SONS & COMPANY

Any account of steam locomotive building in Scotland must make reference to the locomotive builders of Kilmarnock in general, and to the firm of Andrew Barclay Sons & Company in particular. There were four AB built locomotive types taken into BR stock, although several earlier built examples supplied to various UK railways were not.

Early steam age locomotive building in and around the Ayrshire town of Kilmarnock was not necessarily a response to the initial coming of the railways but more a slightly later natural commercial expansion following the development and growth of the coal and iron industry in that part of Scotland.

Andrew Barclay Sons & Company (AB) is perhaps the better known of the Kilmarnock engine builders by virtue of the fact that the trading name (albeit in altered form) survived into the new millennia.

The history of the company dates from the foundation of an engineering workshop circa 1840 by one Andrew Barclay (1814–1900) who is credited with starting the private locomotive building industry in and around Kilmarnock. Because of the large number of AB built industrial locomotives which still survive on preserved railways (over 100 in the UK) the famous 'Caledonia Works' makers plate is perchance almost as recognisable today as it was during the peak of the firm's locomotive building activities.

1902 built Andrew Barclay Sons & Co 2-4-0T LADY MARGARET seen with a line up of railway staff, at Looe station on the Liskeard & Looe Railway (LL) in Cornwall circa 1905. ***National Railway Museum / Science & Society Picture Library***

Andrew Barclay Sons & Co 2-4-0T inside cylinder locomotive built for the Liskeard & Looe Railway (LL) in Cornwall. Seen with a train on the LL circa 1930, note that the 1902 Kilmarnock built loco received a GWR boiler in 1929. The loco was originally named LADY MARGARET and then numbered 1308 in the GWR sequence. *Transport Treasury*

Andrew Barclay Sons & Co works plate dating from 1921. *Keith Langston*

Kilmarnock engineer Andrew Barclay (1814–1900) was only 25 years old when in partnership with Thomas McCulloch he set up a company in order to manufacture mill shafts etc in 1825. Two years later Barclay left that firm to set up his own engineering enterprise at new premises in the town of Kilmarnock, specifically to manufacture winding engines for the coal mining industry (the site for Caledonia Works was acquired in 1847). Additionally Barclay held a patent concerned with the manufacture of gas lamps, he sold the rights to that patent in order to fund his new venture. However, the money from that sale was never paid over and as a consequence Barclay's firm faced sequestration in 1848.

Andrew Barclay continued to trade and after overcoming his financial problems he began to manufacture steam locomotives, the first being completed in 1859. By 1870 the firm had reportedly produced and sold 420 locomotives whilst providing employment for upwards of 150 people.

Circa 1871 Barclay established a second locomotive building company for his younger brother John and his four sons and based at the Riverbank Works in Kilmarnock the firm was called Barclay & Sons, the two enterprises were closely associated. The firm did not trade profitably during the early 1870s and in 1874 and 1882 respectively both firms were declared bankrupt.

In 1886 Andrew Barclay restructured his company and it was renamed Andrew Barclay Sons & Company, but the company Barclay & Sons was not revived. It seemed that fiscal problems continued to impede the new company but nevertheless the firm still took on limited liability in 1892 as Andrew Barclay Sons & Co Ltd. The firm's shareholders saw fit to remove Andrew Barclay from control in 1894. Following his removal Barclay sued the company for unpaid wages but that action was settled out of court in 1899.

In 1930 the company took over the business of engine makers John Cochrane (Barrhead) Ltd and in 1963 the firm acquired the goodwill of the North British Locomotive Co Ltd (NBL). The Leeds based Hunslet Group acquired the Kilmarnock engine manufacturers in 1972 later changing the company name to Hunslet-Barclay Ltd (1989).

After bankruptcy proceedings in 2007 that company became Brush-Barclay Ltd and part of the larger FKI Group. That company was acquired by Wabtec Corporation (name derived from the American firm Westinghouse Air Brake Technologies Corporation) in 2011. Accordingly Brush-Barclay was still operational in January 2013 trading as Wabtec Rail Scotland, Caledonia Works, Kilmarnock.

AB built locomotive classes included in British Railway listings

'L&L' 2-4-0T 1P

The Liskeard & Looe Railway (LL) in Cornwall dates from 1860 with passenger services being introduced in 1879. The branch line, which connects to the Cornish main line, was still in use in 2013. In 1902 the railway placed an order with Andrew Barclay Sons & Company (AB) for the supply of a 2-4-0T locomotive with which to operate its passenger trains, the loco was named LADY MARGARET. The line was taken over by the Great Western Railway (GWR) in 1909 and the AB loco was rebuilt by that company in 1929 and used elsewhere on their network. The engine was numbered 1308 in the GWR series and it was taken into British Railways (BR) stock but was withdrawn from Machynlleth (89C) in West Wales (after frequently working trains on the Tanat Valley Line). No 1308 was scrapped in May 1948.

Driving wheel diameter 4', 2-cylinder engine (inside)

GWR No 1308 LADY MARGARET is seen whilst receiving attention in Swindon Works. *Transport Treasury*

'SHT' 0-4-0ST 0F

The Swansea Harbour Trust Railway (SHT) owned a fleet of small saddle tank engines ostensibly to work the Swansea Dock network of lines. Three of those were built by AB in 1905 and they were the first new locomotives purchased by the railway, a single example survived to be taken into BR stock. That loco, delivered in April 1905 was taken into GWR ownership and originally carried the number 701, later changed to No 1140. The loco was rebuilt at Swindon Works and thereafter sported a GWR style safety valve cover, the diminutive engine was also fitted with a bell which was mounted on top of the firebox (in front of the cab). BR withdrew the loco from service in May 1958 and it was cut up two months later.

Driving wheel diameter 3' 5", 2-cylinder engine (outside)

AB built outside cylinder 0-4-0ST No 1140 (also numbered 701) is seen in BR livery at Swindon in June 1951. Delivered in 1905 this loco was withdrawn by BR May 1958. Note the addition of a bell in front of the cab and the relatively large AB maker's plate on the cab side. ***Rail Photoprints Collection***

'AD' 0-6-2ST

The Alexandra Dock Company of Newport bought 3 outside cylinder 0-6-2T locomotives from AB in 1908. The locos were required for heavy shunting work as coal exports from the docks increased in volume during the early 1900s; the locos were originally numbered 190–192. The engines were rebuilt by the GWR circa 1923 and that 'Swindonisation' resulted in a greatly changed appearance, the side tanks were shortened and GWR style smokeboxes and safety valve covers were fitted. Only one member of the class survived to be taken into BR stock and that engine, No 190 was withdrawn and cut up in April 1948.

Driving wheel diameter 4' 3", 2-cylinder engine (outside)

AB built Alexandra Dock Company 0-6-2T No 192 is seen at Swindon in 1932, note the GWR modifications. One of the original 3 engines in the class No 192 was withdrawn and cut up in 1946. ***Mike Morant Collection***

LMS/SDJR Fowler 0-6-0 4F

The class was built at Derby, Crewe, St Rollox and Horwich works and additionally by contractors Kerr Stuart & Co Ltd, Andrew Barclay Sons & Co Ltd and North British Locomotive Co Ltd.

Andrew Barclay Sons & Co built 25 of the type between 1927 and 1928. The BR numbers of the AB built locomotive were 44357–44381. None of the class remained in traffic beyond the end of 1966, the last Andrew Barclay Sons & Co built examples in traffic were Nos 44373 and 44376 both withdrawn by BR in December 1964.

See also LMS/SDJR Fowler 0-6-0 4F locomotives built at St Rollox Works and also the North British Locomotive Co Ltd.

Driving wheel diameter 5' 3", 2-cylinder engine (inside)

'J94' MOS (WD) 0-6-0ST 4F

The 'J94' class was introduced between 1943 and 1946 to fulfil the need for a powerful shunting engine for war work. The Hunslet Engine Co Ltd (HE) designed the engines under the direction of Robert Riddles and they were built to the order of the Ministry of Supply (MOS) also referred to as the War Department (WD). Several hundred of these highly successful engines were built by a number of private contractors. At the end of the war many of these engines were sold out of service by the MOS to numerous industrial users and additionally the LNER bought a batch of 75 of them.

The BR number series 68006-68080 applies and the AB built examples were numbered 68071-68080 in that series. Withdrawals started in 1960 and by the end of 1966 only two locos remained in service. There are 2 preserved examples and both are from the AB built batch; they are locos No 68077 and No 68078. The last AB built engine in service for BR was No 68079 which was withdrawn in October 1966.

Driving wheel diameter 4' 3", 2-cylinder engine (inside)

The last AB built 'J94' class 0-6-0ST in service with BR, loco No 68079 takes water at Middleton Top on the Cromford and High Peak Line in early 1965. Note the locoman on the top of the engine and the Buxton (9L) shedplate *Rail Photoprints Collection*

Loco No 68079 is again pictured but a year earlier and in an industrial setting thought to be in the Workington area. At that time the loco was carrying a Barrow in Furness (then 12C) shedplate. The 'J94' design proved to be ideal for use on preserved railways. In addition to the two AB built ex-BR examples a total of approximately 50 more engines are now gainfully employed on preserved lines, that impressive total makes 'J94's the largest steam locomotive class in preservation.

AB built Locomotive classes which came into British Railways (BR) ownership

Class/Wheel Arrangement	Designer	Customer (Number to BR stock)	Build dates	BR number series*
'L&L' 2-4-0T	AB Sons & Co	L&L 1 loco	1902	1308
'SHT' 0-4-0ST	AB Sons & Co	SHR 1 loco	1905	701 renumbered GWR 1140
'AD' 0-6-2T	AB Sons & Co	AD 1 loco	1908	190
'4F' 0-6-0	Fowler	LMS/S&DJR 25 locos	1927/28	44358–44381
'J94' MOS 0-6-0ST	Riddles/HE	MOS/LNER 10 locos	1945 1946/7	68071–68074 68075–68080

*The BR numbers are given for identification in BR listings and do not take into account missing numbers due to scrapping or locomotives of the same class built by other companies, but do include locomotives with allocated numbers not carried.

Railway Company abbreviations used in this chapter.

AD – Alexandra Dock Company, **LMS** – London Midland & Scottish Railway, **L&L** – Liskeard & Looe Railway, **MOS** – Ministry of Supply, **LNER** – London & North Eastern Railway, **S&DJR** – Somerset & Dorset Joint Railway, **SHT** – Swansea Harbour Trust Railway

Andrew Barclay Sons & Company – Industrial Locomotives

In addition to supplying the UK national network operators with locomotives Andrew Barclay Sons & Company built significant numbers of industrial locomotives for use within the coal, steel, power generation, chemical, docks and other major industries. A large number of their industrial locomotives were built to the UK 'Standard Gauge' and often operated on private networks with exchange sidings connected to the local freight lines. In addition to moving goods into and around those sites the locomotives would also be used to shunt goods vehicles and make up trains for collection by mainline operators. Amongst the industrial users of AB built engines the coal industry was perhaps the most well known. From their beginning in 1859 Barclays produced over 2000 steam locomotives and they were the last such company to operate in Scotland, building their last steam locomotive in 1962.

Andrew Barclay Sons & Company steam locomotives rightly earned the reputation of being robust and hard wearing machines. The company developed standard designs of four coupled (0-4-0 and 0-4-2) and six coupled (0-6-0 and 0-6-2). They produced side tank (T) and saddle tank (ST) and crane tank (CT) engines, the majority of which were of outside cylinder design and constructed to suit a variety of loading gauges. Interestingly Glasgow locomotive builders, armament manufactures and steelmakers William Beardmore & Company operated a fleet of 8 AB built standard gauge 0-4-0ST locomotives at their various Clydeside sites (supplied 1900–1908).

In addition to UK sales the firm exported a large number of engines to several countries of the former British Empire and beyond.

A large number of restored/preserved AB built steam locomotives are now in the care of preserved railways and many can be seen in operational condition.

Former Ferrybridge Power Station Andrew Barclay Sons & Company 0-4-0ST FERRYBRIDGE No 3 stands at Wirksworth station on the preserved Ecclesbourne Valley Railway on the occasion of its re-launch into traffic, on 25 May 2010. The 1954-built locomotive, AB works number 2360, had just been named 'BRIAN HARRISON' after the man who saved it for preservation. ***Gary Boyd-Hope***

Wearing a fictitious National Coal Board (NCB) West Midland Division livery, Andrew Barclay 0-4-0ST (works number 1964) seen as it runs around its train at the Chasewater Railway on 20 March 2011. *Gary Boyd-Hope*

VICTORY was built by Andrew Barclay in 1945 and delivered new to HM Dockyard Chatham, Kent. In April 2012 the 0-4-0ST (AB works No 2199) returned to the dockyard following a lengthy and comprehensive restoration. The loco is seen there in the company of other Chatham Dockyard resident locomotives, VICTORY was in 2013 based at the Epping Ongar Railway. *Gary Boyd-Hope*

Andrew Barclay 0-6-0T No 2335 built 1953 appears to struggle with a lengthy loaded rake of coal wagons on the NCB Waterside system in Ayrshire, this loco was still in action long after steam on BR had ended, seen in 1972. *Rail Photoprints Collection*

NCB East Wales Area Andrew Barclay 0-6-0ST No 2074, built 1939, and seen outside the running shed at NCB Mountain Ash Colliery, still in steam when this image was taken during November 1972. *Rail Photoprints Collection*

A delightful period image Andrew Barclay 0-4-0ST STANTON 36 (AB works number 2042, built 1937) seen hard at work. The location was at Riddings Foundry, Alfreton, and the date circa 1956. *Rail Photoprints Collection*

A typical Andrew Barclay Sons & Company design of outside cylinder 0-4-0 saddle tank (ST), the locomotive is seen at the head of a staff train on the former private Whittingham Hospital Railway (WHR) circa 1932 (WHR opened 1889 closed 1957). This was Whittingham loco No1 built at Kilmarnock in 1888 to works order number 304, the engine was scrapped in 1947. *Mike Morant Collection*

Andrew Barclay built outside cylinder 0-4-2T is seen as County Mental Hospital Whittingham locomotive No 2, AB works No AB 1026 built in 1904. The loco was supplied new to the line and lasted in service until 1952 when it was replaced by a diesel shunter. *Mike Morant Collection*

Andrew Barclay Sons & Company – Crane Tanks

Amongst the specialist locomotives built by Andrew Barclay Sons & Company were a selection of crane tank (CT) engines built specifically to the customer's requirements and of varying capacity.

AB built crane tank STANTON No 10, this 0-4-0CT works number 855 was built in 1899. Seen at Stanton Ironworks, Ilkeston, in July 1957. *Mike Morant Collection*

Stanton Steel Works locomotive No 26 was a 0-4-0CT built by Andrew Barclay as works number 1928 in 1927. The private works railway locomotive seen at Stanton Ironworks, Ilkeston, circa 1959. *Rail Photoprints Collection*

Andrew Barclay built crane tank built for Glenfield & Kennedy a Kilmarnock based engineering company. This 5-ton lifting capacity 0-4-0CT loco was delivered in 1902. *David Anderson*

Andrew Barclay Sons & Company – Fireless Locomotives

Andrew Barclay Sons & Company became leaders in the development of fireless locomotives for use in industrial locations where the employment of a conventional steam locomotive would be inappropriate (e.g. smokeless environment). Instead of a normal boiler and firebox those locos carried an insulated pressure vessel which was filled with steam from a static source. AB became the largest builder of fireless locomotives in Britain, building 114 of them between 1913 and 1961. Few fireless locomotives are seen in action today. This is mainly due to the low power of the locomotives, and the lengthy process needed to charge a locomotive from a cold start.

The fireless 0-4-0T loco pictured was used to shunt coal wagons within Castle Meads Power Station (1942–1969) this restored engine is now based at the National Waterways Museum in Gloucester. Note the position of the cylinders, this loco was configured to operate with the driver facing in either direction. ***Keith Langston***

Andrew Barclay Sons & Co. – Steam Rail Motors

In 1905 two steam rail motors, to a Pickersgill design, went into service on the Lossiemouth and St Combs branches of the Great North of Scotland Railway (GNoSR). These units were designed with a relatively small engine mounted on a four-wheeled power bogie, and incorporated in a coach body which had a normal bogie at the other end.

The engines were built by Andrew Barclay & Co. and they were supplied steam from vertical boilers made by Cochran & Co. of Annan.

The two engine units were numbered 29 and 31, (Barclay works numbers 1056–7), and the coach units were numbered 28 and 29 respectively. They were introduced into revenue earning service at the St Combs Light Railway and the Lossiemouth branch in November 1905. Although on test the rail motors apparently showed good prospects they were in fact a failure in service.

There was actually nothing wrong with their speed, and after being transferred to work on the Aberdeen suburban services, one unit reportedly attained a speed of 30 mph in 20 seconds and ran at a steady 60 mph between Aberdeen and Inverurie. They were a little more successful on the Aberdeen local services but the units were described as being very noisy and the boilers only steamed moderately. After being taken out of service the boilers were used for a while as stationary units.

Andrew Barclay Sons & Company GNoSR steam rail motor unit No 29. *Mike Stokes Archive*

Chapter 4

DÜBS & CO, QUEEN'S PARK WORKS, GLASGOW

Dübs & Company was a locomotive works in Glasgow founded in 1864 by one Henry Dübs (1816-1876), a gentleman of German extraction. Dübs was born Heinrich Dübs in Darmstadt, Germany and after moving to work in Great Britain in 1842 he anglicised his name to Henry Dübs.

Initially Dübs went to work for the locomotive manufacturers Vulcan Foundry Ltd in St Helens and later moved to the Manchester based firm of Beyer, Peacock & Co Ltd. He was dismissed by that company in 1857 and after only a short while he moved to Glasgow to take up the position of Managing Partner with Neilson & Co, and in doing so he replaced James Reid (later of Neilson Reid & Co fame).

Henry Dübs at first enjoyed success and a good working relationship with that firm's senior director Walter Montgomerie Neilson, but the relationship between the two men effectively broke down and in 1863 they parted company.

In 1864 Dübs made the move in order to set up his own locomotive building business, having reportedly taken with him a number of Neilson's experienced locomotive engineers. The new company based on a site on the south side of Glasgow at Queen's Park Works and was originally known as The Glasgow Locomotive Works, later changing its name to Dübs & Co.

Dübs & Co built Midland Railway Johnson 5' 4" 0-4-4T BR No 58062 is seen looking a little unloved and work weary whilst getting away from Ockendon in 1955, with a local passenger service on a former London, Tilbury & Southend Railway (LTSR) route. This loco was delivered in February 1892 and withdrawn by BR in February 1956, (formerly Midland Railway No 360 and LMS No 1360). ***Dave Cobbe Collection/ Rail Photoprints Collection***

Under the skilled leadership of Dübs the company became extremely successful locomotive manufacturers and were proficient in attracting orders from railway operators in Europe, India, Russia, New Zealand and China. Whilst completing a series of prestigious export orders Dübs & Co also gained a significant amount of business from the domestic market earning a reputation for quality and reliability.

The distinctive Dübs & Company diamond-shaped works plate is believed to have been derived from the mark on the bricks used for building the Queen's Park Works. ***Keith Langston Collection***

It is interesting to note that Dübs & Co won orders for some locomotive classes from UK railway companies which were also simultaneously built by the other main Glasgow firms Neilson & Co/Neilson Reid & Co and Sharp, Stewart & Co.

A large proportion of the Midland Railway and Somerset & Dorset Joint Railway 0-6-0 3F (5' 3") locomotives, were collectively built by all four companies between 1890 and 1902. In 1948 British Railways took into stock a total of 324 of the class, and of those some 221 were Glasgow built!

In 1866 Dübs & Co were credited with being the first major engineering firm in Scotland to employ women as tracers in their drawing offices. Henry Dübs died in April 1876 and he was succeeded by William Lorimer, although the founder's family retained an interest in the firm. It is estimated that the company built in the region of 4,500 steam locomotives over approximately 39 years as sole traders.

By 1903 intense competition from American locomotive builders meant that the smaller companies were unable to compete in the rapidly growing world market. There was a recognised need for amalgamation in order to succeed in the competitive market place. Dübs & Co joined 'The Combine' and with two other established locomotive builders formed the North British Locomotive Co Ltd.

The Queen's Park Works, however, continued to be known locally as 'Dubses' for a long while after the amalgamation had taken place.

Dübs & Co built locomotive classes included in British Railway listings

LSWR '0415' 4-4-2T 1P (Adams Radial*)

This class of 71 engines, specifically intended for passenger work, was designed for the London & South Western Railway (LSWR) by William Adams and built between 1882 and 1885, 28 locomotives were built by Robert Stephenson & Co, 12 by Beyer, Peacock & Co Ltd and 31 were built north of the border, Dübs & Co produced 20 of the class. The SR began withdrawing the class in 1916 as suburban route electrification became operational and by 1928 only two remained in SR ownership and they were used for working the Lyme Regis Branch. In 1948 BR took into stock the 3 remaining 4-4-2T locomotives allocating them the numbers 30582 (LSWR No 125) a Robert Stephenson & Co locomotive, 30583 (LSWR No 488) a Neilson & Co locomotive and 30584 (LSWR No 520) a Dübs & Co locomotive. They were withdrawn in July 1961 with No 30583 being selected for preservation and bought by the Bluebell Railway.

See also LSWR '0415' 4-4-2T 1P (Adams Radial) locomotives built by Neilson & Co.

Driving wheel diameter 5' 7", 2-cylinder engine (outside)

'MSWJR' 2-4-0 1MT

In 1894 Dübs & Co built 3 locomotives of the 2-4-0 wheel arrangement for the Midland & South Western Junction Railway (MSWJR) to work as passenger engines on that railway's main line services they were numbered 10-12 by the MSWJR. In 1924 the Great Western Railway rebuilt the locomotives at Swindon with GWR style fittings, retaining their original cabs.

The 2-4-0s spent most of their working lives on the Lambourne branch and could often be seen at Didcot or Reading motive power depots. All 3 of the engines came into BR ownership with their former GWR numbers being 1334–1336. However, they did not survive long in traffic, with locomotives No 1334 and No 1335 being withdrawn in September 1952 and locomotive No 1336 being withdrawn in March 1954. The engines were amongst the very few 2-4-0 tender engines to be operated by BR.

Driving wheel diameter 5' 6", 2-cylinder engine (inside)

---

* A radial axle is an axle on a railway locomotive or carriage which has been designed to move laterally when entering a curve in order to reduce wear of both the wheel flanges and rails.

Dübs & Co built ex-'MSWJR' 2-4-0 1MT GWR/BR No 1334 is seen at Swindon towards the end of its working life. Someone has hopefully chalked SAVE under the cabside number plate, unfortunately that was not to be the case. *Mike Morant Collection*

Dübs & Co built ex-'MSWJR' 2-4-0 1MT GWR/BR No 1335 is seen on shed at Didcot in 1938. This loco was delivered to the M&SWJR in January 1894 and withdrawn by BR in September 1952. *Rail Photoprints Collection*

Dübs & Co built ex-'MSWJR' 2-4-0 1MT GWR/BR No 1336 is seen in near pristine condition, whilst posed on the turntable at Andover Junction in May 1953. That occasion was a Gloucester Railway Society rail charter named the 'M&SWJR Outing'. No 1336 headed the special on the Gloucester Central - Andover Junction (via Swindon) and the Andover Junction – Swindon sections, with 'Dukedog' 4-4-0 No 9023 taking over for the return trip to Gloucester Central. This loco was delivered to the M&SWJR in January 1894 and withdrawn by BR in March 1954. *Rail Photoprints Collection*

LSWR 'T9' 4-4-0 2P (reclassified 3P by BR in 1953)

This famous class of London & South Western Railway (LSWR) 4-4-0 express passenger locomotives was designed by Dugald Drummond and introduced between 1899 and 1901. The handsome looking engines earned the nickname 'Greyhounds' because of their sleek appearance and speedy qualities.

The class consisted of 66 locomotives and in the early part of the 20th Century they were in the front line as the LSWR strived to compete for passengers with the Great Western Railway (GWR) on the lucrative routes between London and the West of England.

The building was carried out at Nine Elms Works and by the contractor Dübs & Co who built a total of 31 engines, 30 in 1899 delivered as LSWR Nos 702–732 and one locomotive delivered in 1901 as LSWR No 773 and then renumbered by the SR as No 733 in 1924.

All of the locomotives were originally coupled to large 8-wheeled tenders (watercarts) however, later in their working lives some locomotives received smaller six-wheel tenders.

The Dübs built engines had several detailed differences from others of the class and they included the addition of Drummond's patented system of firebox water tubes, which were removed at the behest of SR engineer Robert Urie as later rebuilding of the class took place.

The rebuilding also included the fitting of superheaters, larger diameter cylinders and higher pressure boilers. The rebuilding of the engines was judged to be a great success and despite their modest power classification 'T9' 4-4-0s were often to be found working express services over the heavily graded lines between Salisbury and Exeter, even though larger engines could have been rostered instead.

Locomotives LSWR Nos 713, 722 and 731 were converted to oil burning during the Second World War period and the three were scrapped by BR in 1951, without being converted back to coal burners.

BR took into stock all 66 engines and they were allocated numbers in the series 30113-30122, 30280, 30338 and 30702–30733 (note for LSWR numbers disregard the 30 prefix). None of the class survived beyond the end of 1962 and the last Dübs built engines in service were numbers 30709, 30715 and 30717 which were all withdrawn by BR in July 1961.

Driving wheel diameter 6' 7", 2-cylinder engine (inside)

Dübs & Co, built 'T9' 4-4-0 BR No 30709 is pictured in June 1961 the loco had by then been in service for some 62 years and was withdrawn by BR during the following month. The 'T9' paused at Wadebridge East signal box prior to 'setting back' onto the stock in the station platform. ***David Anderson***

Dübs & Co, built 'T9' 4-4-0 BR No 30711 is seen outside Exeter Central station having just taken water in July 1956. However, the aging 'T9' looks well in the summer sunshine whilst waiting for her next turn of duty. This loco was delivered to the LSWR as No 711 in June 1899 and withdrawn by BR in August 1959. *David Anderson*

LSWR '700' 0-6-0 4F (reclassified 3F by BR in 1953)

Between 1876 and 1883 the North British Railway (NBR) built 133 Dugald Drummond designed 0-6-0 freight engines. The Caledonian Railway (CR) then built a further 244 of the type which became the LMS '2F' class 0-6-0s.

The '700' class 0-6-0 locomotives for the LSWR were almost identical to those built for the Scottish railway operators, and 30 locomotives were supplied by Dübs & Co in 1897, and all were coupled to six wheel tenders.

Dübs & Co built '700' class 'Black Motor' 0-6-0 BR No 30696 is seen over the ash pit at Feltham depot (70B) circa 1960. This loco was delivered to the LSWR as No 696 in March 1897 and withdrawn by BR in August 1961. Note the period Bedford 'CA' van in the right hand distance, a popular Vauxhall built small commercial vehicle also widely used by amateur popular music groups of the era. *Keith Langston Collection*

Between 1921 and 1929 the whole of the class was re-built by Robert Urie and that work included the fitting of superheaters, higher pressure boilers and larger diameter cylinders. The smokebox of the engines was also extended and to accommodate that modification the front end of the frames was increased by 18".

The '700' class were commonly referred to as 'Black Motors', although it is hard to imagine why as for most of their LSWR service lives they were painted dark green!

BR took into stock all 30 of the class in the number series 30306–30368 and 30687–30701 (note for LSWR numbers disregard the 30 prefix). None of the class survived beyond the end of 1962 and the last 6 working '700' 0-6-0s for BR were Nos 30315, 30316, 30325, 30368,30690 and 30695, all withdrawn in December 1962.

Driving wheel diameter 5' 1", 2-cylinder engine (inside)

SECR 'D' 4-4-0 1P

The South Eastern & Chatham Railway (SECR) introduced their Harry Wainwright designed 'D' class 4-4-0 and 51 locomotives which were built between 1900 and 1908. The 4-4-0 express passenger locomotives were built at Ashford Works and by the contractors Robert Stephenson & Co, Vulcan Foundry Ltd, Sharp, Stewart & Co and Dübs & Co. These elegant looking locomotives sported burnished brass domes and as a result they were nicknamed 'Coppertops'. A batch of 21 of the original engines was rebuilt between 1921 and 1927, becoming 'D1' class locomotives (Maunsell).

A total of 28 of the class came into BR ownership in the number series 31057–31750 (note for SECR numbers disregard the 31 prefix). Of the BR batch only 4 engines were Dübs built and they were allocated the BR Nos 31075, 31092, and in the series 31493–31501. The last of the 'Dübs 4' in traffic was No 31075 withdrawn by BR in December 1956.

See also SECR 'D' 4-4-0 1P locomotives built by Sharp, Stewart & Co.

Driving wheel diameter 6' 8", 2-cylinder engine (inside)

Dübs & Co built ex-SECR 'D' 4-4-0 1P, BR No 31075 is seen with a shunter's truck at Clapham Junction in August 1956. This loco was delivered to the SECR as No 75 in March 1903 and withdrawn by BR in December 1956. *Mike Morant Collection*

SECR 'D1' 4-4-0 2P (reclassified as 3P by BR in 1953)
The SECR introduced this class of 4-4-0 passenger locomotives between 1921 and 1927. The 21 engines were rebuilt to a design by Richard Maunsell. The engines were converted from round firebox 'D' class locomotives built at Ashford Works and by the contractors Robert Stephenson & Co, Vulcan Foundry Ltd, Sharp, Stewart & Co and Dübs & Co to become Belpaire boilered engines. One of the locomotives was withdrawn in 1944 but the others came into BR stock and were allocated numbers in the series 31145–31587 (note for SECR numbers disregard the 31 prefix). Of these locomotives 5 were from the original 'D' class Dübs & Co build and the last of those in traffic was No 31489 withdrawn in November 1961.

See also SECR 'D1' 4-4-0 2P locomotives built by Sharp, Stewart & Co.

Driving wheel diameter 6' 8", 2-cylinder engine (inside)

Dübs & Co built ex-SECR 'D1' class 4-4-0 is seen in May 1950 at Stewarts Lane depot (then 73A) note Southern lettering still on the tender but the 1948 BR allocated number on the cabside. This loco was delivered to the SECR as No 502 in May 1903 and withdrawn by BR in March 1951. *Mike Morant Collection*

Dübs & Co, built locomotive classes which came into British Railways ownership

Class	Wheel arrangement	Designer	Customer/ Number to BR	Build dates	BR number series*
'0415'	4-4-2T	Adams	LSWR 1 loco	1885	30584
'MSJW'	2-4-0	Dübs & Co	M&SWJR 3 locos	1894	1334–1336
'T9'	4-4-0	Drummond	LSWR 31 locos	1899/01	30702–30733
'700'	0-6-0	Drummond	LSWR 30 locos	1897	30306–30368 30687–30701
'D'	4-4-0	Wainwright	SECR 4 locos	1902/3	31075, 31092 31493, 31501
'D1'	4-4-0	Wainwright	SECR 5 locos	1902/3	31145, 31489 31492, 31494, 31502

* The BR numbers are given for identification in BR listings and do not take into account missing numbers due to scrapping, or locomotives of the same class built by other companies, but do include locomotives with allocated numbers not carried.

LTSR '3P' 4-4-2T

Between 1905 and 1911 the last remaining 12 engines of the former London, Tilbury & Southend Railway (LTSR) '1' class engines were rebuilt to form the basis of the new '37' class designed by Thomas Whitelegg (BR numbers 41953–41964). The class of engines became commonly known as the 'Tilbury Tanks' and the ex '1' class locomotives all carried names of locations on the LTSR, those locomotives were originally numbered 37–48 in the LTSR series. The engines were built at Derby Works and by the contractors Nasmyth, Wilson & Co, Robert Stephenson & Co, Sharp, Stewart & Co and Dübs & Co (6 engines to BR). In total 72 4-4-2T locomotives of the '1' and '37' class were built for the LTSR.

The ex '1' class ('37 class') batch of 12 engines were re-numbered first by the Midland Railway (MR) Nos 2146–2157 and then again by the LMS Nos 2135–2146.

BR took into stock 51 engines of this combined class in their number series 41928–41978. The 6 of those which were Dübs & Co built carried the BR Nos 41959–41964 (LMS 2141–2146) and they were delivered to the LTSR between December 1898 and January 1900.

None of these engines survived in traffic beyond the end of 1960 and the last Dübs built 4-4-2T was No 41961 withdrawn in October 1952.

See also LTSR '3P' 4-4-2T locomotives built by Sharp, Stewart & Co.

Driving wheel diameter 6' 6", 2-cylinder engine (outside)

MR '3F' 5' 3" 0-6-0 3F

This class of Samuel Waite Johnson designed locomotives was introduced by the Midland Railway (MR) between 1875 and 1902, some of which were rebuilds of the earlier MR '43137' class and also the former MR 2F '58188' class. Selected locomotives were given Belpaire fireboxes and Deeley style cabs by Fowler from 1903 onwards. They were built by Derby Works and contractors Kitson & Co, Sharp, Stewart & Co, Neilson, Reid & Co, Neilson & Co and Dübs &Co.

BR took into stock 324 of these 0-6-0 locomotives of which 48 were Dübs built, in the BR number series 43340–43369, 43410–43459 and 43630–43645. None of the class survived in service beyond 1964 and the last Dübs built example was No 43637 which was withdrawn by BR in February 1964.

See also 'MR Johnson 3F' 0-6-0 3F locomotives built by, Sharp, Stewart & Co, Neilson & Co and Neilson, Reid & Co.

Driving wheel diameter 5' 3", 2-cylinder engine (inside)

Dübs & Co built MR '3F' 5' 3" 0-6-0 3F BR No 43361 is seen approaching Kilnhurst circa 1957 with a mixed goods. This loco was delivered to the Midland Railway (MR) as No 61 in 1891 and withdrawn by BR in November 1960. *Mike Stokes Archive*

HR 'Loch' 4-4-0 2P

This Highland Railway class of 4-4-0 passenger engines was the last to be designed by David Jones and initially 15 of the locomotives were built by Dübs & Co in 1896, later the NBL constructed a further 3 engines bringing the class total to 18. The HR 'Loch' class engines were intended for the working of main line passenger trains and at the time of their introduction they were amongst the most powerful 4-4-0 locomotives in the country. As originally built the engines were fitted with piston valves which were later replaced by slide valves.

Withdrawal of the class began in 1930 consequently only 2 locomotives came into BR ownership they were HR No 119 (LMS No 14379 and BR No 54379) and HR No 125 (LMS No 14385 and BR No 54385). The locomotive allocated BR No 54379 was withdrawn in March 1949 and sister engine allocated BR No 54385 was withdrawn in April 1950, with neither carrying their allocated BR number. Both of those engines were rebuilt by the LMS with larger Caledonian Railway (CR) style boilers.

Driving wheel diameter 6' 3½", 2-cylinder engine (outside)

Highland Railway (HR) 'Loch' class 4-4-0 in its LMSR guise as No 14385 LOCH TAY is seen at Forres in July 1949. This was a Jones design built by Dübs & Co, which entered service as HR No 125 in 1896 and was withdrawn from service at Forres depot in April 1950 still carrying the LMS number 14385. As with a great many locomotive designs of the era it can be seen that the engine's cab afforded very little protection from the elements. *Mike Morant Collection*

HR 'Small Ben' 4-4-0 2P

In 1896 Peter Drummond (the perhaps not so well known brother of Dugald Drummond) succeeded David Jones at the Highland Railway and he introduced his own design of inside cylinder 4-4-0 locomotives, the two classes were named 'Small Ben' class built between 1898 and 1906 and 'Large Ben' class built between 1908 and 1909, the latter were all withdrawn between 1932 and 1937.

These were the first inside cylinder HR tender engines and observers immediately noted that they were in fact very similar in design to the Dugald Drummond 'T9' class. The 'Small Ben' class total was 20 locomotives (HR Nos 397–416 and LMS Nos 14397–14416) with 10 of those engines coming into BR stock, and being allocated numbers in the series 54397–54416.

The BR total included 6 engines built by Dübs & Co, 2 engines built at Lochgorm Works and 2 engines built by the NBL, all of the class carried the names of Scottish Bens. One of the class No 54399 BEN WYVIS was later fitted with a stovepipe style chimney.

None of the class survived beyond the end of 1953 and the last Dübs built engine in BR service was No 54398 BEN ALDER withdrawn in the February of that year, and therein hangs a tale!

Still carrying a Wick (60D) shedplate withdrawn ex Highland 'Ben' class 4-4-0 54398 BEN ALDER is seen at Lochgorm (Inverness) works in May 1953. This is the loco generally referred to as 'The one that got away'. *Mike Morant Collection/ Rail Photoprints*

After being withdrawn the engine was stored out of used in the hope that the HR 4-4-0 locomotive would be preserved. However, after many years No 54398 was removed from store and instead of being preserved was cut up for scrap in 1966. This has since led to Scottish railway enthusiasts often referring to that engine as 'The one that got away'!

See also HR 'Small Ben' 4-4-0 2P locomotives built at Lochgorm Works and by the NBL.

Driving wheel diameter 6' 0", 2-cylinder engine (inside)

CR '812' 0-6-0 3F

The Caledonian Railway (CR) introduced this John Farquharson McIntosh designed class of 0-6-0 freight locomotives between 1899 and 1900. The engines were built at St Rollox Works and by contractors Sharp, Stewart & Co, Neilson Reid & Co and Dübs & Co; they were an enlarged version of the CR 'Jumbo' class engines. BR took into stock 76 of these engines and allocated to them numbers in the series 57550–57628.

The class was originally collectively referred to as mixed traffic (MT) engines however, only 20 locomotives were fitted with Westinghouse brakes and 5 with vacuum brakes for passenger train working. Of the BR total 14 were Dübs & Co built

Dübs & Co built CR '812' 0-6-0 3F BR No 57604 is seen stored at Carstairs as withdrawn and awaiting scrapping in June 1963. This loco was delivered to the CR in May 1900 and withdrawn by BR in December 1962. The 0-6-0 is in the company of withdrawn Derby built ex LMS Fairburn 2-6-4T BR No 42173. *Rail Photoprints Collection*

Dübs & Co built McIntosh designed 0-6-0 for the Caledonian Railway, seen as LMS No 17611, at an unknown location, circa 1934. This loco was delivered in May 1900, became BR No 57611 and was withdrawn in November 1962. *Rail Photoprints Collection*

locomotives numbered 57602–57616 which were delivered between March and April 1900 as CR Nos 864–878 (LMS Nos 17602-17616). None of the class remained in traffic after 1963 and the last surviving Dübs engine was No 57605 withdrawn by BR in March 1963. Locomotives No 57606 and No 57616 were scrapped in 1948 and never carried their allocated BR numbers.

See also CR '812' 0-6-0 3F locomotives built at St Rollox Works, Sharp, Stewart & Co and Neilson, Reid & Co.

Driving wheel diameter 5' 0", 2-cylinder engine (inside)

HR 'Barney' 0-6-0 3F

Peter Drummond designed this Highland Railway, Dübs & Co built freight class of locomotives which were introduced between 1900 and 1907 and it is not entirely clear why they earned the nickname 'Barneys'. Most of the engines in the class were later fitted with Caledonian Railway style boilers but 2 locomotives retained their HR boilers (57695 and 57699) engine No 57697 was later fitted with a stovepipe chimney.

BR took into stock 7 of the class and allocated them numbers in the series 57693–57702 (HR Nos 134–136, 138, 139, 18, 21 and LMS 17693–17699, 17702) however only 3 of the class ever carried their allocated BR numbers 57695, 57697 and 57698. None survived in service beyond January 1952 with No 57695 being the last to be withdrawn.

Driving wheel diameter 5' 0", 2-cylinder engine (inside)

Dübs & Co built Highland Railway 'Barney' class 0-6-0 in its LMSR guise as No 17693 but the date and location of this shot is not documented. This loco entered service as HR No134 in 1900 and was withdrawn from service at Corkerhill depot in June 1949, but never had its allotted BR number applied (57693). Note the diamond shaped maker's plate on the centre splasher in addition to a St Rollox works plate on the leading splasher. *Mike Morant Collection*

Dübs & Co, built locomotive classes which came into British Railways ownership

Class	Wheel arrangement	Designer	Customer/ Number to BR	Build dates	BR number series*
'3P'	4-4-2T	Whitelegg	LTSR 6 locos	1898/99	41959–41964
MR '3F' 5' 3"	0-6-0	Johnson	MR/SDJR 48 locos	1891 1892/93 1900	43340–43369 43410–43459 43630–43645
'Loch'	4-4-0	Jones	HR 2 locos	1895/96	54379, 54385
'Small Ben'	4-4-0	Drummond	HR 6 locos	1898/99	54397–54399 54301 54303–54304
'812'	0-6-0	McIntosh	CR 14 locos	1900	57602–57616
'Barney' 3F	0-6-0	Drummond	HR 7 locos	1900	57693–57695 57697–57699 57702

* The BR numbers are given for identification in BR listings and do not take into account missing numbers due to scrapping, or locomotives of the same class built by other companies, but do include locomotives with allocated numbers not carried.

MR '1P' 6' 6" 2-4-0

Samuel W. Johnson designed this class of 6' 6" driving wheel diameter passenger locomotives for the Midland Railway (MR) and 40 of them were introduced between 1876 and 1880. Dübs & Co built 30 of these engines as MR '1282' class which were originally numbered in the MR series 157–186 and later renumbered 1282–1311. Some of the class were later rebuilt with Belpaire boilers by the LMS.

In 1934 the survivors of the class were transferred to the LMS Duplicate List with 20000 being added to their numbers but only one locomotive came into BR stock that being a Belpaire boilered variant which was allocated (but never carried BR No 58021) and that engine was scrapped in 1948.

Driving wheel diameter 6' 6½", 2-cylinder engine (inside)

MR '1P' 5' 4" 0-4-4T

This class was made up of locomotives from the MR second and third batches of this locomotive type which were originally numbered 1266–1430. Of the original total of 165 engines built by Derby Works, Neilson & Co and Dübs & Co only 56 came into BR stock in the number series 58039–58091, and of those several never carried their BR allocated numbers.

The Dübs & Co built examples introduced from 1889 onwards were constructed with boilers of a higher working pressure rating (150 psi, other locomotives 140 psi), and several engines were amongst a batch of variants fitted with condensing apparatus for working through the Metropolitan tunnels on the London suburban services.

The Dübs engines were allocated BR numbers in the series 58059–58067 (LMS 1353–1370), 58073–58077 (LMS 1382–1397), 58080–58091(LMS 1411–1430). However, Dübs locomotives LMS Nos 1361, 1365, 1366, 1370, 1385, 1389, 1402, 1406 and 1413 never carried their allocated BR numbers.

None of the class survived in service beyond 1960 and the last Dübs & Co engine to remain in BR service was No 58065 withdrawn in November 1959.

See also MR '1P' 5' 4" 0-4-4T locomotives built by Neilson & Co.

Driving wheel diameter 5' 4", 2-cylinder engine (inside)

GNR/M&GNJR 'J3' 'J4' 0-6-0 2F

Between them Patrick Stirling and Henry A. Ivatt introduced 302 freight locomotives of the 0-6-0 configuration for the Midland & Great Northern Joint Railway (M&GNR) and the Great Northern Railway (GNR) between 1892 and 1901. The locomotives were built at Doncaster Works and by the contractors Vulcan Foundry Ltd, Kitson & Co and Dübs & Co. The Stirling designed engines originally had round domeless boilers and round topped cabs. The engines were later designated as 'J3' and 'J4' class respectively.

The LNER 'J3' engines previously being the GNR 'J4' class engines rebuilt by Gresley between 1912 and 1928 with larger diameter boilers (4' 8"), in total 153 of the class were rebuilt. The LNER 'J4' class previously being the GNR 'J5' class Ivatt engines built as a development of an earlier Stirling design. In 1937 the LNER took over the M&GNR and that railway's 0-6-0 'J3' and 'J4' engines were added to the total.

BR took into stock 33 'J3' class engines and allocated them numbers between 64105 and 64163 and 8 'J4' class engines allocating those engines numbers between 64109 and 64167. Of those combined class totals only 17 locomotives ever carried their allocated BR numbers, the balance being withdrawn without re-numbering between 1948 and 1951.

Of the 17 'J3'/'J4' engines in BR service 8 were Dübs & Co built, BR Nos 64116, 64118, 64119, 64122, 64125, 64129, 64153 and 64160, and the last of those in traffic being No 64125 which was withdrawn in December 1953.

Driving wheel diameter 5' 2", 2-cylinder engine (inside)

Dübs & Co built GNR/M&GNJR 'J3' 0-6-0 2F LNER No 4124 (BR No 64124 never carried) is pictured at Retford Great Central depot (36E) in 1949, note the badly scorched smokebox door doubtlessly caused by a build up of hot ash. This loco was delivered to the GNR in March 1899 as No 113 and officially withdrawn by BR in September 1951. *Rail Photoprints Collection*

Dübs & Co, built locomotive classes which came into British Railways ownership

Class	Wheel arrangement	Designer	Customer/ Number to BR	Build dates	BR number series*
'1P' 6' 6"	2-4-0	Johnson	MR 1 loco	1876	58021
'1P' 5' 4"	0-4-4T	Johnson	MR 28 locos	1892	58059–58067 58073–58077 58080–58091
'J3'	0-6-0	Stirling/Ivatt	GNR/M&GNJR 19 locos	1896 1898/99 1900/01	64106–64110 64114–64129 64152–64167
'J4'	0-6-0	Stirling/Ivatt	GNR/M&GNJR 5 locos		64109–64110 64120–64121 64160

* The BR numbers are given for identification in BR listings and do not take into account missing numbers due to scrapping, or locomotives of the same class built by other companies, but do include locomotives with allocated numbers not carried.

MR '58110' Double Framed 2F 0-6-0

The Midland railway (MR) built the first of Matthew Kirtley's double framed 0-6-0 locomotives in 1863. Several hundred locomotives of the design were built between that date and 1874 and they were successful in traffic with many of them recording a long service life and originally referred to as the '700' class. Some were withdrawn before 1907 and a batch of locomotives was temporarily transferred to the Railway Operating Division (ROD) of the British army before and during the First World War, all later returning safely to the MR.

This class of engines were built at Derby Works (26 engines) and by the contractors John Fowler & Co (10 engines), Kitson & Co (10 engines), Vulcan Foundry Ltd (80 engines), Neilson & Co (40 engines) and Dübs & Co (150 engines).

Post 1907 they carried numbers in the MR series 2592–2617 and 2672–2681 but only one of the class survived long enough to become BR stock, that locomotive was from the Dübs & Co built batch of 1870. Formerly MR No 2630 it became LMS Duplicate List locomotive No 22630 and was allocated the BR number 58110. When No 58110 was withdrawn in November 1951 it was 81 years old!

Driving wheel diameter 5' 3", 2-cylinder engine (inside)

MR '58111' Double Framed (Belpaire Boilered) 2F 0-6-0

These Matthew Kirtley designed engines were all members of the '58110' class (ex MR '700' class) which had been rebuilt with Belpaire boilers. The survivors were transferred to the LMS Duplicate List with 20000 added to their numbers. There were 3 Dübs & Co 1873/74 built examples, engines Nos 22846, 22853 and 22863 which were allocated BR Nos 58111–58113, the engines never carried their BR numbers and were scrapped 1949/51.

Driving wheel diameter 5' 3", 2-cylinder engine (inside)

Kirtley ex-MR/LMS 2F 0-6-0 No 22863 built by Dubs and Co in 1874 and later converted to a Belpaire boiler type. The engine was allocated to Bournville (21B) from where it regularly worked trains over the weight restricted Halesowen branch. The engine is seen late in its working life just prior to being withdrawn and scrapped at Derby Works in 1949. The Kirtley 0-6-0 never carried its BR allocated number (58113). ***John Day Collection/Rail Photoprints***

MR '2F' 4' 11" 0-6-0

This class of Johnson designed locomotives was a development of the MR designer's 'Class 2' engines which dated from 1875. They were the forerunners of several classes of 0-6-0 inside framed engines. The 4' 11" '2F' 0-6-0 were introduced between 1875 and 1902 and were built by Derby Works and the contractors Kitson & Co, Beyer, Peacock & Co, Neilson & Co and Dübs & Co. BR took into stock 96 of the class allocating to them numbers in the series 58114–58187 and 58229–58248 amongst those the Dübs built examples were numbered 58129–58145 and they were all delivered during 1875 (earlier numbers LMS Duplicate List 22931–22959). The majority of these engines were rebuilt with Belpaire fireboxes from 1917 onwards however, Nos 58134 and 58141 (both withdrawn in 1948) retained their round topped Johnson fireboxes.

None of the class survived in service beyond 1964 and the last Dübs & Co built engine to remain in BR service was No 58143 which was withdrawn in November 1963.

See also MR '2F' 4' 11" 0-6-0 locomotives built by Neilson & Co,

Driving wheel diameter 4' 11" 2-cylinder engine (inside)

Dübs & Co built MR '2F' 4' 11" 0-6-0 BR No 58143 is seen shunting stock at Bournville, circa 1959. This loco was delivered in 1875 and was the last Dübs & Co built member of the class to be withdrawn by BR. *Rail Photoprints Collection*

MR '2F' 5' 3" 0-6-0

This class of Johnson designed 0-6-0 locomotives for the Midland Railway was introduced between 1878 and 1902 and they were a 5' 3" diameter driving wheel version of the 58114–58248 series of engines. They were built at Derby Works and additionally by the contractors Robert Stephenson & Co, Beyer, Peacock & Co, Sharp, Stewart & Co, Kitson & Co, Vulcan Foundry, Neilson, Reid & Co, Neilson & Co and Dübs & Co. During the period of the Second World War 40 engines of this class were loaned to the Great Western Railway (GWR).

BR took into stock 109 of the class allocating to them numbers in the series 58188–58228 and 58249–58310. None of the class survived in service beyond 1962.

The Dübs built examples were numbered 58188–58194, 58256, 58260–58265, 58297 and 58298 (MR numbers in the series 3021–3039, 3360, 3420–3451, 3632 and 3648) and the last of those in BR service was No 58260 which was withdrawn by BR in December 1960. It should be noted that 5 of the Dübs & Co built engines never carried their allocated BR numbers, all being scrapped in 1948.

See also MR '2F' 5' 3" 0-6-0 locomotives built by Sharp, Stewart & Co, Neilson & Co and Neilson, Reid & Co.

Driving wheel diameter 5' 3", 2-cylinder engine (inside)

Dübs & Co built MR '2F' 5' 3" 0-6-0 BR No 58298 at Glenfield on the Leicester West Bridge branch during a Leicester Railway Society event in 1952 in May 1952. This loco was delivered to the MR in 1900 and withdrawn by BR in November 1960. ***Rail Photoprints Collection***

Dübs & Co, built locomotive classes which came into British Railways ownership

Class	Wheel arrangement	Designer	Customer/ Number to BR	Build dates	BR number series*
'2F' double frame	0-6-0	Kirtley	MR 1 loco	1870	58110
'2F' double frame Belpaire Boilered	0-6-0	Kirtley	MR 3 locos	1873	58111-58113
'2F' 4' 11"	0-6-0	Johnson	MR 17 locos	1875	58129-58145
'2F' 5' 3"	0-6-0	Johnson	MR 17 locos	1878 1878 1892 1899/00	3021(MR) 58188-58194 58260-58265 58297, 58298

* The BR numbers are given for identification in BR listings and do not take into account missing numbers due to scrapping, or locomotives of the same class built by other companies, but do include locomotives with allocated numbers not carried.

Railway Company abbreviations used in this chapter.

CR – Caledonian Railway, **GNR** – Great Northern Railway**, HR** – Highland Railway **MR** – Midland Railway, **LSWR** – London & South Western Railway, **LTSR** London, Tilbury & Southend Railway, **M&GNJR** – Midland & Great Northern Joint Railway, **M&SWJR** – Midland & South Western Joint Railway, **SECR** – South Eastern & Chatham Railway, **S&DJR** – Somerset & Dorset Joint Railway

Chapter 5

GRANT, RITCHIE & COMPANY

The Kilmarnock based company of Grant, Ritchie & Co (GR) was founded circa 1879 reportedly following what was described at the time as a 'disastrous fire' at the Caledonia Works of locomotive builders Andrew Barclay. Former Andrew Barclay works manager Thomas Grant left that company and together with another former employee William Ritchie set up a new engineering venture. They chose a premises previously occupied by the firm Grant Brothers which was situated just down the road from their former employers.

Rumours to the effect that both men were seen leaving the Barclay works under the cover of darkness and whilst carrying bundles of engineering drawings circulated at the time. Whether the allegation was true or false remains unproven! However, it would be fair to say that the saddle tank locomotives which the new enterprise went on to produce did exhibit more than a passing resemblance to similar locomotives of a Barclay design. However, distinctive features of the Grant, Ritchie engines included double-lever safety valves on the steam dome and outside cylinders which incorporated single slide bars.

Between 1879 and 1920 GR built in the region of 47 steam locomotives which were in the main supplied to operators serving the Scottish coal and steel industry (43 engines built to the standard gauge) at Townholme Engine Works, Kilmarnock. The company were also recognised in their own right as leading manufacturers of colliery winding gear.

Former Fife Coal Company Ltd 0-4-0ST which operated at Kinglassie Colliery as loco LESLIE No 21 was the 14th engine built by GR and outshopped in 1894 (GR works number 272). That locomotive was rescued for restoration to working order and during 2013 it was still a work in progress at the Ribble Steam Railway, Preston. *See* www.ribblesteam.org.uk/

Grant Ritchie locomotive number 536 dating from 1914 is a 0-4-2ST engine which was built for the Lothian Coal Company and operated at Newbattle Colliery, as loco No 7. That engine is preserved in working order and is in the care of the Scottish Society for the Preservation of Industrial Machinery and in 2012 it was based at Prestongrange Museum, East Lothian. See www.prestongrange.org.

No GR built locomotives passed via any of the 'Big Four' railway companies into BR stock.

Former Fife Coal Company Ltd 0-4-0ST LESLIE No 21, a Kinglassie Colliery outside cylinder loco built by Grant Ritchie & Co and outshopped in 1894 (GR works number 272). This locomotive was rescued for restoration to working order and during April 2013 it was still a work in progress at the Ribble Steam Railway, Preston. *Fred Kerr*

Chapter 6

DICK, KERR & CO

Dick, Kerr & Company (DK) was an engineering company formed circa 1883 who originally occupied the Britannia Engineering Works, Kilmarnock, Scotland (and later at a factory in Preston, England). The firm was formed by the amalgamation of W.B. Dick & Co with John Kerr & Co thereafter trading as Dick, Kerr & Company. Circa 1883 DK took over the company of locomotive builders Barr, Morrison & Company who formerly traded as Alan Andrews & Co.

From its inception until 1919 the company, which was also associated with tramway activities and gas engine production, built in the region of 50 tramway and industrial type steam locomotives to various loading gauges. A good proportion of the firm's engines were made for export.

Following the formation of a trading partnership with the English Electric Manufacturing Company DK gained access to an additional manufacturing facility in Preston, Lancashire. In 1919 the Kilmarnock works were sold to the Kilmarnock Engineering Company and the activities of the company Dick, Kerr & Co were then concentrated at the Preston site. That company was later taken over by the English Electric Co. Until the late 1890s the company had largely produced steam tramway engines however, in the years that followed it became one of Britain's largest manufacturers of electric tramway cars.

The British based customers to whom DK supplied standard gauge shunting locomotives included Joseph Rank Ltd Flour Millers of Birkenhead, John Cashmore Newport Ltd, Cadbury Brothers Ltd Bournville, the Ministry of Munitions, the Admiralty and several and municipal power companies. No DK built locomotives passed via any of the 'Big Four' railway companies into BR stock.

Dick, Kerr built 0-6-0T dating from 1915 is seen at Stanton Ironworks in July 1957, as that owner's STANTON 22 locomotive. No 22 was built as an outside 2-cylinder engine with 3 foot 6 inch diameter driving wheels. This engine was originally supplied to the Ministry of Munitions, Chilwell, Nottingham. *Rail Photoprints Collection*

Chapter 7

SHARP, STEWART & CO, GLASGOW

Sharp, Stewart & Company was a steam locomotive manufacturer initially based in Manchester, England. The company was formed in 1843 upon the demise of a former company Sharp, Roberts & Co. The company established at Atlas Works in the Great Bridgewater area of Manchester and in addition to locomotive manufacturing they were active as boiler makers, ironfounders, machine makers, millwrights, toolmakers and dealers.

The firm moved to Glasgow in 1888. At that time they were also dealing in general brass, ironmongery, and machine tools and a change of premises was necessary mainly for two reasons, firstly they were seriously short of manufacturing space and secondly the lease on their Manchester site had expired.

To facilitate the move north they took over the premises of the company previously trading there and known as the Clyde Locomotive Works in Glasgow. In acknowledgement to their 45 year history in Manchester they renamed the Glasgow site Atlas Works.

In 1889 the company began manufacturing a number of compound type locomotives for the Argentine Central Railway, the locomotives were built in 4-4-0 and 2-8-0 configurations and were reportedly very successful in traffic.

Sharp, Stewart & Co famously built the first 4-6-0 wheel arrangement locomotives for use by a British railway company. Ex Highland Railway 'Jones Goods' 4-6-0 is seen as LMS No 17929 (formerly HR No 116) on the turntable at Inverness shed. Note that the loco is fitted with a tablet catcher and snowplough. ***Mike Morant Collection***

A Sharp, Stewart & Co works plate dating from 1894. *Keith Langston*

In 1892 the firm received an order from the Midland Railway (MR) for a total of 75 4-4-0 and 0-6-0 locomotives and continued to build a number of 4-6-0 locomotives for export.

In 1894 the Highland Railway ordered 15 freight engines of the then ground breaking 4-6-0 wheel arrangement which had been designed by David Jones. The class was a big advance on anything else operated by the Highland Railway and the outside cylinder engines with 5' 3" diameter driving wheels were very successful and were later power rated at 4F by the LMS. They were also the first tender locomotives for the railway not to have 'Allan' double frames and inclined cylinders beside the smokebox.

In 1903 the company amalgamated with two other Glasgow based established locomotive manufacturers in order to form the North British Locomotive Co. By the time the company became part of the 'Combine' they had reportedly built over 5000 steam locomotives in their own right.

Sharp, Stewart & Co built locomotive classes included in British Railway (BR) listings

North London Railway, Crane 0-4-2ST 0F

This locomotive was built in 1858 as a 0-4-0ST for the North & South West Junction Railway which later became the North London Railway and it was the oldest engine to be inherited by BR. In 1872 this locomotive was re-built as a 0-4-2ST when it was given square saddle tanks and fitted with a crane. Originally NLR No 29A it then became LNWR No 2896 and later LMS No 7217. In 1948 it was allocated the BR No 58865 in 1949 and withdrawn in February 1951.

Driving wheel diameter 3' 10", 2-cylinder engine (inside)

Barry Railway 'B' and 'B1' 0-6-2T 3F

Designed for the Barry Railway in South Wales by J.H. Hosgood the 'B' and 'B1' class of 0-6-2T locomotives were introduced between 1888 and 1900. The 'B1' class engines were effectively enlarged versions of an earlier 'B' class tank engine which were themselves enlarged versions of Barry Railway 'A' class 0-6-2T.

The 'B' class numbered some 25 engines and those which survived into GWR ownership were re-boilered at Swindon circa 1924. A total of 4 'B' class tank engines were taken into BR stock but all of those were withdrawn by BR early in 1948 and 1949, and the last in traffic was No 231 withdrawn in November 1949.

Sharp, Stewart & Co built ex Barry Railway 0-6-2T No 258 is seen at Swindon Works in late September 1950, still a serviceable engine almost a year after being withdrawn. This loco was delivered in December 1894 and officially withdrawn in November 1949 but was not scrapped until January 1953. *Rail Photoprints Collection*

The 'B1' class numbered 42 engines the majority of which were built by Sharp, Stewart & Co but a smaller number were constructed to the same design by Vulcan Foundry Ltd. After taking ownership of the class the GWR re-boilered all but 5 of the class in 1924, in total 20 'B1' class engines came into BR stock with all of them being withdrawn during BR's first 3 years, the last surviving examples in traffic being No 270 and No 271, which were both withdrawn in May 1951. Several examples survived for a short while after being officially withdrawn and they worked as works shunters at Swindon.

Driving wheel diameter 4' 3", 2-cylinder engine (inside)

Cambrian Railways 2-4-0T (Not power rated)
In 1866 Sharp, Stewart & Co built 3 2-4-0T type locomotives for the Cambrian Railways. When taken into GWR stock the locomotives were numbered and named 1192 MAGNOLIA, 1196 GLADYS and 1197 SEAHAM. Loco No 1192 was scrapped by the GWR in 1929 but the other two members of the class were re-built using standard Swindon fittings and new boilers in 1923/24 and became listed as 'Small Side Tanks'. The locomotives were delivered in May 1866 and both operated for a time on the Tanant Valley Line, the 2-4-0Ts were withdrawn by BR in April 1948.

Driving wheel diameter 4' 6", 2-cylinder engine (inside)

Port Talbot Rly 0-8-2T (Not power rated)
The Port Talbot Railway in South Wales famously operated a total of 5 locomotives with the 0-8-2T wheel arrangement the first two of which were built in the USA and scrapped by the railway in 1928/29. Sharp, Stewart & Co built a further 3 of the type and delivered them to the PTR during 1902. The design was based on a Barry Railway class of 7 similarly configured engines originally introduced by that company in 1896.

Only one of the engines survived into BR stock and that loco GWR No 1358 was scrapped in February 1948. Earlier in GWR ownership the loco was fitted with a Swindon style boiler and smokebox.

Driving wheel diameter 4' 3", 2-cylinder engine (outside)

Sharp, Stewart & Co built locomotive classes which came into British Railways ownership

Class	Wheel arrangement	Designer	Customer/ Number to BR	Build dates	BR number series*
Crane	0-4-2ST	Sharp, Stewart	NLR	1858 rebuilt 1872	58865
'B'	0-6-2T	Hosgood	BR 1 loco	1890	231
'B1'	0-6-2T	Hosgood	BR 12 locos	1894/00	258–272
'Cam2'	2-4-0T	Sharp, Stewart Co	CR 2 locos	1866	1196–1197
'PT2'	0-8-2T	Sharp, Stewart Co	PTR 1 loco	1902	1358

*The BR numbers are given for identification in BR listings and do not take into account missing numbers due to scrapping, or locomotives of the same class built by other companies, but do include locomotives with allocated numbers not carried.

SECR 'C' 0-6-0 3F (re-classified 2F in 1953)
The South Eastern & Chatham Railway introduced a Harry Wainwright designed 0-6-0 freight/mixed traffic engine which was designated that railway's 'C' class, between 1900 and 1908. A total of 109 0-6-0 'C' class engines were built at Ashford Works, Longhedge Works and by the contractors Neilson, Reid & Co, Sharp, Stewart & Co, and BR took into stock 106 of the class allocating to them numbers in the series 31004–31725, and of those locomotives Nos 31711–31725 (SECR Nos 711–725) were Sharp, Stewart & Co built between December 1900 and January 1901.

Apart from 2 engines which were transferred to the service stock pool none of the class remained in traffic with BR after 1963, the last Sharp, Stewart & Co built example being No 31719 withdrawn in May 1962.

See also SECR 'C' 0-6-0 3F locomotives built by Neilson, Reid & Co.

Driving wheel diameter 5' 2", 2-cylinder engine (inside)

Sharp, Stewart & Co built 'C' class 0-6-0 BR No 31719 is seen at Stewarts Lane (73A) in May 1961. This locomotive was delivered in January 1901 and withdrawn by BR in May 1962. *Rail Photoprints Collection*

Sharp, Stewart & Co built Wainwright 'C' class 0-6-0 BR No 31724 seen with a snowplough attached at Brighton (75A) circa 1955. This locomotive was delivered in January 1901 and withdrawn by BR in April 1962. *Rail Photoprints Collection*

SECR 'D' and 'D1' 4-4-0 1P

The South Eastern & Chatham Railway (SECR) introduced their Harry Wainwright designed 'D' class 4-4-0 and 51 locomotives which were built between 1900 and 1908. The 4-4-0 express passenger locomotives were built at Ashford Works and by the contractors Robert Stephenson & Co, Vulcan Foundry Ltd, Dübs & Co and Sharp, Stewart & Co. A batch of 21 of the original engines was rebuilt between 1921 and 1927, becoming 'D1' class locomotives (Maunsell).

A total of 28 of the class came into BR ownership in the number series 31057–31750 (note for SECR numbers disregard the 31 prefix). Of the BR batch 7 engines were Dübs built and they were allocated BR numbers in the series 31728–31734. The last of those in traffic was No 31734 withdrawn by BR in November 1955.

See also SECR 'D' 4-4-0 1P locomotives built by Dübs & Co.

Driving wheel diameter 6' 8", 2-cylinder engine (inside)

Sharp, Stewart & Co built Wainwright 'D' class 4-4-0 BR No 31733 at Bricklayers Arms (73B) in March 1952. This locomotive was delivered in April 1901 and withdrawn by BR in December 1963. *Rail Photoprints Collection*

Sharp, Stewart & Co built Wainwright 'D' 4-4-0 BR No 31727 seen as a rebuilt 'D1' class engine with a down South Eastern Division local service, circa 1952 in an uncertain location. This locomotive was delivered in January 1901 and withdrawn by BR in March 1961. *John Day Collection/Rail Photoprints Collection*

Sharp, Stewart & Co built Wainwright 'D' class engine seen as re-built 'D1' class 4-4-0 BR No 31735 emerges from the tunnel on the approach to Chatham with a down local service, circa 1953. This locomotive was delivered in November 1901 and withdrawn by BR in April 1961. ***John Day Collection/Rail Photoprints Collection***

SECR '01' 0-6-0 1F

Between 1878 and 1899 the South Eastern Railway introduced their first James Stirling designed class of 0-6-0 freight engines, which were designated as 'O' class. The 0-6-0s were built at Ashford Works and by Sharp, Stewart & Co of Glasgow, as designed the engines had a Stirling type domeless boiler and rounded top cabs.

The SECR took delivery of 122 of the class of which 65 were Glasgow built to the following order numbers E758 for 20 locomotives, E984 for 10 locomotives, E1024 for 20 locomotives and E 1100 for 15 locomotives, all 65 engines were delivered between October 1878 and October 1897.

Between 1903 and 1927 58 of the class were re-built to a Harry Wainwright design with domed boilers and new cabs those engines were then designated 'O1' class.

BR took into stock 55 'O1' class locomotives of which 33 were Sharp, Stewart & Co built. They were allocated numbers in the BR/SR series 31369 to 31439 (SECR Nos 369–349) however, only 6 of those remained in traffic long enough to carry their allocated numbers, those engines were Nos 31370, 31378, 31383, 31425, 31430 and 31434. The last of the Sharp, Stewart & Co examples to remain in traffic was No 31370 which was withdrawn by BR in February 1960. Ashford Works built example No 31065 which is preserved.

Driving wheel diameter 5' 2", 2-cylinder engine (inside)

Sharp, Stewart & Co built SECR '01' class 0-6-0 1F BR No 31434 is seen at Eythorne on the former East Kent Railway with a London, Chatham & Dover Railway (LCDR) rail tour on the 19 May 1957. This was actually a top 'n' tailed train with another Glasgow built '01' BR No 31425, which is out of sight in this picture, and that locomotive delivered in August 1897 was withdrawn by BR in August 1958. Featured locomotive No 31434 was delivered in September 1897 and was withdrawn by BR in August 1959. ***Mike Morant Collection***

Sharp, Stewart & Co built locomotive classes which came into British Railways ownership

Class	Wheel arrangement	Designer	Customer/ Number to BR	Build dates	BR number series*
'C'	0-6-0	Wainwright	SECR 15 locos	1900/01	31711–31725
'D'	4-4-0	Wainwright	SECR 7 locos	1903	31728–31734
'D1'	4-4-0	Wainwright	SECR 2 locos	1901	31727, 31735
'O1'	0-6-0	Stirling	SECR 33 locos	1891/97	31369–31439

*The BR numbers are given for identification in BR listings and do not take into account missing numbers due to scrapping, or locomotives of the same class built by other companies, but do include locomotives with allocated numbers not carried.

LCDR (SECR) 'R' and 'R1' 0-4-4T 1P

The London, Chatham & Dover Railway (LCDR) introduced a class of 0-4-4T passenger tank locomotives from a design by William Kirtley in 1891/92 and those 18 locomotives were built by Sharp, Stewart & Co. The whole of the class was later rebuilt with 'H' class boilers and the first of those was withdrawn in 1929. In 1900 a further 15 engines to an almost identical design were introduced by the SECR and those engines were designated 'R1' class.

BR took into stock 15 of the class, allocating them numbers in the series 31658 to 31675 (SECR Nos 1658–1675) and all but 2 of the engines carried their allocated BR numbers in traffic. Most of the later surviving members of the class were fitted for push pull working however none survived beyond December 1955 the last to be withdrawn being No 31666.

Driving wheel diameter 5' 6", 2-cylinder engine (inside)

Sharp, Stewart & Co built ex-LCDR/SECR 'R1' class BR No 31671 is seen with the RCTS 'Invicta Special' on 12 September 1954. The tour was predominantly an East Kent affair, but rather strangely started from Liverpool Street behind a pair of ex-GER 'J69' 0-6-0T's which took the train under the Thames to Blackheath No 1 siding where the Southern took over proceedings for the rest of the day. This shot's location is in all probability Faversham and features the Kirtley 0-4-4T BR No 31671 which was in charge of the legs from Rainham to Sheerness and thence to Sittingbourne and Faversham. Delivered in November 1991 No 31671 was one of the last of the class in service and was withdrawn by BR in November 1954. *Mike Morant Collection*

Sharp, Stewart & Co built ex LCDR/SECR 'R1' class BR No 31665 is seen pre-1951 whilst coupled with 'Articulated Coach Set No 514' and van at Leysdown on the Sheppey Light Railway. This locomotive was delivered in October 1891 and was withdrawn by BR in October 1952. *Mike Morant Collection*

LBSCR 'B4' 1P and 'B4X' 3P 4-4-0

The London, Brighton & South Coast Railway (LBSCR) introduced 33 new 4-4-0 passenger locomotives between 1899 and 1902 as that railway's 'B4' class. They were designed by Robert John Billinton and built at Brighton Works and by Sharp, Stewart & Co who built 25 of the class in 1901 and a further 5 in 1902. In total 33 of the design were built and the locomotives were named.

Between 1922 and 1924 a total of 12 of the class were re-built by L B Billinton and those locomotives were designated 'B4X' class. In 1948 BR took into stock 7 of the original 'B4' class engines of which 5 were Sharp, Stewart & Co built. Although the 7 were allocated BR numbers in the series 32044 to 32074 they did not survive in traffic long enough to carry them in service.

The 'B4X' engines were re-designed as powerful express passenger engines and as such carried a 3P power classification. BR took into stock all 12 of the class, allocating them numbers in the series 32043 to 32073 and 9 of those locomotives, 32050 and 32055–32073 were constructed from original Glasgow built 'B4' engines. However, the class did not survive long in BR service and of the Sharp, Stewart & Co built examples only 2 carried their allocated numbers in service, Nos 32071 and 32072, and both of those engines were withdrawn by BR in December 1951.

Driving wheel diameter 6' 9", 2-cylinder engine (inside)

Sharp, Stewart & Co built 'B4X' class 4-4-0 LBSCR No 2060 (originally named KIMBERLEY) is seen leaving Barnham Junction with a Portsmouth–London Bridge service, Easter 1938. This locomotive which was allocated but never carried the BR number 32060 was completed in August 1901 and withdrawn by BR in December 1951. *Dave Cobbe Collection – C. R. L. Coles/Rail Photoprints Collection*

'B4X' class 4-4-0 LBSCR No 2073 (originally named WESTMINSTER) leaves Havant with a Cardiff–Brighton service, circa 1937. This locomotive which was allocated but never carried BR No 32073 was completed in October 1901 and withdrawn by BR in September 1951. *Dave Cobbe Collection – C. R. L. Coles/Rail Photoprints Collection*

'B4X' 4-4-0 LBSCR No 2055 (originally named EMPEROR) is depicted passing Vauxhall whilst hauling a rake of GER air-braked suburban stock. The working was a Farnborough air show special on 7 July 1950. Billinton 4-4-0 No 2055 was stored out of use at Eastbourne shed (75G) when the call came to resume duties. However, No 2055 rapidly returned to storage at Eastbourne and faced the axe in November 1951 never having carried its allocated BR number 32055. *Mike Morant Collection*

'MR Johnson/Fowler 4-4-0' 2P

The Midland Railway (MR) first introduced this Samuel Waite Johnson designed 4-4-0 class of 2-cylinder (inside) locomotives between 1882 and 1901. In total some 265 of the class were built for the MR and additionally 40 for the Midland & Great Northern Railway (M&GNR). Over the years a great deal of modification and re-building took place to the instructions of MR engineers Richard Deeley and Henry Fowler. Notable modifications included differing driving wheel diameters, Stephenson slide valves (in place of Stephenson piston valves), superheating, Belpaire fireboxes and extended smokeboxes.

Derby Works built the majority of the class with other locomotives being supplied by contractors Beyer, Peacock & Co Ltd, Neilson & Co and Sharp, Stewart & Co Ltd (48 engines).

In 1948 BR took into stock 160 of the class allocating to them numbers in the series 40332–40562, which included Sharp, Stewart & Co engines Nos 40403–40422, 40430–40439 and 40503–40522 (for earlier MR numbers discount the 40 prefix). However, 8 of the Sharp, Stewart & Co built engines never carried their allocated BR numbers and they were locomotives Nos 40403, 40406, 40408, 40437, 40506, 40510, 40512 and 40517 which were all scrapped 1948/49.

The last of Sharp, Stewart & Co built engines to remain in service were No 40411 and No 40502 which were withdrawn in February 1961.

See also 'MR Johnson/Fowler 4-4-0' 2P locomotives built by Neilson & Co.

Driving wheel diameter 7' 0½", 2-cylinder engine (inside)

Sharp, Stewart & Co built MR Johnson/Fowler 4-4-0 '2P' LMS No 414 heads a local passenger train south near Hasland circa 1936. This locomotive was delivered in May 1892 and withdrawn by BR in January 1957. *Rail Photoprints Collection*

Sharp, Stewart & Co built MR Johnson/Fowler 4-4-0 '2P' BR No 40411 is seen at Wirksworth station with a rail charter. The special train was run as part of a Gloucester Railway Society 'Cromford and High Peak Tour' on 21 May 1955. No 40416 was delivered in May 1893 and withdrawn by BR in May 1959 in her 66th year of service. *Hugh Ballantyne/Rail Photoprints Collection*

Sharp, Stewart & Co built MR Johnson/Fowler 4-4-0 '2P' BR No 40509 seen with No 4F 44333 at Bath Green Park, in May 1955. No 40509 was delivered in November 1899 and withdrawn by BR in June 1957. *Hugh Ballantyne/Rail Photoprints Collection*

MR '1F' 0-6-0T

The Midland Railway introduced a large class of shunting engines between 1878 and 1899 and they were the first tank engines designed for the railway by Samuel W. Johnson. The large majority of the '1F' 0-6-0T engines were built at Derby Works but contractors Vulcan Foundry, Robert Stephenson Ltd and Sharp, Stewart & Co also built examples of the class.

Some of the class were fitted with totally enclosed cabs whilst others were of an open backed 'half cab' design. This class became the standard Midland Railway shunting engine and as such they were a familiar sight all over the network. Some 280 of the type were constructed and BR took into stock 95 examples, and they were allocated numbers in the series 41660–41895.

The 4 Sharp, Stewart & Co built engines which came into BR stock were numbered 41855–41857 and 41859 (MR Nos 855–857 and 859) but locomotive number 41856 never carried its BR number being withdrawn in June 1951. Sharp, Stewart & Co built No 41855 was the last of the four to be withdrawn in May 1960.

Driving wheel diameter 4' 7", 2-cylinder engine (inside)

Sharp, Stewart & Co built locomotive classes which came into British Railways ownership

Class	Wheel arrangement	Designer	Customer/ Number to BR	Build dates	BR number series*
'R' and 'R1'	0-4-4T	Kirtley	LCDR 15 locos	1891/92	31658–31675
'B4'	4-4-0	Billinton	LBSCR 5 locos	1901	32051–32074
'BX4'	4-4-0	Billinton	LBSCR 9 locos	1901	32050 32055–32073
'MR 2P'	4-4-0	Johnson	MR 48 locos	1892 1893 1899	40403–40422 40430–40439 40503–40522
'MR 1F'	0-6-0T	Johnson	MR 4 locos	1895	41855–41857 41859

*The BR numbers are given for identification in BR listings and do not take into account missing numbers due to scrapping, or locomotives of the same class built by other companies, but do include locomotives with allocated numbers not carried.

LTSR 'Intermediate' 4-4-2T 2P

To operate its heavy outer suburban services, the London, Tilbury & Southend Railway made extensive use of outside cylinder tank locomotives with the 4-4-2 wheel arrangement. Accordingly between 1900 and 1903 the railway introduced its '51' class which was designed by Thomas Whitelegg, who was the father of LTSR engineer Robert Whitelegg. Originally these engines carried the names of London area locations but the names were later removed. The locomotives were amongst the last to be built by Sharp, Stewart & Co before they became part of the North British Locomotive Co.

BR took into stock 16 engines from the original class and allocated to them numbers in the series 41910–41926 (LMS 2092–2103). Locomotives numbered 41910–41921 were Sharp, Stewart & Co built during September and October 1900, however none of those remained in traffic long enough to carry their BR numbers.

The last Sharp, Stewart & Co built example in traffic was LMS No 2093 which was allocated the number BR No 41911, which it never carried and was withdrawn in March 1953.

See also LTSR Whitelegg 'Intermediate' 4-4-2T '2P' locomotives built by the NBL.

Driving wheel diameter 6' 6", 2-cylinder engine (outside)

Sharp, Stewart & Co built Whitelegg '2P' 'Intermediate' 4-4-2T seen at Nottingham after withdrawal as LMS No 2101; this engine was allocated, but never carried BR No 41919. The date of the picture is listed as being March 1951. *Rail Photoprints Collection*

LTSR '3P' 4-4-2T

Between 1905 and 1911 the last remaining 12 engines of the former London, Tilbury & Southend Railway (LTSR) '1' class engines were rebuilt to form the basis of the new '37' class designed by Thomas Whitelegg. The class of engines became commonly known as the 'Tilbury Tanks' and the ex '1' class locomotives all carried names of locations on the LTSR, those locomotives were originally numbered 37–48 in the LTSR series. The engines were built at Derby Works and by the contractors Nasmyth, Wilson & Co, Robert Stephenson & Co, Dübs & Co and Sharp, Stewart & Co (6 engines to BR). In total 72 4-4-2T locomotives of the '1' and '37' class were built for the LTSR.

The ex '1' class ('37 class') batch of 12 engines were re-numbered first by the Midland Railway (MR) Nos 2146–2157 and then again by the LMS Nos 2135–2146.

BR took into stock 51 engines of this combined class in their number series 41928–41978. The 6 of those which were Sharp, Stewart & Co built carried the BR Nos 41953–41958 (LMS 2135–212140) and they were delivered to the LTSR during March and April 1897.

None of these engines survived in traffic beyond the end of 1960 and the last Sharp, Stewart & Co built 4-4-2T was No 41958 withdrawn in December 1951.

See also LTSR '3P' 4-4-2T locomotives built by Dübs & Co.

Driving wheel diameter 6' 6", 2-cylinder engine (outside)

MR '3F' 5' 3" 0-6-0 3F

This class of Samuel Waite Johnson designed locomotives was introduced by the Midland Railway (MR) between 1875 and 1902, some of which were rebuilds of the earlier MR '43137' class and also the former MR 2F '58188' class. Selected locomotives were given Belpaire fireboxes and Deeley style cabs by Fowler from 1903 onwards. They were built by Derby Works and contractors Kitson & Co, Neilson, Reid & Co, Neilson & Co, Dübs & Co and Sharp, Stewart & Co.

BR took into stock 324 of these 0-6-0 locomotives (BR numbers in the series 43191–43753) of which 36 were Sharp, Stewart & Co built, in the BR number series 43370–43408, 43546–43568 and 43690–43709, for LMS numbers discount the 4 prefix. None of the class survived in service beyond 1964 and the last Sharp, Stewart & Co, built examples were No 43637 and No 43709 which were withdrawn by BR in August 1962.

See also 'MR Johnson 3F' 0-6-0 3F locomotives built by Neilson & Co, Neilson, Reid & Co and Dübs & Co.

Driving wheel diameter 5' 3", 2-cylinder engine (inside)

Sharp, Stewart & Co built MR '3F' 5' 3" 0-6-0 BR No 43395 (LMS 3395) is seen with a short tank train on the outskirts of Kilnhurst in 1958. This locomotive was delivered in 1892 and withdrawn by BR in March 1961. *Mike Stokes Archive*

CR '812' 0-6-0 3F

The Caledonian Railway (CR) introduced this John Farquharson McIntosh designed class of 0-6-0 freight locomotives between 1899 and 1900. The engines were built at St Rollox Works and by contractors, Neilson, Reid & Co, Dübs & Co and Sharp, Stewart & Co, they were an enlarged version of the CR 'Jumbo' class engines.

BR took into stock 76 of these engines and allocated to them numbers in the series 57550–57628 (17550–17628).

The class was originally collectively referred to as mixed traffic (MT) engines however, only 20 locomotives were fitted with Westinghouse brakes and 5 with vacuum brakes for passenger train working.

Of the BR total 14 were Sharp, Stewart & Co built locomotives numbered 57587–57601 which were delivered during August and September 1900 as CR Nos 587–601 (for LMS numbers prefix with 17). None of the class remained in traffic after 1963 and the last surviving Sharp, Stewart & Co engine was No 57600 withdrawn by BR in September 1963.

See also CR '812' 0-6-0 3F locomotives built at St Rollox Works, Dübs & Co and Neilson, Reid & Co.

Driving wheel diameter 5' 0", 2-cylinder engine (inside)

Sharp, Stewart & Co built CR '812' class 0-6-0 BR No 57597 (LMS 17597 and CR 859) is seen between shunting turns whilst adjacent to the signalbox at Dingwall (Southside) in September 1958. The locomotive was delivered in August 1900 and withdrawn by BR in November 1959. Note the huge stock of coal in the tender and the fireman who looks to be pushing coal down onto the shovelling plate. *David Anderson*

MR '2F' 5' 3" 0-6-0

This class of Johnson designed 0-6-0 locomotives for the Midland Railway was introduced between 1878 and 1902 and they were a 5' 3" diameter driving wheel version of the 58114–58248 series of engines. They were built at Derby Works and additionally by the contractors Robert Stephenson & Co, Beyer, Peacock & Co, Kitson & Co, Vulcan Foundry, Neilson, Reid & Co, Neilson & Co, Dübs & Co and Sharp, Stewart & Co.

BR took into stock 109 of the class allocating to them numbers in the series 58188–58228 and 58249–58310. None of the class survived in service beyond 1962.

The Sharp, Stewart & Co built examples were numbered 58257–58259, and 58287–58292 (MR numbers in the series 3372–3385 and 3545–3566) and the last of those in BR service was No 58305, which was withdrawn by BR in June 1961. Locomotive No 58292 was scrapped in 1948 and never carried its allocated BR number.

See also MR '2F' 5' 3" 0-6-0 locomotives built by, Dübs & Co, Neilson & Co and Neilson, Reid & Co.

Driving wheel diameter 5' 3", 2-cylinder engine (inside)

Sharp, Stewart & Co built locomotive classes which came into British Railways ownership

Class	Wheel arrangement	Designer	Customer/ Number to BR	Build dates	BR number series*
Intermediate	4-4-2T	Whitelegg	LTSR 12 locos	1900/03	41910–41921
'3P'	4-4-2T	Whitelegg	LTSR 6 locos	1897/98	41953–41958
MR '3F' 5' 3"	0-6-0	Johnson	MR/S&DJR 36 locos	1892 1897 1901	43370–43408 43546–43568 43690–43709
'812'	0-6-0	McIntosh	CR 14 locos		57587–57601
MR '2F' 5' 3"	0-6-0	Johnson	MR 13 locos	1892 1897 1901	58257–58259 58287–58292 58302–58305

*The BR numbers are given for identification in BR listings and do not take into account missing numbers due to scrapping, or locomotives of the same class built by other companies, but do include locomotives with allocated numbers not carried.

LYR Rebuilt '23' 0-6-0ST

When John Aspinall became CME of the Lancashire & Yorkshire Railway he commenced a programme of rebuilding 0-6-0 locomotives into 0-6-0ST configuration in order to meet a need by that railway for shunting engines. A total of 230 such engines were rebuilt between 1891 and 1900 at Horwich Works, Miles Platting Works, and by contractors Kitson & Co, Beyer, Peacock Ltd, Vulcan, Foundry Ltd and Sharp, Stewart & Co. Withdrawal of the class commenced in 1926 and consequently only 96 general traffic examples (in the number series 51307–51530) and 5 departmental engines (Nos 11304–11394) came into BR stock. Of the BR general traffic locomotives only 6 were Sharp, Stewart & Co built Nos 51319, 51320 (LMS 11319 and 11320) and 51323 (LMS 11323) 51325 (LMS 11325) 51336 (LMS 11336) and 51338 (LMS 11338) the last of those in service being No 51336 which was withdrawn by BR in November 1960.

Of the 5 departmental engines (which all retained LMS numbers in BR service) 3 examples numbered 11304, 11305 and 11324 were Sharp, Stewart & Co built and the last of those in service was No 11305 a Horwich Works shunter withdrawn in September 1964, and at that time being for a short period the oldest working engine on BR.

Driving wheel diameter 4' 6", 2-cylinder engine (inside)

HR 'Jones Goods' 4-6-0 4F

Designed by David Jones for the Highland Railway (HR) this class of engines earned its place in the British locomotive hall of fame by being the first 4-6-0 tender engine to run in Great Britain. Sharp, Stewart and Co built 15 of the class and they were delivered between September and November 1894, numbered 103 to 117 in the HR series, none came into BR ownership but one example is preserved. At the time, these were the most powerful main line engines in Britain. Principally intended for use as freight engines, they were often called upon to perform passenger duties by the HR.

Driving wheel diameter 5' 3", 2-cylinder engine (outside)

Sharp, Stewart & Co built HR 'Jones Goods' No 103 is seen at Carstairs Junction before working an enthusiast's charter train to Auchinleck, Ayrshire in June 1963. *David Anderson*

'Jones Goods' 4-6-0 No 103 entered service on the Highland Railway in September 1894. This preserved example became No 17976 under LMSR ownership and was withdrawn from active service in July 1934 as a candidate for preservation. The engine is seen outside St Rollox works shortly after being returned to mainline condition in 1959, after which it regularly worked special trains for several years before being retired to Glasgow Museum of Transport/ Riverside Museum. *Mike Morant Collection*

Preserved 'Jones Goods' 4-6-0 No 103 is seen double heading with '812' class 0-6-0 No 57581 (a Neilson Reid built engine) on Sunday 30th June 1963. The pair are pictured leaving Carstairs on the leg to Auchinleck via Lanark, Muirkirk and Cronberry, of the RCTS 'Three Summits Rail Tour' (1X36 throughout). The tour originated in Leeds with 'A4' No 60023 GOLDEN EAGLE heading the first leg to Carlisle (via S&C) thereafter Stanier Pacific No 46255 CITY OF HEREFORD took the 10 coach train forward to Carstairs via Beattock. After the double headed leg 'A4' No 60004 WILLIAM WHITELAW then took the return leg to Carlisle via Dumfries where 'A4' 60023 GOLDEN EAGLE took over for the journey back to Leeds via Sedbergh and Settle Junction. *David Anderson*

GCR 'D9' 4-4-0 2P

John G. Robinson designed what many considered to be an extremely handsome looking class of 4-4-0 express passenger engines for the Great Central Railway 40 of which were introduced into traffic between 1901 and 1904. There were originally slight variations in design of the class with engines designated variously as GCR classes '11B', 11C' and '11D'. Later they were fitted with larger superheated boilers becoming collectively LNER 'D9' class. Of the original build 30 engines were Sharp, Stewart & Co built and 10 engines were Vulcan Foundry & Co built.

BR took into stock 26 engines and they were allocated numbers in the series 62300–62333 and of those 22 engines BR Nos 62300–62325 (GCR Nos 1013–1041) were Sharp, Stewart & Co built and delivered between October 1901 and March 1903.

The 4-4-0s were originally intended for use by the GCR for 'London Expresses' but were actually replaced on those services by GCR Atlantics very early in their working lives. Under BR ownership the engines often worked fast express services on the Cheshire Lines route between Manchester and Liverpool. Names were originally given to 4 of the class but only No 62307 QUEEN MARY retained its name in BR service. The last Sharp, Stewart & Co built 'D9' in BR service was No 62305 which was withdrawn by BR in July 1950.

Driving wheel diameter 6' 9", 2-cylinder engine (inside)

Sharp, Stewart & Co built ex-Great Central Railway '11B' class (LNER D9) 4-4-0 No. 1018 (LNER No. 6018 and 2305), delivered in February 1902 by Sharp, Stewart & Co and withdrawn as BR No 62305 in July 1950. The 4-4-0, as pictured, still carries the full GCR livery as it heads an up Aberdeen-Penzance train away from York, circa 1925. *Mike Morant Collection*

Sharp, Stewart & Co built 'D9' 4-4-0 LNER No 2306 seen in ex-works condition at Gorton motive power depot. This locomotive was at that time allocated to Liverpool Brunswick depot from where it was withdrawn in January 1949; as a consequence it did not carry its allocated BR No 62306. *Mike Morant Collection*

NBR 'C' 0-6-0 2F – 'J36'

Designed for the North British Railway by Matthew Holmes the 'C' class 0-6-0 locomotives were the most numerous on the NBR, the original build total being 168 engines, the class was designated 'J36' by the LNER. The locomotives were built at Cowlairs Works and by the contractors and Neilson & Co and Sharp, Stewart & Co. BR took into stock 123 'J36' class engines allocating to them numbers in the series 65210–65346.

Of that BR total only 13 locomotives were Sharp, Stewart & Co built and they carried the Nos 65249–65261 (NBR Nos 249–261).

The class achieved a modicum of fame when a batch of 25 engines was selected to be sent overseas during the 1917–1918 period of the First World War. On their return to the UK those locos were given the names of famous military leaders and locations associated with the war. Sharp, Stewart & Co built example BR No 65253 carried the name JOFFRE for a short period. The names were painted on the centre driving wheel splasher, but at the time of nationalisation and for periods in BR ownership the locomotives often ran un-named.

None of the class remained in service beyond the end of 1967 and the last Sharp, Stewart & Co built engine in BR service was No 65345 which was delivered in December 1900 and withdrawn by BR in November 1963.

See also NBR 'C' 0-6-0 2F – 'J36' locomotives built at Cowlairs Works and also by Neilson & Co.

Driving wheel diameter 5', 2-cylinder engine (inside)

Sharp, Stewart & Co built NBR 'C' 0-6-0 2F (J36) BR No 65261 with a tender cab is seen at Bathgate (64F) in the company of other locomotives of the class during April 1958. This locomotive was delivered to the NBR as No 690 in March 1892 and withdrawn by BR in June 1963. *David Anderson*

NBR 'D' 0-6-0T ('J83')

The North British Railway (NBR) introduced a class of 40 Matthew Holmes designed 0-6-0T engines between 1900 and 1901. The locomotives were designated NBR 'D' class which was later changed to 'J83' class by the LNER. The engines were originally intended for shunting and freight transfer duties on the NBR and they were the most powerful 0-6-0T engines to be used on that railway.

They were built by Neilson, Reid & Co (20 engines) and Sharp, Stewart & Co (20 engines). Only one engine was scrapped prior to 1948 and therefore BR took into stock 39 engines allocating to them numbers in the series 68442–68481 (LNER Nos 8442–8481 and 9795–9814. The Sharp, Stewart & Co built engines were numbered 68463–68481.

Under LNER/BR a number of these engines were fitted with Westinghouse brakes and thereafter were often used for station pilot duties at both Glasgow Queen Street and Edinburgh Waverley stations, with the Haymarket based engines re-painted in light green livery by the LNER in 1947.

None of the class survived in traffic beyond 1962 and the last serving Sharp, Stewart & Co built engine was No 68477, which was withdrawn by BR in December 1962.

See also NBR 'D' 0-6-0T ('J83') locomotives built by Neilson, Reid & Co.

Driving wheel diameter 4' 6", 2-cylinder engine (inside)

Sharp, Stewart & Co built 'J83' class 0-6-0T BR No 68463 is seen at Craigentinny sidings, which were situated a short distance east of Edinburgh Waverley station. This locomotive was delivered in April 1901 and was withdrawn by BR in November 1958. *David Anderson*

Sharp, Stewart & Co built 'J83' class 0-6-0T BR No 68474 is seen whilst working on station pilot duty at Edinburgh Waverley in August 1956. This locomotive was delivered in April 1901 and was withdrawn by BR in April 1958. ***Hugh Ballantyne/Rail Photoprints Collection***

GNR 'J13' 0-6-0ST 3F - 'J52'

Great Northern Railway CMEs Patrick Stirling and Henry Alfred Ivatt both adopted the 0-6-0 saddle tank design as their standard GNR shunting engine. Between 1868 and 1909 a total of 264 of the 0-6-0ST engines designated 'J13' class were built. The engines attributed to Stirling were built with domeless boilers whilst those originated by Ivatt were built with domed boilers. Under the GNR/LNER rebuilding of both types under Gresley took place between 1922 and 1932.

The Stirling engines were designated 'J52/1' class by the LNER whilst the Ivatt locomotives were designated 'J52/2' class. The majority of these saddle tanks were built at Doncaster Works but the contractors Robert Stephenson & Co Ltd, Neilson & Co, Sharp, Stewart & Co also participated in the build.

BR took into stock 132 of the engines allocating to them numbers in the series 68757–68889 (LNER 8757–8889) of those Nos 68825–68849 (earlier numbers 8825–8849) were Sharp, Stewart built between April and May 1899, all being 'J52/2 variants. None of the class survived beyond the end of 1961 and the last NBL built 'J52/2' in service with BR was No 68834, which was withdrawn in February 1960. Sharp, Stewart & Co built locomotive BR No 68846 is preserved.

See also GNR 'J13' 0-6-0ST 3F (LNER 'J52') locomotives built by Neilson & Co.

Driving wheel diameter 4' 8", 2-cylinder engine (inside)

Preserved Sharp, Stewart & Co built GNR 'J13' class 0-6-0ST is seen as LNER 'J52' No 68846 at a Doncaster Works open day in July 2003. This locomotive is preserved as a part of the National Railway Museum collection. ***Keith Langston Collection***

Sharp, Stewart & Co built locomotive classes which came into British Railways ownership

Class	Wheel arrangement	Designer	Customer/ Number to BR	Build dates	BR number series*
'23'	0-6-0ST	Aspinall/Barton Wright	LYR 6 locos	1848/50	51319–51320 51323–51325 51336, 51338
'Jones Goods'	4-6-0	Jones	HR 1 loco	1894	103
'D9'	4-4-0	Robinson	GCR 22 locos	1901/02	62300–62309 62311–62325
'J36'	0-6-0	Holmes	NBR 13 locos	1892	65249–65261
'J83'	0-6-0T	Holmes	NBR 19 locos	1901	68463–68481
'J52'	0-6-0ST	Stirling/Ivatt	GNR 25 locos	1899	68825–68849

*The BR numbers are given for identification in BR listings and do not take into account missing numbers due to scrapping, or locomotives of the same class built by other companies, but do include locomotives with allocated numbers not carried.

Railway Company abbreviations used in this chapter.

BR – Barry Railway, **CR** – Caledonian Railway, **GCR** – Great Central Railway, **GNR** – Great Northern Railway**, HR** – Highland Railway, **MR** – Midland Railway, **NBR** – North British Railway, **NLR** – North London Railway, **L&Y** – Lancashire & Yorkshire Railway, **LBSCR** – London, Brighton & South Coast Railway, **LCDR** – London, Chatham & Dover Railway, **LTSR** London, Tilbury & Southend Railway, **PTR** – Port Talbot Railway, **SECR** – South Eastern & Chatham Railway, **S&DJR** – Somerset & Dorset Joint Railway

Chapter 8

WILLIAM BEARDMORE & COMPANY

William Beardmore & Co was a well known Scottish engineering and shipbuilding conglomerate based mainly in the Clydeside area of Glasgow. The company was active in its own right from 1886 to the mid-1930s and at its peak was thought to have employed in the region of 40,000 people. The founder of the company was William Beardmore, after whom the 'Beardmore Glacier' in Antarctica was named and that gentleman later became Lord Invernairn.

The history and development of the company is as interesting as it is diverse from the company's earlier years of operation centred on steel forging and rolling in general and the production of shipbuilding products in particular. The manufacture of road, rail vehicle and aviation products were also undertaken. However, Beardmore & Company will of course be remembered for the manufacture of high quality armour plate and naval guns.

Several acquisitions and partnerships accelerated the growth of the company so much so that in 1900 William Beardmore purchased a further works site and shipyard at Dalmuir on the Clyde initially for the purpose of building warships and

William Beardmore & Co (BM) built 'Jinty' 3F 0-6-0T No 47524 is seen at Crewe station with a local service circa 1963. This loco was delivered to the LMS in March 1928 and withdrawn by BR in September 1964. ***Keith Langston Collection***

ordnance. In 1902 the company formed an association with Vickers, Sons & Maxim by way of a reciprocal exchange of shareholding.

In order to briefly detail the firms earlier years, under the chairmanship of the founder's son William Beardmore junior we need only to look at a 1914 listing of their sphere of activities which were;

Armour Plate and Ordnance Manufacturers, Forge masters, Shipbuilders, Engineers. Specialities: 'Armour Plates, Ordnance, War Vessels, Cargo Vessels, Steamers, Forgings, Shafting, Castings, Steel Plates, Boiler Plates, Nickel Steel Plates, Beardmore Gas Engines, Beardmore Oil Engines, Motor Car Frames, Tyres, Axles, Wheels and Axles, Flanging of all kinds, Furnaces, corrugated or plain'.

WM. BEARDMORE & CO.
(CONTRACTORS TO ADMIRALTY),
Parkhead Forge, Rolling Mills, & Steel Works, GLASGOW,
MANUFACTURERS OF
STEEL AND IRON FORGINGS,
HOLLOW STEEL SHAFTING,
SHIP AND BOILER PLATES, ANGLES, BARS, AND RIVETS.
(ALL STEEL BY SIEMENS' PROCESS).
Admiralty, Lloyds', Board of Trade, Bureau Veritas, Indian State Railway, and other Tests at Works. 7083

Employees then reportedly totalled 12,000 to 15,000. The main Beardmore steel works were at Parkhead, Glasgow and Mossend with ancillary works at Dalmuir, Coatbridge, Paisley and Anniesland.

During 1918 the company purchased the shares of Stephen Alley whose company Alley & Maclallan owned the Polmadie works of the Sentinel Company and the associated Shrewsbury based steam-wagon manufacturing facility. The Glasgow works were separated from the rest of the Sentinel operation with vehicle production being concentrated in Shrewsbury.

During the First World War Beardmores were involved with aircraft production being licensed manufacturers of the famous 'Sopworth Pup' bi-plane. They went on to develop a version of that aircraft for use as an aircraft carrier based fighter and that successful machine was known as the 'Beardmore WD III'.

As the war years came to an end Beardmores started to make taxi cabs at a London based branch of the company. Through associations with other companies they also manufactured motorcycles, motorcars and wagons, further illustrating the firm's apparent love affair with diversification. In 1919 the Dalmuir premises were refurbished in order to make them suitable for the manufacture of steam locomotives.

In 1926 Vickers sold its shareholding in the firm back to William Beardmore.

In the period between the World Wars the company also produced several aircraft engines including in 1930 the power units for the ill-fated airship 'R101'.

The company was not during that period in the best of financial health a fact that in 1928 had triggered an investigation chaired by financier Montague Norman (later became Baron Norman of St Clere) who famously served as Governor of the Bank of England between 1920 and 1944.

The committee ousted William Beardmore (junior) from his position and then over the following two years closed down or sold off many of the diversifications of the company, including the locomotive building facility (1928–30).

However, the company name continued with steel making and after the passing of the 1951 Iron & Steel Act (Nationalisation) it became part of Iron & Steel Corporation of Great Britain and then was in turn sold to the Thomas Firth and John Brown conglomerate circa 1957.

Steam Locomotive Construction

In 1920 steam locomotive production commenced at the Dalmuir site and whatever the companys plans were for developing that side of its diverse business activities, they were in truth never to become a big force in the market place in comparison classes of locomotive specifically for the British market.

On the export front they manufactured several notable locomotive types for railways in India and Burma which included conventional 2-8-0, 2-8-2, 4-6-0, 4-6-2 configured engines and also a 5 engine batch of metre gauge 'Mallett' type 0-6-6-0 locomotives. In total William Beardmore & Company built 168 steam locomotives for export in 8 different classes between 1920 and 1931.

For the home market Beardmores in 1920 built 20 'S69' class (LNER/BR 'B12' class) 4-6-0 engines for the Great Eastern Railway (GER). That order was followed in 1921/22 by a prestigious order from the London & North Western Railway (LNWR) for 4-6-0 engines of the 'Prince of Wales' class. Beardmore built 60 locomotives with tenders and 30 locomotives only for the LNWR (90 engines). That batch was followed in 1924 by another inside cylinder 'Prince of Wales' class engine but this time configured with outside valve gear as a so called 'Tishy'*. That engine was sent to the 1924 'Wembley Exhibition' as Loco No 5845.

* The 'Tishy' nickname was given to the 6 'Prince of Wales' class 4-6-0 engines which were constructed with outside valve gear configured to operate valves on the inside cylinders. The nickname was taken from a race horse of the era which had a propensity for falling over its own legs and was made famous by cartoon drawings in a daily newspaper.

In 1927 the company completed an order from the London & North Eastern Railway (LNER) for 20 'N7/3' 0-6-2T locomotives. The last UK order received was from the London Midland Scottish Railway (LMS) for 90 'Jinty' type 0-6-0T engines which was completed between 1928 and 1929. William Beardmore & Company built a total of 221 standard gauge steam locomotives for British companies.

Interestingly, William Beardmore & Company reportedly played a prominent part in the development of Caprotti Valve gear for both marine and railway use. Records from the 1930s show that 125 sets of the valve gear had been supplied for locomotives 'in England and other parts of the world'.

GER 'S69' 4-6-0-'B12' 4P

The Great Eastern Railway (GER) first introduced the James Holden designed 'S69' class in 1911 and thereafter the LNER continued to build the class up to 1928. The Holden engines were designated 'B12' by the LNER with four variants. British Railways (BR) took into stock 69 of the class (BR number series 61500–61580) of which 17 were from the original 20 engines which had been supplied by William Beardmore & Company (BM). The BM batch of engines was built between 1920 and 1921 and their works serial numbers were in the series 135–154 (BR numbers allocated were in the series 61541–61560). A total of 14 BM built examples were designated as 'B12/3' after being rebuilt with larger diameter round topped boilers to a Gresley inspired modification. However, 3 of the total remained in their original condition with smaller Belpaire boilers and they were designated 'B12/1'. None of the class survived in traffic beyond the end of 1961 and the last BM built example to be withdrawn was No 61546 in May 1959.

Driving wheel diameter 6' 6", 2-cylinder engine (inside)

William Beardmore & Co built LNER 4-6-0 'B12' class (GER 'S69' class) No 61547 is seen as it draws the stock for the 5.48pm service to Cromer over Melton West Junction on 29 August 1958. This loco was delivered in September 1920; it was rebuilt by the LNER with a Gresley type larger round topped boiler (B12/3) and withdrawn by BR in October 1958. *Hugh Ballantyne/Rail Photoprints Collection*

William Beardmore & Co built LNER 4-6-0 'B12' class (GER 'S69' class) No 61554 seen with the RCTS 'East Midlander No.1 Railtour' (Nottingham Midland-Crewe-Nottingham Midland) on the 8 May 1955. This loco was delivered to the Great Eastern Railway (GER) in January 1921; it was rebuilt by the LNER with a Gresley type larger round topped boiler (B12/3) and withdrawn by BR in September 1958. *Rail Photoprints Collection*

William Beardmore & Co built LNER 4-6-0 'B12' class (GER 'S69' class) No 61558 seen at Stratford depot (30A) on the 18 August 1956. This loco was delivered to the Great Eastern Railway (GER) in February 1921; it was rebuilt by the LNER with a Gresley type larger round topped boiler (B12/3) and withdrawn by BR in April 1959. *Rail Photoprints Collection*

LNWR 'Prince of Wales' 4-6-0 4P (LMS 3P)

The London & North Western Railway (LNWR) introduced the Charles Bowen-Cooke designed 'Prince of Wales' 4-6-0 class locomotives in 1911. A total of 246 of these express passenger locomotives were built between 1911 and 1922, the majority at Crewe Works. Due to constraints on works capacity at the time LNWR contracted out the construction of two batches of 'Prince' 4-6-0 engines.

William Beardmore & Company received an order to construct 90 locomotives only and 60 tenders during 1921–1922, and the BM serial numbers 174–263 applied.

Because of the ruling Caledonian Railway loading gauge bridge clearance leaving the BM works site was reportedly a problem for the larger LNWR locos which were delivered with their chimneys and steam dome tops removed (fitted later). Although many of the 'Prince of Wales' locomotives carried names the BM built examples did not. The LMS commenced withdrawals in 1933 and only 6 of the class were taken into BR stock in 1948. The BR batch included 2 BM built engines, one built October 1921 and being LMS number 25787, which was allocated the BR numbered 58003. The other BM example was LMS No 25827 which was not allocated a BR number. None of the 6 'Prince' engines taken into BR stock entered traffic and were subsequently withdrawn and cut up in 1948/49, without ever carrying their allocated numbers.

The final 'Prince of Wales' locomotive built was by William Beardmore & Company in February 1924.That engine was one of 6 'Tishy' type 'Prince of Wales' inside cylinder 4-6-0s and it was built for display at the British Empire Exhibition that year. The London Midland & Scottish Railway (LMS) bought that engine in November 1924, and numbered it 5845 in the LMS series.

Driving wheel diameter 6' 3", 2-cylinder engine (inside)

LNWR Beardmore built 'Prince of Wales' 4-6-0 No 551 is seen on the turntable at Camden depot circa 1924. A BM works plate is carried on the locomotive smokebox. *Edward Talbot Collection*

Following a batch of 90 'Prince of Wales' class 4-6-0 engines in 1921/22 William Beardmore & Company built another loco to a special order in 1924. The engine was sent to the 1924 'Wembley Exhibition' as Loco No 5845 which carried the class name on the wheel splasher. The so called 'Tishy' is pictured at Crewe Works prior to being sent to Wembley. *Edward Talbot Collection*

GER 'L' 0-6-2T 3MT – 'N7'

The 'L' class tank locomotives were designed by Alfred John Hill for suburban passenger work on the Great Eastern Railway routes out of London, Liverpool Street station and the first of the class was introduced in January 1914. The 'N7' engines were built at Stratford Works, Gorton Works and Doncaster Works and also by the contractors Robert Stephenson & Co Ltd and Beardmore Ltd.

Building continued by the GER and eventually the LNER until 1928. The LNER designated the class 'N7' of which there were five variants. BR took into stock 134 of the class in the number system 69600-69733 of which 20 locomotives in the BR number series 69682–69701 were built by William Beardmore & Company in 1927 (BM serial numbers 305–324).

The BM built engines were originally included in the 'N7/2' variant i.e. locomotives fitted with long travel valves, Walschaert valve gear and Belpaire fireboxes. Additionally those engines were fitted with pony trucks (instead of radial axle boxes) and higher bunkers without 'greedy rails'. All but two of the BM locos were later rebuilt with Gresley round topped boilers and designated as 'N2/3' engines. None of the class survived beyond 1962 and the last BM examples to be withdrawn were No 69692 and No 69697 both in September 1962.

Driving wheel diameter 4' 10", 2-cylinder engine (inside)

BM built 'N7/2' class 0-6-2T No 69695, in original condition calls at Ockendon on the former London, Tilbury & Southend route with local service, circa 1957. This engine was delivered in August 1927 and withdrawn by BR in December 1958. ***Dave Cobbe Collection/Rail Photoprints Collection***

LMS/SDJR Fowler 'Jinty' 0-6-0T 3F

A relatively large number of the 'Fowler' designed 0-6-0T 3F locomotives, which over time became known as the 'Jinty' class, were built between 1924 and 1931 and they were a development of the earlier Midland Railway (MR) Johnson 'Jinty' class engines. In 1948 British Railways (BR) took into stock 417 Fowler 0-6-0T 'Jinty' locos (BR number series 47260–47681) the majority of which were built for the LMS/SDJR by various outside contractors which included the North British Locomotive Co Ltd and Beardmore & Company.

Beardmores built 90 engines of the popular class between 1928 and 1929 under the BM works serial numbers 325–414. Of the 90 Fowler 0-6-0Ts in the BM built batch 87 were taken into BR stock and carried numbers in the BR series 47517–47541 and 47602–47666.

In 1940 a batch of 8 BM built 'Jinty' class engines were transferred to the War Department (WD) and subsequently saw service overseas.

From that total 5 locos returned at the end of the Second World War hostilities and were taken into BR stock they were Nos 47589, 47607, 47611, 47659 and 47660. The engines did not survive the war in Europe completely unscathed as reportedly they returned with evidence of bullet holes in the side tanks and cabs etc, and 3 engines did not return at all. Additionally when repatriated loco No 47589 returned sporting a chimney from a GWR/WD 'Dean Goods' engine. Whilst serving in France loco No 47659 carried the name CORSAIR.

The class served BR well with large numbers remaining in service up to the end of 1960. The number of locos in traffic then reduced steadily until 1966 when only 4 engines remained in service at the end of that year. The last BM 'Jinty' in service with BR was No 47629 which was withdrawn in October 1967. None of the BM built engines are amongst the 10 preserved examples.

See also LMS/SDJR Fowler 'Jinty' 0-6-0T 3F built by the North British Locomotive Co Ltd.

Driving wheel diameter 4' 7", 2-cylinder engine (inside)

BM built 'Jinty' 3F 0-6-0T No 47530 at seen between duties at Crewe South (5B) in March 1958. This loco was delivered to the LMS in March 1928 and withdrawn by BR in October 1966. *Alan H. Bryant ARPS/Rail Photoprints Collection*

Beardmore built locomotives which came into British Railways (BR) ownership

Class/Wheel Arrangement	Designer	Customer (Number to BR stock)	Build dates	BR number series*
'S69' 4-6-0 ('B12')	Holden	GER 17 locos	1920	61541–61560
'Prince of Wales' 4-6-0	Bowen-Cooke	LNWR 2 locos	1921 1922	58003 Un-numbered
'N7' 0-6-2T	Gresley	LNER 20 locos	1927	69682–69701
'Jinty' 0-6-0T	Fowler	LMS/S&DJR 87 locos	1928 1928 1929	47517–47541 47602–47640 47641–47666

*The BR numbers are given for identification in BR listings and do not take into account missing numbers due to scrapping or locomotives of the same class built by other companies, but do include locomotives with allocated numbers not carried.

Railway Company abbreviations used in this chapter.

GER – Great Eastern Railway, **LMS** – London Midland & Scottish Railway, **LNWR** London & North Western Railway, **S&DJR** – Somerset & Dorset Joint Railway. **LNER** – London& North Eastern Railway

Chapter 9

THE LOCOMOTIVE BUILDERS

North British Locomotive Company Limited (NBL)

Locomotive builders to the World

This Glasgow based locomotive manufacturer really did aspire to the title 'Locomotive Builders to the World'. The firm came into being following the amalgamation of three established railway locomotive builders in 1903 and traded in its own right until 1962. In the April of that year the directors of the company were left with no alternative but to recommend that the shareholders accept a proposal to put the by then seriously ailing company into liquidation. The loss of the NBL was a major blow to engineering employment prospects in Scotland which the then Provost of Glasgow, Mrs Jean Roberts, described as being tragic.

The company was already receiving financial support in order to continue trading but appeals for further help and support of the Westminster Government, via the Board of Trade, came to nothing. It was thus inevitable that the once giant engineering company would cease to trade in its own right. In truth and with the benefit of hindsight it can be seen that

Preserved Stanier 6P5F 'Jubilee' class 4-6-0 No 5593 (BR 45593) KOLHAPUR was one of 50 members of the 3-cylinder class built by the North British Locomotive Co Ltd. No 5593 was outshopped by the NBL Queen's Park Works in December 1934 (the engine carries a diamond shaped maker's plate). The Scottish built 'Jubilee' class locomotives were built in two batches of 25 engines each at Hyde Park Works and Queen's Park Works during 1934/5. The preserved 'Jubilee' class 4-6-0 is pictured in an LMS livery style. *Keith Langston*

The NBL diamond shaped makers plate as fitted to preserved 2-10-0 'Austerity' locomotive No 600 GORDON. Note, the diamond shaped NBL plate was fitted to locomotives built at the company's Queen's Park Works in Polmadie, which was a continuation of a tradition started by Dübs and Company. ***Keith Langston***

the writing had been on the wall for some time; orders were falling and between 1959 and 1962 the NBL was forced to cut its work force from over 5,000 employees to around 1,500.

Perchance the NBL may have only struggled on during its last decade because of the support of its three major creditors, General Electric Company, a consortium of banks and HM Treasury. The company was judged as being unable to continue operating without sustaining further major losses and sadly the Chairman and his board of directors therefore saw no alternative but to liquidate the 59-year- old firm.

Thomas Coughtrie, the NBL Chairman said that he identified the failure of the company, and the 'big losses sustained in its last decade or so of trading' as being 'attributable to the company's unsuccessful switch to the building of non-steam locomotives'. Reportedly the NBL had supplied British Railways (BR) with many diesel and electric locomotives at uneconomical prices hoping that bigger orders would follow, unfortunately they did not! During the liquidation of the company's assets the so called 'Goodwill' of the firm was sold to the Kilmarnock based locomotive manufacturing company of Andrew Barclay Sons & Co.

The worldwide reputation of the NBL had been earned by building high quality steam locomotives. The company successfully constructed locomotives to suit various loading gauges in a multiplicity of designs and exported them to the world's railway operators, indeed exports amounted to a little over 70 per cent of the company's production. No less a distinguished person than Sir Nigel Gresley is known to have praised NBL designs ranking them as being amongst the best in the world. The famous diamond shaped North British Locomotive Co Ltd maker's plate became a world renowned symbol of quality.

This Pickersgill designed class of 4-4-0 locomotives for the Great North of Scotland Railway were built by Neilson, Reid & Co (4 locomotives GNoSR class 'V') in 1899, by the North British Locomotive Co Ltd (5 locomotives in 1920) as modified by Heywood with superheated boilers (GNoSR class 'F') and by Inverurie Works (9 locomotives 1909-1921) of which one example built in 1921 was also a Heywood modified engine. They became LNER 'D40' class and in 1948 all 18 locomotives came into BR stock. One example GNoSR No 49 GORDON HIGHLANDER (BR No 62277) is preserved. That engine was the last survivor of the class and was restored to full working order in 1958 after which it worked many special charter trains. The handsome 4-4-0 was later retired to Glasgow Museum of Transport/Riverside Museum as a static exhibit. No 49 is pictured at Auchterless on a Stephenson Locomotive Society/RCTS special train on 13 June 1960. ***Mike Morant Collection***

'The Combine'

The North British Locomotive Co Ltd was formed in 1903 by the amalgamation of three existing Scottish locomotive manufacturers. They were Neilson, Reid & Company (originally founded as Neilson & Company in 1863 and becoming Neilson Reid & Company in 1898) who were based at Hyde Park Works, Springburn Glasgow, Dübs & Co who were based at Queen's Park Works, Polmadie Glasgow which was founded in 1863. The third member of the locomotive building trio was Sharp, Stewart & Co (founded in Manchester in 1828). That engineering firm moved to Glasgow in 1888, when they took over the Clyde Locomotive Co. in Springburn, Glasgow. Sharp, Stewart & Co changed the name of their newly acquired factory to Atlas Works mirroring the name of their former Manchester facility.

As stated all three companies were established in their own right as steam locomotive engineers and all had traded successfully prior to the amalgamation. The thinking behind the creation of North British Locomotive Co Ltd was to help compete in the worldwide market with other companies in general and in particular with the Baldwin Co. of the U.S.A. As a consequence of the mergers the resultant company became the largest steam locomotive manufacturer in Europe capable of producing approximately 600 engines a year. The new company, often referred to as 'The Combine' at its peak employed some 8,000 people and its manufacturing facilities occupied approximately 60 acres within the boundary of the City of Glasgow.

The new company was initially represented by agents in London, England, Buenos Aires, Argentina, Sydney and Perth, Australia, Hong Kong and Shanghai, China, Santiago, Chile, Bilbao, Spain and Lisbon, Portugal. The North British Locomotive Company name became trusted and was rightly considered to be a recognised symbol of quality with both industrial and national system railway operators worldwide. Glaswegians would regularly have sight of exported steam locomotives on low loader road vehicles being taken through the city on the way to the docks.

Industrial locomotive '0-4-0T (still carrying former Worthington Co numberplate), originally 'Bass No 4' is seen outside the locomotive shed at Bass Brewery, Burton- on-Trent, circa 1960. This locomotive was built at Hyde Park Works as works number 19848 in 1912 to order number L493. *Rail Photoprints Collection*

North British steam locomotives being loaded for export at Prince's Dock Govan in 1910. Note the William Kerr & Co steam road tractors CLYDE (at the front) and LORD ROBERTS top and tailing the low loader vehicle. The locomotives are of 2-8-2 configuration built for the Argentinean Government to a 'Henschel' design, 25 engines built at Hyde Park Works to order L432 and 25 engines built at Queen's Park Works to order L433. *NBL/GMRC*

Depression and War

Any consideration into the eventual demise of steam locomotive construction at the NBL must take into account factors other than the growing global decline in the use of steam traction. The Atlas Works site was closed in 1923 with production being concentrated at the firm's Queen's Park and Hyde Park locations. The market was unable to award big orders to the Glasgow based company during the period of the 'Depression' and indeed the NBL was fortunate to survive through the 1920s and 1930s, as many other large engineering firms were forced out of business. The total number of people employed at all sites by the NBL had by 1932 been reduced to only 389, a dismal statistic which was perhaps directly attributable to the effects of the depression.

Thereafter things did not improved markedly and it should be noted that no orders at all were received from UK railways during the years 1931, 1932, 1934 and 1936. Between 1929 and 1939 the 'Big Four' British railways (LMS, LNER, GWR and SR) actually placed five orders with the NBL but the combined total of locomotives ordered was only 193. However, as Britain faced the certainty of war more people were employed as production was stepped up. At the outbreak of war in 1939 the number of people employed by the NBL had risen to 2,333.

Locomotive manufacturers, North British Locomotive Company Limited was a totally separate entity to the similarly named former Edinburgh based train operators, North British Railway Company.

Built for the UK

This publication principally concerns UK based standard gauge steam locomotives which came into British Railways (BR) ownership in January 1948, and separate tables are included showing the listings of those Scottish built engine classes. However, it should be noted that not all of those survived beyond the end of that year and many more never even carried their allocated BR numbers.

Notwithstanding the stated brief it should be remembered that Scottish based locomotive builders supplied considerably large numbers of various locomotive types to UK railway companies many which were withdrawn before the formation of British Railways (BR).

An NBL example worthy of note being two 10 locomotive batches of the Charles Bowen Cooke designed 'Prince of Wales' class 4-6-0 type for the London & North Western Railway (LNWR). The 20 engines were built during 1915 to order number L658, 10 locomotives at Hyde Park Works and to order number L659, 10 locomotives at Queen's Park Works. In those orders locomotives only were supplied by the NBL, with the associated tenders being manufactured and fitted at Crewe Works.

A circular style NBL Hyde Park works maker's plate as fitted to Stanier '8F' No 48773. *Keith Langston Collection*

LNWR No 446 PEGASUS was one of the North British Locomotive Co Ltd (NBL) built 'Prince of Wales' class 2-cylinder 4-6-0 engines supplied in 1915. The locomotive is seen at Stockport circa 1917. None of the NBL built 'Prince of Wales' locomotives came into BR stock. Note that there is an NBL circular maker's plate fixed to the side of the smokebox. ***Edward Talbot Collection***

NBL built locomotive classes included in British Railway (BR) listings

LTSR 'Intermediate' 4-4-2T 2P

During its first year of operation (1903) the newly formed company completed orders for the London, Tilbury & Southend Railway (LTSR) to designs by Thomas Whitelegg, who was the father of LTSR engineer Robert Whitelegg. The outside cylinder tank locomotives were in fact inherited/continuation orders for engines previously supplied by an NBL founding partner Sharp, Stewart & Co., originally these engines carried the names of London area locations but the names were later removed.

Officially 16 of these engines came into BR stock and were allocated the numbers 41910–41926, the NBL built example carried BR numbers 41922-41926 (LMS 2104-2109). Of the 5 NBL built engines only 3 actually carried their nationalisation numbers, locomotives No 41922, No 41923 and 41925, therefore effectively became operational BR engines. The last to be scrapped was No 41922 (LMS No 2104) which was withdrawn in March 1953.

See also LTSR Whitelegg 'Intermediate' 4-4-2T 2P locomotives built by Sharp Stewart & Co.

Driving wheel diameter 6' 6", 2-cylinder engine (outside)

LTSR 'Corringham/69' 0-6-2T 3F

BR took into stock 14 engines of this Thomas Whitelegg class and allocated them numbers in the series 41980–41993 of that total 10 engines were NBL built, and they included the first 6 of the class built in 1903 (LMS 1980–1985 and BR 41980–41985). Although built by NBL these 6 engines were covered by an original Dübs & Co order number, 4468E. A batch of 4 more was built in 1908 (LMS 1986–1989 and BR 41986–41989) to order number L298. Some of these engines originally carried names of locations on the London, Tilbury & Southend Railway when in LTSR ownership. Scrapping of the class did not begin until 1956 with the last in service being an NBL built example BR number 41981. These engines were built specifically for freight work on the LTSR system.

Driving wheel diameter 5' 3", 2-cylinder engine (inside)

Whitelegg designed NBL built 0-6-2T No 41985 (later LMS 2185) to Dübs & Co order number 4468E for the LTSR is pictured at Tilbury in April 1954. This locomotive entered LTSR service in July 1903 and was withdrawn by BR in February 1959. ***Rail Photoprints Collection***

Whitelegg designed NBL built 0-6-2T No 41988 (later LMS 2188) was built to NBL order number L298) the engine is pictured on shed at Plaistow (33A) in 1956. This locomotive entered LTSR service in August 1908 and was withdrawn by BR in April 1958. ***Rail Photoprints Collection***

GCR '8B' and '8J' Atlantic (4-4-2) 2P - 'C4'

Details of this historically important John George Robinson (later C.B.E.) designed 4-4-2 (Atlantic type) express passenger locomotive for the Great Central Railway are included as no less than 20 of the type were actually taken into BR stock (in two variants i.e. 'C4/4' piston valve and 'C4/2' slide valve type). The engines were allocated numbers in the series 62900–62925 but never carried them as all of the class were either scrapped immediately or effectively stored for a short period until being sent for scrap between 1948 and 1951. The 'C4' class engines were built at Gorton Works, Beyer, Peacock Ltd and North British Locomotive Co Ltd. The NBL batch of 12 GCR 'Atlantic' type locomotives were built during 1905 at Hyde Park Works to order number L130. The Class members built by the NBL and allocated BR numbers were 62908–62910, 62912, 62914–62917.

Driving wheel diameter 6' 9", 2-cylinder engine (outside)

Cylinder size variants 19" dia x 26" stroke BR 62908, 62912 and 62917 additionally 21" dia x 26"stroke BR 62909/10, 62914–62916.

NBL built Great Central Railway (GCR) 'C4' Atlantic No 1090 is pictured in GCR livery circa 1920, the location is thought to be Guide Bridge station. Note the superb signal array. This locomotive became LNER No 6090 and was withdrawn in 1939 after sustaining severe damage in a collision at Banbury. Earlier No 6090, along with three other members of the class, had been rebuilt as a 4-cylinder compound. *Rail Photoprints Collection*

NBR 'B' 0-6-0 3F – 'J35'

This class of 2-cylinder 3F 0-6-0 engines, designed by William Paton Reid was introduced by the North British Railway (NBR) between 1906 and 1913. In total 76 locomotives were built, 40 by the NBL and an additional 36 at Cowlairs Works.

The NBL built four batches of 10 locomotives the first during 1906 to order number L167 at Atlas Works, the second batch during 1909 to order number L347 at Queen's Park Works, a third batch in 1909 to order number L357 at Atlas Works and a final batch also during 1909 to order number L382 at Hyde Park Works.

There were 5 class variants 'J35/1, 'J35/2' and 'J35/3' were all pre-superheater designations, 'J35/4' were slide valve engines whilst 'J35/5' were piston valve engines. A total of 70 locomotives came into BR stock and were allocated numbers in the series 64460–64535. Of those engines BR Nos 64460–64468 and 64484–64513 were the surviving NBL built examples.

Although designed for freight work the class was often to be seen working secondary passenger train duties. The LNER designated the NBL locomotives Nos 64460–64468 as 'J35/5' and they were piston valve types. The later batch Nos 64484–64513 were designated 'J35/4 and that variant were slide valve engines. The majority of the class remained in service until the early 1960s, the last NBL built examples in BR service was No 64491 withdrawn in December 1962.

See also NBR Reid 'B' 0-6-0 3F – 'J35' locomotives built at Cowlairs works.

Driving wheel diameter 5', 2-cylinder engine (inside)

North British Locomotive Co Ltd built NBR Reid 'B' class 0-6-0 seen as 'J35/5' class BR No 64463 (NBR 851, LNER 9581 and 4463) seen at St Boswells circa 1954. The locomotive stands over one of the two servicing pits at St Boswells, on the former Waverley Route which was a sub shed of Hawick (64G). This 'J35/5' locomotive was delivered to the NBR in August 1906 and withdrawn by BR in September 1960. *Rail Photoprints Collection*

NER 'P3' 0-6-0 4F – 'J27' (BR reclassified as 5F in 1953)

The North Eastern Railway first introduced this Wilson Worsdell class in 1906 and they continued to be supplied up to 1923 with the last 35 locomotives being constructed under the direction of Vincent Raven at Darlington Works and by contractors Robert Stephenson & Co Ltd, Beyer, Peacock & Co Ltd and by the NBL. BR took into stock 115 of the class allocating them numbers in the series 65780–65894, of that total 20 were built by the NBL to order number L281 and were delivered in 1907/8 from Atlas Works. The LNER designated the engines as 'J27' class and the NBL built examples which came into BR stock were numbered in the series 65810-65829 (NER 1014–1048). The 'J27' class was a familiar sight in the North East of England. None of the class survived in traffic beyond the end of 1967, and of those the last NBL built locomotive in service was No 65811, withdrawn in September 1967.

Driving wheel diameter 4' 7 ¼", 2-cylinder engine (inside)

NBL built Worsdell 'P3' class 0-6-0 seen as LNER 'J27' class No 65811 (NER 1015 and LNER 1015 and 5811) at Heaton (52B) in 1963. The locomotive is in the company of stored 'J72' class No 69028. *Martyn Hunt/Rail Photoprints Collection*

HR 'Small Ben' 4-4-0 2P

In 1896 Peter Drummond (the perhaps not so well known brother of Dugald Drummond) succeeded David Jones at the Highland Railway and he introduced his own design of inside cylinder 4-4-0 locomotives, the two classes were named 'Small Ben' class built between 1898 and 1906 and 'Large Ben' class built between 1908 and 1909, the latter were all withdrawn between 1932 and 1937.

These were the first inside cylinder HR tender engines and observers immediately noted that they were in fact very similar in design to the Dugald Drummond 'T9' class. The 'Small Ben' class total was 20 locomotives (HR Nos 397–416 and LMS Nos 14397–14416) with 10 of those engines coming into BR stock, and being allocated numbers in the series 54397–54416. Dübs & Co and Lochgorm Works also participated in the construction of the class. All of the class carried the names of Scottish Bens.

The BR total included 2 engines built by the NBL (BR Nos 54415 and 54416). None of the class survived beyond the end of 1953 and the last NBL built engines in service were Nos 54415 BEN BHACH ARD (HR No 415 and LMS 14415) and 54416 BEN A'BHUIRD (HR No 416 and LMS 14416), both withdrawn in 1948 without ever carrying their allocated BR numbers. Those engines were built as part of a 3 locomotive batch at Queen's Park Works to order number L177.

See also HR 'Small Ben' 4-4-0 2P locomotives built at Lochgorm Works and by Dübs & Co.

Driving wheel diameter 6' 0", 2-cylinder engine (inside)

NBR 'Scott/J' 4-4-0 3P – 'D29'

The 'Scott' class was a famous locomotive type designed especially for hauling passenger trains on the North British Railway (NBR) routes. There was 16 of the class originally built and the North British Locomotive Co Ltd (NBL) built a batch of 6 engines to order number L344 at Hyde Park Works in 1909, Cowlairs Works also built other examples of this class. The engines carried names derived from characters in Sir Walter Scott's novels; the LNER designated the class 'D29'.

British Railways (BR) took into stock 12 of the class in the number series 62400–62406 and 62409–62413. The 6 locomotives BR Nos 62400–62405 were NBL built (NBR 895–900, LNER 9895–9900 and also 2400–2405). However, only No 62405 and Nos 62410–62413 actually carried their allocated BR numbers.

The class were considered to be strong reliable locomotives and they retained their very distinctive NBR appearance throughout their working lives. None of the class survived beyond the end of 1952 and the last NBL built example to be withdrawn was No 62405 THE FAIR MAID, in February 1951.

See also NBR Reid 'Scott/J' 4-4-0 3P – 'D29' locomotives built at Cowlairs Works.

Driving wheel diameter 6' 6", 2-cylinder engine (inside)

NBL built NBR Reid 'Scott' class 4-4-0 No 62405 THE FAIR MAID (formerly NBR 900) is seen at Edinburgh St Margaret's (64A) shortly before being withdrawn. This locomotive was delivered to the North British Railway in September 1909 and withdrawn by BR in February 1951. ***Rail Photoprints Collection***

TVR 'A' 0-6-2T 4P

In 1948 British Railways (BR) took into stock a total of 58 ex Great Western Railway (GWR) former Taff Vale Railway (TVR) 0-6-2T locomotives which were designed by John Cameron and introduced between 1914 and 1921, the class was designed principally for passenger work. Some of the class had round tops to the tanks whilst others were later rebuilt with square tops. Of that total 8 locomotives were NBL built circa 1915 at Atlas Works to order number L647. The engines were numbered in the GWR sequence between 303 and 399 and 402 and 440. However, engines No 439 and No 440 were later renumbered by BR as No 312 and No 316 respectively. None of the class remained in traffic after the end of 1957 and the last NBL built example to be withdrawn was No 316 withdrawn in July 1956.

Driving wheel diameter 5' 3", 2-cylinder engine (inside)

NBL built Taff Vale Railway (TVR) 'A' class 0-6-2T No 356 seen at Abercynon circa 1954. This locomotive entered service in August 1915 and was withdrawn by BR in January 1955. *John Day Collection /Rail Photoprints Collection*

NBL built Locomotive classes which came into British Railways (BR) ownership

Class/Wheel Arrangement	Designer	Customer (Number to BR stock)	Build dates	BR number series*
'Intermediate'4-4-2T	Whitelegg	LTSR 5 locomotives	1903	41922–41926
'Corringham' 0-6-2T	Whitelegg	LTSR 10 locomotives	1903/08	41980–41989
'C4' 4-4-2	Robinson	GCR 8 locomotives	1905	62908–62917
'J27' 0-6-0	Worsdell	NER 20 locomotives	1908	65810–65829
'J35' 0-6-0	Reid	NBR 35 locomotives	1906 1910	64460–64488 64484–64513
'D29' 4-4-0	Reid	NBR 6 locomotives	1909	62400–62405
'N14' 0-6-2T	Reid	NBR 3 locomotives	1909	69120–69125
C7 4-4-2	Raven	NER 1 locomotive	1911	62954
'A' 0-6-2T	John Cameron	TVR 8 locomotives	1915	312,316,346, 352,356,357, 439,440

*The BR numbers are given for identification in BR listings and do not take into account missing numbers due to scrapping or locomotives of the same class built by other companies, but do include locomotives with allocated numbers not carried.

CR '944' 4-6-2T 4P

This 12 locomotive class was built for the Caledonian Railway to a Pickersgill design by North British Locomotive Co Ltd at their Glasgow Hyde Park Works to order No L672, and the engines were allocated the NBL works numbers 21480–91. Confusingly some listings show the class as being an 'in house build' by the Caledonian Railway at St Rollox Works. The engines were basically a smaller tank loco version of the CR '54630' class tender engines.

The large passenger tanks were the only engines of that type ever built for the Caledonian Railway and they were specifically designed for use on the semi-fast services out of Glasgow to the Ayrshire coast. For that reason the powerful Pacific Tanks were referred to colloquially as 'Wemyss Bay Tanks'. Following their removal from passenger duties the remaining members of the class were allocated to banking duties at Beattock, a roster they easily coped with.

Locos allocated LMS numbers 15357 and 15358 were withdrawn prior to Nationalisation and of the remaining 10 taken into BR stock only 8 were given their allocated BR numbers with loco Nos 55351 and 55355 being cut up in 1948 and 1949 respectively. Loco No 55356 fared little better it being withdrawn in June 1950, the last loco in service being 55359 which survived until October 1953.

Driving wheel diameter 5' 9", 2-cylinder engine (outside)

NBL built CR Pickersgill '944' class 4-6-2T BR No 55352 is seen on shed at Beattock (68D). This locomotive was delivered in January 1917 as CR No 946 and withdrawn in March 1952. *Mike Stokes Archive*

NBR 'C16' 4-4-2 2P

The North British Railway (NBR) introduced 21 locomotives of this class, a William Paton Reid designed passenger tank engine between 1915 and 1921, and they were a superheated version of that railway's earlier 'C15' class, all were built by the NBL (NBR numbers 438–516). The 'C15' and 'C16' were similar in appearance but the 'C15' engines had larger domes and chimneys than the 'C16' class. Both classes were at the time considered to be the standard passenger tank engines of the NBR. Order number L652 covered the building of a first batch of 15 engines at Atlas works in 1915 which were described as being 'to a Yorkshire Engine Co Ltd design'. The final 6 engines were also built at Atlas Works to order number L740 in 1920. All 21 came into BR stock in the number series 67482–67502, and No 67484 was the last 'C16' class locomotive in BR service, it being withdrawn in April 1961.

Driving wheel diameter 5' 9", 2-cylinder engine (inside)

NBL built NBR 'C16' class 4-4-2T No 67494 (NBR 450, LNER 9450 and 7494) is seen heading away from Polmont with a two coach service to Falkirk and Grangemouth, circa 1958. This locomotive entered service in April 1916 and was withdrawn by BR in February 1961. ***David Anderson***

The design details of NBL built NBR 'C16' class 4-4-2T No 67502 (NBR 516, LNER 9516 and 7502) are seen to good effect in this study taken at Dundee Tay Bridge depot (62B) circa 1958, note also the maker's plate. This handsome tank engine was the last of the class to be built; it was delivered in March 1921 and withdrawn by BR in April 1960. ***David Anderson***

NBR 'A' 0-6-2T 4MT – 'N15' (BR reclassified as 3MT in 1953)
This class of mixed traffic tank engines was designed by William Paton Reid for the NBR as a development of that railway company's earlier 'A' class 0-6-2T engines. The LNER designated the class 'N15'. There was a total of 99 of the class built between 1910 and 1924 and 69 of the locomotives which came into BR stock were NBL built between 1910 and 1920. Other locomotives in the class built by Robert Stephenson & Co Ltd (BR 69196–69205) and also at Cowlairs Works (BR 69206–69224).

The NBL build details are, 1910 Hyde Park Works to order number L394, BR numbers 69126–69143 (18 locomotives), 1912 at Queen's Park Works to order number L492, BR numbers 69144–69163 (20 locomotives), 1913 at Queen's Park Works to order number L528, BR numbers 69164–69171 and No 69185 (9 locomotives), 1916 at Atlas Works to order number L653, BR numbers 69172–69177 and 69179–69184 (12 locomotives), and 1920 at Atlas Works to order number L717, BR numbers 69186–69195 (10 locomotives).

There were 2 variants, the 'N15/1' (93 locomotives), was a version of the 'N15/2' class intended for normal freight duties and fitted with a smaller (3½ ton) capacity bunker. The 'N15/2' (6 locomotives), variants were fitted with a larger (4½ ton) capacity bunker and were mainly intended for use as banking engines on the Cowlairs incline. Withdrawals commenced in 1957 but 7 NBL built examples were amongst those which remained in traffic until October 1962.

Driving wheel diameter 4' 6", 2-cylinder engine (inside)

See also NBR Reid 'A' 0-6-2T 4MT – 'N15' locomotives built at Cowlairs Works.

NBL built NBR 'N15/2' 0-6-2T No 69131 (NBR No 282) is seen at Glasgow Eastfield shed (65A) in June 1956. This locomotive was one 6 engines fitted with larger capacity 4½ ton capacity coal bunkers. Note the 'slip coupling' apparatus attached to the smokebox door. Delivered in June 1910 No 69131 was withdrawn by BR in February 1962. ***David Anderson***

NBL built NBR 'N15/1' 0-6-2T No 69186 (NBR No 9022) is one of 93 engines fitted with the normal smaller 3½ ton coal bunker than the 6 'N15/2' variants. A total of 63 of these locomotives were built between 1910 and 1920, thereafter the LNER ordered that another 30 be built between 1923 and 1924. The locomotive is seen whilst receiving attention at St Margaret's depot (64A), note that the centre set of driving wheels are removed and that the NE lettering can still be seen. ***David Anderson***

FR 'Pettigrew' 0-6-0 3F

The Furness Railway (FR) was one of the UKs smaller independent companies. A total of 19 FR 0-6-0 locomotives designed by William Frank Pettigrew (Glasgow born) was built between 1913 and 1920. The two builders involved were Kitson & Co Ltd who built 4 engines and the NBL who built a further 15 engines. The NBL locomotives were built in two batches, the first 6 engines between 1913 and 1914 (order L592) and a second batch of 9 between 1918 and 1920 (orders L701 and L733). A total of 6 of the class were taken into BR stock in the number series 52494-52510 of which locomotives No 52494 and No 52499 were from the NBL 1913 batch and locomotives 52508/9 and 52510 from the firm's 1920 built batch. The LMS rebuilt most of the class fitting boilers with Belpaire fireboxes and lengthened smoke boxes. The NBL built FR '3Fs' were all withdrawn in the 1950s with No 52510 being the last in August 1957.

Driving wheel diameter 4' 7½", 2-cylinder engine (inside)

A 1913 NBL built FR 'Pettigrew' 3F 0-6-0 seen as BR No 52494 (formerly FR No1 and LMS 12494). Withdrawn from service in May 1956 the 0-6-0 3F is seen prior to that date at its last allocated shed Barrow (11B). This was the one member of the class with a Furness Railway (FR) type round topped boiler which after No 52494 was scrapped was fitted first to No 52508 and later to No 52494. *Keith Langston Collection*

G&SWR '3F' 0-6-2T

The Glasgow & South Western Railway (G&SWR) introduced 28 locomotives of the 0-6-2T wheel arrangement, which were based on an earlier 0-6-4T type designed by Dugald Drummond for the Highland Railway. One locomotive of the class had the distinction of being the last surviving ex G&SWR engine to come into BR stock. During the LMS era almost all of the workings on the former G&SWR section were rostered for locomotives of Midland Railway design, and so the fact that LMS No 16905 survived beyond the inception of BR was probably due to locomotive shortages during the Second World War period.

The last 10 engines of the class were all re-built by Whitelegg with larger water tank capacity. That batch included the sole survivor which was allocated, but never carried, the BR number 56905. The loco was delivered to the G&SWR in June 1919 having been built at Queen's Park Works as part of a 10 engine batch to order number L706, the engine was withdrawn by BR in April 1948.

Driving wheel diameter 5', 2-cylinder engine (inside)

GCR/ROD 2-8-0 7F

In 1911 Robinson introduced a 2-8-0 design for the Great Central Railway (GCR) and the 2-cylinder freight locomotive motive classified '8K' was hailed as a great success. North British Locomotive Co Ltd built a batch of 50 such engines under order number L496. The Robinson 2-8-0 design proved to be robust in build and reliable in traffic and accordingly the Railway Operating Division (ROD) of the Royal Engineers selected the type for war service (primarily in France) the build total being 521 of the 7F(BR classification) engines.

The NBL built a further 369 of that total between February 1917 and October 1919 under order numbers L689, L692, L693, L703, L704, L707, L710, L711, L712, L713 and L714. It can be seen from the build dates that production was still under way when hostilities came to an end (11th November 1918) and consequently not all of the ROD locomotives saw service in France. The NBL divided production between its three Glasgow manufacturing facilities with Queen's Park Works building 183 engines, Hyde Park Works 142 engines and Atlas Works 44 engines.

The LNER operated Robinson ROD 2-8-0 types in 8 variants which collectively became the '04' class under British Railways (numbers 63570–63920); from that number 173 ex NBL engines became BR stock with numbers in the series 63570–63571, 63573–63576, 63578–63579, 63581, 63583–63584, 63587–63593, 63595–63597, 63599, 63735–63901. Of those none saw service beyond the end of 1966 and the last NBL built example in traffic was No 63858 withdrawn in April 1966.

In 1944 Thompson rebuilt 58 engines fitting 'B1' type boilers, side window cabs and Walschaert valve gear, those 2-8-0s were separately designated as '01' class, 42 NBL built engines became members of the '01' class.

The Great Western Railway (GWR) also purchased a quantity of these engines (circa 1919) which were modified to suit GWR practice; 36 locomotives of that batch came into BR stock with numbers in the series 3002–3048. None of the GWR engines survived beyond the end of 1958, with the last NBR built operational examples being Nos 3011, 3015 and 3024 all withdrawn in October 1958.

Worthy of mention is the fact that a quantity of the ex ROD 2-8-0 engines were acquired by the London & North Western Railway (LNWR) and London Midland & Scottish Railway (LMS numbers 9616-65) around the time of grouping, but all were scrapped circa 1932.

Driving wheel diameter 4' 8", 2-cylinder engine (outside)

Locomotive No 3037, NBL built ROD 2-8-0 allocated to the GWR in 1919 is seen in splendid condition in GWR livery just having been outshopped from Swindon Works circa 1945. The NBL diamond shaped maker's plate can clearly be seen on the splasher note also the 'as built' boiler with Belpaire firebox also the non side window cab. This locomotive was withdrawn by BR in August 1948. *Rail Photoprints Collection*

NBL built Ex London & North Eastern Railway (LNER) '04/7' class 2-8-0 No 63848, rebuilt circa 1939, note the shortened '02' type boiler and round topped firebox. The locomotive is pictured leaving Northwich on the 'Cheshire Lines' with a coal train for the nearby Imperial Chemical Industries Ltd works at Winnington in May 1961. The converging line to the right of the locomotive is one side of the 'Northwich Triangle' which connects the CLC with the branch line to Sandbach via Middlewich. This locomotive was outshopped in June 1919 and withdrawn by BR in July 1965. *Keith Langston Collection*

Western Region ROD 2-8-0 No 3024, is pictured at Didcot circa 1955. This locomotive was built by the NBL at their Hyde Park Works and entered GWR stock in 1917 being withdrawn by BR in October 1958. Note the GWR style safety valve cover and the circular maker's plate on the splasher. *Rail Photoprints Collection*

NBR 'S' 0-6-0 4F – 'J37' (BR reclassified as 5F in 1953)

The North British Railway (NBR) introduced the Reid designed 'S' class 0-6-0 between 1914 and 1921, they were designated 'J37' class by the LNER. These locomotives were reportedly the most powerful 0-6-0 tender engines ever built for use on a Scottish railway. A total of 104 of the class came into BR stock and 60 of those engines were NBL built at Atlas works between 1918 and 1921 to order numbers L695, L716 and L739, and also a further batch by Cowlairs Works between 1914 and 1921. The class proved both capable and reliable in service whilst hauling mainline freight trains. The locomotives often worked both passenger and freight services over the West Highland Line and in addition were regularly rostered to work heavily loaded coal trains from the Fife collieries.

The NBL locomotives carried numbers in the BR series 64556–64566, 64568, 64571–64573 and 64576–64629 (NBR numbers were allocated in a non-consecutive sequence from 88–508, for LNER numbers disregard the 6 prefix).

Engines of the class remained in service almost to the end of steam on BR with the last NBL examples Nos 64576, 64602, 64611 and 64620 being withdrawn in October 1967. See also NBR Reid 'S' 0-6-0 4F – 'J37' locomotives built at Cowlairs Works.

Driving wheel diameter 5', 2-cylinder engine (inside)

NBL built NBR Reid 0-6-0 No 64566 looks to be in ex-works condition and the 'J37' is seen shunting wagons at Seafield shed in this 1960s image. Seafield was a sub shed of St Margaret's, note that some of the wagon doors are open whilst ash removal takes place. The NBL maker's plate can be seen on the centre wheel splasher. Delivered in August 1918 this engine was withdrawn by BR in April 1962. *David Anderson*

NBL built NBR 'J37' class 0-6-0 No 64618 seen at Leslie having worked from Markinch with the 'Scottish Rambler No 2 Railtour', 13 April 1963. This locomotive was delivered in December 1920 and withdrawn by BR in October 1966. *Rail Photoprints Collection*

NBL built 'J37' class 0-6-0 No 64614 quietly simmers to itself whilst parked on the approach roads to Bathgate (64F) shed, in May 1964. This locomotive was delivered to the NBR in January 1920 and withdrawn by BR in December 1964. *Rail Photoprints Collection*

NBL built Locomotive classes which came into British Railways (BR) ownership

Class/Wheel Arrangement	Designer	Customer (Number to BR stock)	Build dates	BR number series*
'944'	Pickersgill	CR 10 locomotives	1917	55350–55351
'C16' 4-4-2T	Reid	NBR 21 locomotives	1915/21	67482–67502
'N15' 0-6-2T	Reid	NBR 69 locomotives	1910/13 1913 1916/17 1920	69126–69171 69185 69172–69184 69186–69195
'FR' 3F 0-6-0	Pettigrew	FR 5 locomotives	1913 1920	52494–52499 52508–52510
'3F' 0-6-2T	Drummond/ Whitelegg	G&SWR 1 loco	1915/19	56905
ROD 7F 2-8-0	Robinson/ GCR	GWR/ROD 36 locomotives	1919	3002–3049
'04' 2-8-0	Robinson	GCR/MOD 173 locomotives	1912 1913 1917/19	63570–63597 63599 63735–63901
'J37' 0-6-0	Reid	NBR 60 locomotives	1918 1919 1920/21	64556–64590 64591–64608 64609–64629

* The BR numbers are given for identification in BR listings and do not take into account missing numbers due to scrapping or locomotives of the same class built by other companies, but do include locomotives with allocated numbers not carried.

GNR 'H2' 2-6-0 4MT - 'K2'

The Gresley designed 'K2' class Mogul (2-6-0) was first introduced by the Great Northern Railway (GNR) in 1912 as that railway's 'H2' class, changed to 'H3' class in 1914. The class designation later became LNER 'K1' class but that classification was later changed to 'K2' class and building of the Mogul variants continued until 1921. Introduced during the so called 'Ragtime' era the locomotives were often referred to as 'Ragtimers'. The 'K2' class locomotives were built at Doncaster Works and by the contractors Kitson & Co Ltd and NBL.

In 1948 BR took into stock 75 engines allocating them numbers in the series 61720–61794 and of that total 20 were built by the NBL during 1918. Hyde Park Works built 10 locomotives to order L698 and Queen's Park Works built a further 10 locomotives to order number L699 (BR number series 61750-61769).

After 1925 a number of the class were transferred to work in Scotland (specifically on the West Highland Line). The NBL built members of that 13 locomotive batch were Nos 61755, 61758, 61764 LOCH ARKAIG and 61769. Those engines were later fitted with side window cabs. Interestingly the NBL listed their 'K2/2' variant engines as being to a design which had been 'modified by Beyer, Peacock Ltd'. All of the class were withdrawn before the end of 1962 and the last NBL built example in traffic was No 61756 withdrawn in June 1962.

Driving wheel diameter 5' 8", 2-cylinder engine (outside)

NBL built GNR 'H1'/'H2' class 2-6-0 seen as ex-LNER BR 'K2/2' No 61754 (formerly 4664 and 1754) seen at an unknown location, circa 1950. This locomotive entered service in August 1918 and was withdrawn by BR in September 1959. *Rail Photoprints Collection*

GNR '01' 2-8-0 8F – '03'

In 1919 the NBL constructed two batches of a Nigel Gresley designed 2-cylinder 2-8-0 locomotive for the Great Northern Railway (GNR), 5 further locomotives of this class were built at Doncaster Works. NBL Hyde Park Works built 10 under order number L705 and Atlas Works a further 5 under order L709. The engines entered service between March and November of that year. In 1944 the class name was changed to 'O3' in order that designation 'O1' could be used for rebuilds of the 'O4' 2-8-0 class. In 1948 a total of 17 'O3' class engines came into BR stock and were allocated numbers in the series 63475–63494, of those 12 were NBL built locomotives which were allocated numbers in the series 63480–63494. All of the class were withdrawn before the end of 1952 and the last NBL built locomotive to be withdrawn was No 63484 which was retired by BR in December 1952.

Driving wheel diameter 4' 8", 2-cylinder engine (outside)

NBL built '01' class (later '03' class) LNER locomotive No 3482 (BR 63482) is pictured on shed in LNER livery pre 1948. This locomotive was delivered to the GNR in May 1919 and was withdrawn by BR in January 1952. *Keith Langston Collection*

CR '113', '918', and '72' 4-4-0 3P

Between 1916 and 1922 William Pickersgill introduced his own version of the 'Dunalastairs' which were the last express passenger engines built for the Caledonian Railway, and were commonly referred to as 'Caley Bogies' (BR numbers 54461–54508).

The express passenger 4 cylinder 4-4-0 locomotives were identified by three class designations, all in the '3P' classification. In 1948 BR took into stock 48 of the type of which 22 were NBL built engines. In addition St Rollox Works (16 engines) and Sir W. G. Armstrong Whitworth & Co Ltd (10 engines) also built locomotive of this class(s). The '72' class locomotives which were introduced from 1920 onwards were fitted with slightly larger cylinders than the other two variants.

Atlas Works produced the first NBL batch in 1916 building 10 engines to order number L664 (CR numbers 928–937) which were '113' and 918' variants. An additional batch of 12 engines was built at Hyde Park Works in 1922 to order number L768 (CR numbers 66–71 and 92–97) as '72' variants. In total 22 NBL built engines of the '113', '918' and '72' classes came into BR stock and were allocated numbers in the series 54467–54476 and 54497–54508. None of the class saw service beyond the end of 1962 and the last NBL built example to be withdrawn was No 54502 in October 1962.

See also Caledonian Railway '113', '918', and '72' 4-4-0 3P built at St Rollox Works.

Driving wheel diameter 6' 6", 2-cylinder engine (inside) Cylinder size variants 20" dia x 26"stroke BR 54467-54476, 20½" dia x 26"stroke BR 54497–54508.

NBL built Pickersgill '72' class 4-4-0, formerly Caledonian Railway (CR) No 69 is seen soon after being renumbered 14500 and given LMS livery. The Down mainline express is passing over Floriston water troughs (north of Carlisle) and a Caledonian Railway Carlisle–Glasgow Central semaphore route indicator is carried on the buffer beam. The locomotive became BR No 54500 and was withdrawn in February 1962. *Mike Bentley Collection*

The first NBL built Pickersgill Caledonian Railway '113'/ '918' class 4-4-0 seen as BR No 54467 (CR No 928 and LMS No 14467) outside the locomotive shed at Forfar (then 63C) in 1959. Introduced in March 1916 this locomotive was withdrawn by BR in October 1959. Note the snow plough. *Rail Photoprints Collection*

The clean lines of the sturdy looking Pickersgill Caledonian Railway class of 4-4-0 locomotive are well illustrated in this mid-1950s image of BR No 54473 between duties at Keith (61C). No 54473 (CR No 934 and LMS No 14473) was delivered in June 1916 and withdrawn by BR in October 1959. *David Anderson Collection*

The ex Highland Railway two road shed building at Forres (60E) is the setting for this September 1958 image of 'Caley Bogie' 4-4-0 No 54470 (CR No 931 and LMS 14470), at that time the depot was home to 6 former Caledonian Railway locomotive. Forres was the first of the main ex HR depots to close to steam with its then locomotive allocation being transferred to Inverness, St Rollox and Polmadie sheds. *David Anderson*

GNR '02' 2-8-0 8F

The Nigel Gresley designed 3-cylinder '02' class 2-8-0 locomotives were built between 1921 and 1943; the 'Big Four' came into being 1 January 1923. The majority of these 3-cylinder engines were constructed at Doncaster Works (The Plant), with the later built examples of the Great Northern Railway (GNR) design being supplied to the London & North Eastern Railway (LNER). BR showed a total of 67 in their January 1948 stock figure (BR numbers 63921–63987) and included in that total were 10 NBL built engines ordered in March 1919 and delivered in 1921, they were classified as '02/1' variants.

This was Gresley's first 3-cylinder design and as such it employed his patented conjugated valve gear. The NBL built examples carried the BR numbers 63922–63931 (originally designated '02/1' variants).The first engine of the class (BR No 63921 withdrawn 1948) was the only one built with inclined cylinders and Gresley conjugated valve gear, it was designated '02' but there were 4 other variants. In 1921 the '02/1' variant with horizontal cylinders and a modified form of conjugated valve gear was introduced. The '02/2 type appeared in 1924, '02/3' in 1932 and from 1943 onwards Thompson rebuilt some engines with 'B1' type boilers they became '02/4' variants and the rebuilds included 6 NBL built engines (BR Nos 63925/26, 63928–63931).

The engines were well received by the depots and because of their 8F rating they were able to haul 80 wagon coal trains between Peterborough and London. None of the class survived in traffic beyond the end of 1963, the NBL built engines were withdrawn by BR between 1962 and 1963 the last of those being No 63924 in October 1963.

Driving wheel diameter 4' 8", 3-cylinder engine

NBL built GNR Gresley '02/1' class 2-8-0 No 63928 is seen in '02/4' form whilst on shed at Doncaster (36A) during 1960. This locomotive entered service with the Great Northern Railway (GNR) in May 1921 and was withdrawn by BR in September 1963. *Rail Photoprints Collection*

NBL built GNR Gresley '02/1' class 2-8-0 No 63930 is seen with a rake of iron ore empties heading down the mineral only branch from High Dyke to Stainby, in June 1960. The loco was delivered to the GNR in May 1921 and withdrawn by BR in December 1962. *Hugh Ballantyne/Rail Photoprints Collection*

GNoSR 'V' 4-4-0 2P – 'D40' (BR reclassified as 1P in 1953)
Between 1899 and 1921 the Great North of Scotland Railway (GNoSR) introduced a William Pickersgill designed class of 2-cylinder 4-4-0 locomotive which were designated 'V' class (BR number series 62260–62262, 62264–62265, 62267–62273). In addition to the NBL 'D40' class variants were built by Neilson, Reid & Co Ltd and at Inverurie Works.

In 1920/21 Thomas Heywood introduced a superheated version of the class with piston valves and extended smoke boxes (BR number series 62274-62279) those locomotive were designated GNoSR 'F' class, those 4-4-0 engines were the first of the GNoSR fleet to be officially given names. In total BR took into stock 18 locomotives of this class.

The NBL batch of 5 with BR numbers 62275–62279 (GNoSR Nos 47–50, 52), were built at Hyde Park Works as part of an GNoSR 'F' class batch of 6 locomotives to order number L730 and one of that batch LNER No 2280 (GNoSR No 54) was scrapped prior to 1948.

This class is perhaps better known by the LNER designation of 'D40' class from which one locomotive, No 62277 GORDON HIGHLANDER (GNoSR No 49) is preserved. None of the class remained in traffic beyond the end of 1958 and the last NBL built example to be withdrawn was the aforementioned preserved example which was withdrawn by BR in June 1958.

See also GNoSR Pickersgill 'V' 4-4-0 2P – 'D40' locomotives built by Neilson, Reid & Co Ltd and also at Inverurie Works.

Driving wheel diameter 6' 1", 2-cylinder engine (inside)

NBL built 'D40' class 4-4-0 No 62276 ANDREW BAIN is seen with Ivatt 'Class 2' Mogul No 46460 outside the former GNoSR engine shed at Fraserburgh in 1953. Note the cowcatcher fitted to No 46460 for working over the St Combs branch. No 62276 entered service in October 1920 and was withdrawn by BR in October 1955. *Rail Photoprints Collection*

Preserved NBL built GNoSR 'V' class (LNER 'D40' class) No 49 (BR 62277) 'GORDON HIGHLANDER' together with preserved Caledonian Railway 'Single' No 123 is seen heading the RCTS 'Solway Ranger' railtour during a stop at Silloth on 13 June 1964. The venerable Scottish pair double headed the Carlisle–Port Carlisle Junction–Silloth–Carlisle section. GNoSR No 49 was retired as BR No 62277 in June 1958 and thereafter restored to main line working condition in order to haul special trains for a number of years before being finally retired to Glasgow Museum of Transport/ Riverside Museum as a static exhibit. *Rail Photoprints Collection*

The former CR motive power depot at Dawsholm (65D) was situated in the Kelvindale area of Glasgow and it was a brick-built 6-track dead-ended shed with a twin track repair shop. This image of No 49 in GNoSR livery was taken at the site in February 1962. The shed became a base for locomotive No 49 and other preserved engines which frequently worked mainline special trains during the late 1950s and early 1960s. The shed closed on 3 October 1964; a housing estate was built on the site in 1989. *Keith Langston Collection*

'D40' class 4-4-0 No 62277 GORDON HIGHLANDER is seen between duties and in light steam at Keith (61C) circa 1954, note the cast nameplate and works plate on the splasher. *Rail Photoprints Collection*

LNER 'A1' 4-6-2 7P, later became 'A3'/'A10' (1928–1947)

The London & North Eastern Railway (LNER) placed an order in 1923 for 20 Gresley designed Pacific locomotives of the type which eventually all became designated 'A3' class, the NBL batch were delivered between July and December 1924. All of the Scottish built 'A1' ('A3'/ 'A10') class 3-cylinder engines were built at NBL Hyde Park Works under order number L787 (LNER 2563-2582) and all passed into British Railway's ownership (60064–60083). This was Nigel Gresley's first 3-cylinder Pacific design, delivered first to the Great Northern Railway (GNR) and from January 1923 to the LNER.

NBL built No 60068 SIR VISTO was the only 'A10' class engine to come into BR stock but was rebuilt as an 'A3' in December 1948. In keeping with others of the class, and conforming to BR policy some, but not all the ex NBL examples were fitted with German style smoke deflectors between 1959 and 1962. During the same period several others were fitted with double chimneys.

The very reliable NBL built examples of the class survived in traffic well into the BR era, two of the batch being the last to be withdrawn in October 1964; they were No 60071 TRANQUIL and No 60080 DICK TURPIN.

Driving wheel diameter 6' 8", 3-cylinder engine

NBL built Gresley 'A3' class Pacifics at work north of the border circa 1960, both are seen leaving Edinburgh Haymarket shed (64B) on the way to join southbound trains at Waverley station (seen before the addition of double chimney 04/1959 and smoke deflectors 07/1961). Above is No 60077 THE WHITE KNIGHT completed in December 1924 and withdrawn by BR in November 1964, below is No 60078 NIGHT HAWK (also seen before the addition of double chimney 02/1959 and smoke deflectors 03/1962) which was also completed in December 1924 and was withdrawn by BR in June 1963. *Both images David Anderson*

NBL built Gresley 'A3' class Pacific No 60079 BAYARDO, a Carlisle Canal (12C at that time) based engine is seen at Hawick on the former Waverley Route in August 1960 with a train from Edinburgh, the locomotive is standing at the station platform part of which was on a viaduct. No 60079 was delivered to the LNER in October 1924 and withdrawn by BR in September 1961. Note the double chimney which had been fitted in April 1960, this locomotive did not receive German style smoke deflectors. ***Hugh Ballantyne/ Rail Photoprints Collection***

NBL built Gresley 'A3' class Pacific No 60079 BAYARDO is seen between duties at Edinburgh Haymarket shed yard (64B) the locomotive is fully coaled and ready for its next express passenger turn, circa 1959. This locomotive was regularly used on Waverley Route services during the late 1950s and 1960s. ***David Anderson***

LMS/SDJR Fowler 0-6-0 4F

The combined total of Fowler 0-6-0 '4F' freight engines introduced to the Somerset & Dorset Joint Railway (SDJR) in 1922 and the LMS between 1924 and 1940 and taken into BR stock was 580 engines in the number series 44027–44606. The large number built is testament to the success of the uncomplicated design and although the 0-6-0s were primarily designed as freight locomotive they were often to be seen on both local passenger services and double heading duty. The class was built at Derby, Crewe, St Rollox and Horwich works and additionally by contractors Kerr, Stuart & Co Ltd, Andrew Barclay Sons & Co Ltd and North British Locomotive Co Ltd.

The NBL built 80 of the type in four batches, 25 engines at Queen's Park Works to order number L802 (1924) also 25 engines to order number L821 (1926) 15 engines at Hyde Park Works to order number L835 (1927) and a further 15 engines at Queen's Park Works to order number L836 (1927). The BR numbers of the NBL built locomotive were 44057–44081, 44382–44406 and 44477–44506. None of the class remained in traffic beyond the end of 1966 however, NBL built engines Nos 44394 and 44500 were amongst the last to be withdrawn in October 1966.

See also LMS/SDJR Fowler 0-6-0 4F locomotives built at St Rollox Works and also Andrew Barclay Sons & Co Ltd.

Driving wheel diameter 5' 3", 2-cylinder engine (inside)

NBL built Fowler '4F' 0-6-0 BR No 44394 was outshopped from Queen's Park Works in October 1926. This locomotive is seen at Barrow shed in 1965 (then 12C) from where the '4F' was withdrawn by BR in July 1966. ***Keith Langston Collection***

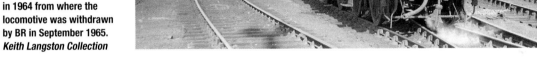

NBL built Fowler '4F' 0-6-0 BR No 44505 was outshopped from Queen's Park Works in October 1927. The '4F' is seen with fellow class members at Workington (then 12D) in 1964 from where the locomotive was withdrawn by BR in September 1965. ***Keith Langston Collection***

NBL built Locomotive classes which came into British Railways (BR) ownership

Class/Wheel Arrangement	Designer	Customer (Number to BR stock)	Build dates	BR number series*
'K2' 2-6-0	Gresley	GNR 20 locomotives	1918	61750–61769
'03' 2-8-0 The class was known as '01' until 1944	Gresley	GNR 12 locomotives	1919	63480–63494
'113'/'918'/'72' 4-4-0	Pickersgill	CR 22 locomotives	1916 1922	54467–54476 54498–54508
'3F' 0-6-2T	Whitelegg	GSWR 1 locomotive	1919	56905
'F' class 4-4-0 (D40)	Pickersgill	GNoSR 5 locomotives	1920	62275–62279
'02' 2-8-0	Gresley	GNR 10 locomotives	1921	63922–63931
'A1' 4-6-2 became 'A3'	Gresley	LNER 20 locomotives	1924	60064–60083
'4F Fowler' 0-6-0	Fowler	LMS/SDJR 80 locomotives	1925 1926/27 1927	44057–44081 44382–44406 44477–44506

* The BR numbers are given for identification in BR listings and do not take into account missing numbers due to scrapping or locomotives of the same class built by other companies but do include locomotives with allocated numbers not carried.

LMS Fowler 'Compound'* 4-4-0 4P

This Midland Railway (MR) 4-4-0 'Compound' (3-cylinder) type was designed by Samuel Waite Johnson in 1902. That design was later modified by his successor Richard Mountford Deeley, who ordered a further batch of similar locomotives to be built between 1905 and 1909.

The MR was absorbed by the LMS in the 1923 reorganisation of the railways after which the LMS locomotive designer Henry Fowler (later Sir) having evaluated the performance of the Johnson inspired 4-4-0 4P engines, ordered an LMS modified batch of 195 to be built between 1924 and 1927. The majority of those engines were built at Derby. However, others were built by Horwich Works and contractors Vulcan Foundry Ltd and North British Locomotive Co Ltd. In 1924/5 a batch of 25 engines with LMS numbers 1135–1159 (BR numbers 41135–41159) were built at Queen's Park Works to order number L801.

In 1928 locomotive LMS No 1054 (Derby built) after being fitted with a modified tender made history by running non-stop over the 400 mile journey between London Euston and Edinburgh Princes Street. The run was perhaps a low key LMS answer to the LNER's announcement of a non-stop 'Flying Scotsman' service between the two capital cities.

BR took into stock 195 of these successful and popular locomotives allocating them numbers in the series 40900–40939 and 41045–41199, a series which included all of the NBL built engines. None of the class remained in service beyond the end of 1961 and the last NBL example to be withdrawn was No 41157 in May 1960.

Driving wheel diameter 6' 9", 3-cylinder engine

* *'Compound' Locomotives*

In this MR compound design 3-cylinders were used with the smaller volume inside cylinder (19" dia x 26") stroke operating on high pressure steam whilst the larger volume (21" dia x 26") stroke outside pair operated on the low pressure steam exhausted by the inside cylinder.

Fowler designed 'Midland Railway Compound' built at the NBL Queen's Park Works in 1925 is seen in London Midland & Scottish Railway (LMS) livery whilst working a local passenger train in the Glasgow area. The LMS 4P became BR No 41137 and was withdrawn from service in April 1956. *Mike Morant Collection*

LMS/SDJR 'Jinty' 0-6-0T 3F

A relatively large number of the 'Fowler' designed 0-6-0T 3F locomotive, which over time became known as the 'Jinty' class, were built between 1924 and 1931 and they were a development of the earlier Midland Railway (MR) Johnson 'Jinty' class engines. In 1948 British Railways (BR) took into stock 412 Fowler 0-6-0T 'Jinty' locomotives allocating to them numbers in the series 47260 – 47681, the majority of which were built for the LMS/SDJR by various outside contractors which included the North British Locomotive Co Ltd and Beardmore Ltd. During 1948 the BR increased their number of 'Jinty' engines by 5 adding locomotives returned to them by the War Department, which were in fact Glasgow built Beardmore Ltd engines.

The NBL constructed a total of 75 of the class. Queen's Park Works built the NBL's first 15 engines to order number L788 during 1923/4 (BR number series 47280–47294). In 1926 Hyde Park Works built 30 engines to order number L819 whilst Queen's Park Works built a further 30 to order number L820. The 60 NBL 1926 built engines carried numbers in the BR series 47317–47376. None of the 'Jinty' class survived in traffic beyond the end of 1967. Three of the NBL built engines Nos 47324 (delivered June 1926 and withdrawn December 1966), 47327 (delivered July 1926 and withdrawn December 1966) and 47357 (delivered July 1926 and withdrawn December 1966) survived into preservation (in total 10 'Jinty' tank engines escaped the cutter's torch).

See also LMS/SDJR Fowler 'Jinty' 0-6-0T 3F locomotive built by Beardmore Ltd.

Driving wheel diameter 4' 7", 2-cylinder engine (inside)

NBL built LMS Fowler 'Jinty' 3F 0-6-0 No 47338 is seen on shed at Crewe South (5B) in July 1965. This locomotive entered service in August 1926 and was withdrawn by BR in October 1965. *Keith Langston Collection*

Preserved NBL built LMS Fowler 'Jinty' 3F 0-6-0 No 47357 (LMS 7357) is seen at the Midland Railway Centre whilst double heading with preserved Fowler 0-6-0 No 44027 (LMS 4027). For a short period the locomotive carried a Midland Railway (MR) style number and fictional livery (MR No 16440). The world famous NBL diamond maker's plate can be seen on the coal bunker side below the MR crest. *Keith Langston Collection*

SR 'N15' 4-6-0 5P

This class of 5P express passenger engines was introduced by the London & South Western Railway (LSWR) and the Southern Railway (SR) between 1918 and 1927, to a Robert Urie/Richard Maunsell design. They were numbered 448–457, 736–755 and 763–806 in the SR number series. During 1925 a total of 30 'N15' 'King Arthur' class 4-6-0 engines were built by the NBL for the Southern Railway (SR) (SR Nos 763–792, BR Nos 30763–30792) that batch of engines were affectionately referred to as 'Scotch Arthurs'. The 2-cylinder 5P engines were all built at Hyde Park Works, 20 under order number L800 (SR 763-782) and 10 under order number L803 (SR 783–792). BR took into stock all 74 engines in the class and they were allocated numbers in the series 30448–30457, 30736–30755 and 30763–30806.

The NBL built locomotives were well received by the SR and in performance terms they compared favourably with others built at the SR Eastleigh Works. The 'Scotch Arthurs' were fitted with modified cabs to facilitate working over the Eastern Section of the SR and they were coupled to 8-wheel bogie tenders. None of the class survived in traffic beyond the end of 1962, however NBL built locomotive No 30777 SIR LAMIEL was saved for preservation. SR No 777 was delivered to the Southern Railway (SR) in June 1925 and retired by BR as 30777 in October 1961.

Driving wheel diameter 6' 7", 4-cylinder engine.

The Southern Railway (SR) 'King Arthur' class 4-6-0 engines were considered to be successful express passenger locomotive which served that company and BR Southern Region well, the NBL built 30 of the class during 1925. The NBL built 5P 4-6-0s were fitted with modified cabs to suit the loading gauge of the SR Eastern Section, the eight wheeled bogie tender can clearly be seen. Above BR No 30765 SIR GARETH (SR No 765 delivered May 1925 and withdrawn September 1962) is seen at Basingstoke working hard on the Eastern Section of the SR, note the fireman feeding the firebox. ***David Anderson***

BR No 30791 SIR UWAINE (SR 791 delivered September 1925 and withdrawn May 1960) is seen at Eastleigh shed (71A) circa 1957. ***Keith Langston Collection***

Preserved 'Scotch Arthur' SR No 777 (BR 30777) SIR LAMIEL seen in the environs of Chester whilst on 'North Wales Coast Express' duty, August 1991.
Keith Langston

GWR '5700' 0-6-0PT 4F

The 0-6-0 Pannier Tank design, although operated by several railways is mainly associated with the Great Western Railway (GWR). Charles Benjamin Collett (later O.B.E.) introduced a 4ft 7½ diameter driving wheel version in 1929. So successful was the 'Pannier Tank' general design that examples were still being built as British Railways (BR) took over the running of the national network (from 1948).The total BR stock of the '5700' class at the end of 1949 was an impressive 772 engines. The majority of the class was built at Swindon Works but in order to keep up with demand the GWR also sub-contracted other companies to build them. Those companies were Kerr Stuart & Co Ltd, Sir W.G. Armstrong Whitworth & Co Ltd, Beyer, Peacock & Co Ltd, W.G. Bagnall Ltd and the North British Locomotive Co Ltd.

The class was designed for light goods and shunting work but were also used on passenger traffic. They replaced worn out saddle tank (ST) and pannier tank (PT) engines, many of which dated from the late 1880s. Distinctively the '5700' class locomotive had tapered chimneys and large steam domes. The engines were allocated numbers in GWR/BR series 3600–3799, 4600–4699, 5700–5799, 7700–7799, 8700–8799, 9600–9682 and 9711–9799.

The NBL built 100 of the class in four batches which included the first of the class to enter service. A total of 25 engines each were built to orders L852, L853, L863 and L872. The NBL built locomotives carried GWR/BR numbers in the series 5700–5748 and 7725–7774.

None of the class remained in traffic with BR beyond the end of 1966. However, all but one of the 12 '5700' class engines employed by London Transport survived longer, with NBL built LT locos L90 (BR 7760) and L94 (BR 7752) remaining in service until June 1971. Three of the NBL 1930 built examples survived into preservation GWR/BR No 7752 which also became London Transport No L94, GWR/BR No 7754 and GWR/BR No 7760 which also became London Transport L90.

Driving wheel diameter 4' 7½", 2-cylinder engine (inside)

Great Western Railway (GWR) class '5700' 0-6-0PT (BR 7754) is one of three preserved NBL built examples of the class. The locomotive is pictured approaching Glyndyfrdwy station whilst en-route from Llangollen to Carrog on the scenic Llangollen Railway. This locomotive entered GWR service in December 1930 and was withdrawn by British Railways (BR) in January 1959. ***Keith Langston***

NBL built GWR class '5700' 0-6-0PT 0-6-0 No 7729 draws away from Portbury Shipyard signalbox with the 1.45 Portishead - Bristol Temple Meads passenger service in February 1962. This locomotive was delivered in December 1929 and withdrawn by BR in July 1962. ***Hugh Ballantyne/Rail Photoprints Collection***

LMS 'Royal Scot' 4-6-0 6P (BR reclassified as 7P in 1951)
A total of 50 London Midland & Scottish Railway Fowler 'Royal Scot' 4-6-0 locomotives were ordered from the NBL for delivery in 1926. Those 3-cylinder engines were built in two batches, 25 engines at Queen's Park Works under order number L833 and 25 engines at Hyde Park Works under order number L834. During 1930 the LMS Derby Works built a further 20 'Royal Scot' class locomotives.

A study of the NBL works records will show that the company actually built the 'Royal Scot' locomotives with LMS numbers 6100–6124 at Queen's Park Works and the engines with LMS numbers 6125–6149 at Hyde Park Works. However, post 1933 records rightly show the locomotive with LMS number 6100 (BR 46100) as a Derby Works built engine.

The explanation being that in 1933 the LMS swopped the identities (names and numbers) of No 6100 (July 1927 NBL built engine) and No 6152 (July 1930 Derby built engine) so that the later newer built locomotive could be sent on a visit to the USA as No 6100 ROYAL SCOT. The locomotive visited the Chicago World Fair and thereafter went on a successful 11,194 mile long tour of North America. The engines never reverted back to their original identities after No 6100 returned to the UK.

The Fowler designed locomotives were extremely successful in traffic and for over 10 years they were the mainstay of the LMS Anglo-Scottish express passenger services, until ousted by Stanier's 4-cylinder Pacific engines. The whole of the class was rebuilt with larger boilers (tapered) double chimneys and new cylinders between 1943 and 1955.

The LMS ordered an experimental 'Royal Scot' from the NBL in 1928 under order number L585 the 4-6-0 originally carried the LMS number 6399 and was named FURY. Built at Hyde Park Works that engine was built with a high pressure boiler designed by the Superheater Co. During the engine's trial run a tube in the locomotive's high pressure steam circuit failed. That occurrence caused a blow back which resulted in a fatal injury being sustained by one of the Superheater Company employees who was travelling on the footplate. The experiment was immediately discontinued and No 6399 was thereafter rebuilt as a conventional 'Royal Scot' class engine becoming No 6170 BRITISH LEGION (BR 46170) and increasing the class build total to 71 locomotives. BR took into stock the whole of the class, allocating the 'Royal Scots' numbers in the series 46100–46170.

None of the class remained in traffic after the end of 1965. Derby built 46100 ROYAL SCOT (originally LMS No 6152) and importantly NBL built No 46115 SCOTS GUARDSMAN (LMS 6115) both survived into preservation albeit in rebuilt form.

Driving wheel diameter 6' 9", 3-cylinder engine

NBL built 'Royal Scot' class 4-6-0 BR No 46134 THE CHESHIRE REGIMENT is seen being coaled at Dalry Road shed (64C) Edinburgh, prior to working a through Birmingham express in July 1953. This locomotive was delivered to the LMS in September 1927, re-built in December 1953 and withdrawn by BR in November 1962. ***David Anderson***

NBL built 'Royal Scot' class 4-6-0 BR No 46137 THE PRINCE OF WALES'S VOLUNTEERS (SOUTH LANCASHIRE) was delivered to the LMS in September 1927, re-built in March 1955 and withdrawn by BR in October 1962. The locomotive is seen at Dalry Road shed circa 1953. ***David Anderson***

It is appropriate to include images of NBL built 'Royal Scot' class 4-6-0 BR No 46112 SHERWOOD FORESTER in the Stanier rebuilt form if only for comparison with the original build appearance. Locomotive No 46112 was delivered by the NBL in September 1927. An interesting scene at St Pancras station in 1961, as since 2008 that totally refurbished area of the famous ex Midland Railway London terminus has been designated for the use of Eurostar services. ***Keith Langston Collection***

NBL built 'Royal Scot' class 4-6-0 BR No 46148 THE MANCHESTER REGIMENT is seen whilst being assisted by a Fairburn 2-6-4T on the climb past Harthope with a Carlisle–Glasgow service, in July 1953. This locomotive was delivered to the LMS in November 1927 and later re-built; No 46148 was withdrawn by BR in November 1964. *Dave Cobbe/Rail Photoprints Collection*

NBL built 'Royal Scot' class 4-6-0 BR No 46133 THE GREEN HOWARDS seen in re-built form whilst hard at work on Beattock Bank, with a Carlisle–Glasgow stopping train in August 1955. This locomotive was delivered to the LMS in September 1927 and withdrawn by BR in February 1963. *David Anderson*

SECR 'L' 4-4-0 2P – 'L1'

In 1926 the South Eastern & Chatham Railway (SECR) introduced a 4-4-0 class from a design by Maunsell which was designated SECR 'L' class. The Southern Railway developed the 18½ ton axle load design further and it became their 'L1' class. The 2-cylinder class totalled 15 locomotives which were all built by the NBL to order number L814 at Hyde Park Works in 1926, they were similar in appearance to the SR 'D1' and 'E1' type engines. All 15 engines of the class came into BR stock in the number series 31753–31759 and 31782–31789 they were subsequently withdrawn between August 1959 and February 1962, the last in service being No 31757 withdrawn by BR in December 1961.

Driving wheel diameter 6' 8", 2-cylinder engine (inside)

NBL built Southern Railway/BR Southern Region 'L1' class 4-4-0 No 31787 seen with 'H' class No 31512 at Gillingham (73D) shed in March 1959. Outshopped in April 1926 and withdrawn by BR in January 1961. *Hugh Ballantyne/Rail Photoprints Collection*

NBL built Locomotive classes which came into British Railways (BR) ownership

Class/Wheel Arrangement	Designer	Customer (Number to BR stock)	Build dates	BR number series*
4P 'Compound' 4-4-0	Fowler	LMS 25 locomotives	1925	41135–41159
'Jinty' 0-6-0T	Fowler	LMS/SDJR 75 locomotive	1924 1926	47280–47294 47317–47376
'King Arthur' N15 4-6-0	Maunsell	SR 30 locomotives	1925	30763–30792
'5700' 0-6-0PT	Collett	GWR 100 locomotives	1929 1930/31	5700–5749** 7725–7774**
'Royal Scot' 4-6-0	Fowler	LMS 51 locomotives	1927 1927 1929	46101–46149 46152 46170
'L1' 4-4-0	Maunsell	SR 15 locomotives	1926	31753–31789

* The BR numbers are given for identification in BR listings and do not take into account missing numbers due to scrapping or locomotives of the same class built by other companies but do include locomotives with allocated numbers not carried. **Several NB built '5770' class engines became London Transport stock with appropriate 'L' numbers, 7760 (L90) 7752(L94) 7741(L96) 7749(L97) 7739(L98).

LNER 'B17' 4-6-0 4P (BR reclassified as 5P in 1953)

In 1928 the LNER placed with the NBL an order for 'B17' 'Sandringham' 3-cylinder 4-6-0 locomotive to a Gresley design. The first 10 locomotives of that class were built at Hyde Park Works under order number L850 (BR 61600–61609). Class leader No 61600 SANDRINGHAM was in fact the third of the popular 4-6-0 class to enter service. The NBL batch, in general with others of the first 48 engines in the class were designated 'B17/1' and were originally fitted with Great Eastern Railway (GER) type tenders. Over time there evolved 6 variants of the class and the 10 NBL examples became 'B17/6' after being rebuilt with 'B1' type boilers.

BR took into stock 73 of the class in 4 variants; they were allocated numbers in the series 61600–61672.

None of the class remained in traffic beyond the end of 1960 and the last NBL built engines to be withdrawn were No 61603 FRAMLINGHAM and No 61606 AUDLEY END, both in September 1958. No member of the class was preserved but a project to build a new LNER 'Sandringham' class 4-6-0 locomotive was launched in May 2008.

Driving wheel diameter 6' 8", 3-cylinder engine

NBL built 'B17' class 4-6-0 No 61600 SANDRINGHAM, seen on shed at Stratford (30A) in 1956. Outshopped in December 1928 this locomotive was withdrawn by BR in July 1958. *Rail Photoprints Collection*

LMS 'Jubilee' 4-6-0 5XP (BR reclassified as 6P5F in 1951)

In November 1933 NBL received instructions to build 50 'Jubilee' class 6P5F 4-6-0 engines to an LMS William Stanier design (class total to BR 191 engines in the number series 45552–45742). The NBL 3-cylinder 'Jubilee' class 4-6-0s were built in two batches of 25 engines each at Hyde Park Works and Queen's Park Works, under order number L885 (LMS 5557–5606 BR 45557–45606). The class was also built at Crewe Works. After modifications carried out on the earlier built members of the class the 6P5F tapered boiler engines became reliable performers and were often to be seen hauling express passenger trains on the routes of the former Midland Railway (MR). All of the class carried names and the first 'Jubilee' class engine to be withdrawn was Crewe built No 45637 WINDWARD ISLANDS, after that locomotive was damaged beyond repair in the horrific 1952 Harrow & Wealdstone accident.

The majority of the class remained in traffic until almost the end of 1960 when withdrawals began. The last NBL example in traffic was No 45562 ALBERTA which was taken out of traffic by BR in November 1967. Two NBL built examples survived into preservation, No 45593 KOLHAPUR (withdrawn October 1967) and No 45596 BAHAMAS (withdrawn July 1966).

Steam locomotive building was a capital and labour intensive operation, thus profits were not always guaranteed. For example the NBL bid a total price of £286K for building the batch of 50 engines (£5720 each) later agreed extras of £7K were added to the contract. The cost of raw materials and 'bought in' components totalled £152,345. It was later calculated that the remaining £140,037 from the contracted price was insufficient to cover wages and overheads, and as a result the NBL suffered a loss on the 'Jubilee' contract.

Driving wheel diameter 6' 9", 3-cylinder engine

NBL built LMS 'Jubilee' class 4-6-0 No 45588 KASHMIR is pictured at Castle Douglas with the 'Scottish Rambler No 2 Railtour', on 15 April 1963. Built in 1934 this locomotive was withdrawn by BR in May 1965. The railtour was operated over the Easter weekend of 1963 using this impressive selection of motive power, CR No 123, NBR No 256 GLEN DOUGLAS, HR No 103, GNSR No 49 GORDON HIGHLANDER, No 45588 KASHMIR, No 46474, No 57375, No 60041 SALMON TROUT, No 61324, No 64603, No 64618, No 65323, No 80023 and No 80093. *Rail Photoprints Collection*

NBL built LMS 'Jubilee' class 4-6-0 BR No 45563 AUSTRALIA is seen leaving Chester with a train of vans for Holyhead in August 1965. The yellow stripes on the cab sides indicate that the locomotive could not work 'under the wires', south of Crewe. This locomotive was delivered to the LMS in August 1934 and withdrawn by BR in November 1965. *Keith Langston*

Preserved NBL built LMS 'Jubilee' class 4-6-0 No 45596 BAHAMAS seen in BR livery during a visit to the East Lancashire Railway. Note the addition of a double chimney. *Keith Langston*

GNR 'H4' 2-6-0 6MT – 'K3'

The Great Northern Railway (GNR) designated 'H4' class and later London & North Eastern Railway (LNER) designated 'K3' class Mogul 3 cylinder 2-6-0 class designed by Gresley was introduced between 1920 and 1937. In 1948 BR took 192 of the type into stock in the number series 61800–61992. Included in that total were 20 engines in the BR number series 61939–61958 which were constructed by the NBL at Hyde Park Works during 1935 to order number L890 and were later designated as sub-class 'K3/2'. The powerful and reliable 'K3' class were considered to be excellent 'Mixed Traffic' engines however, their large physical size restricted route availability. Coincidentally the last 'K3/2' class engines were withdrawn by BR in 1962 the same year that the once proud North British Locomotive Co Ltd (NBL) was being wound up. None of the class survived beyond the end of 1962 and the last NBL built example to be withdrawn was No 61952 in December 1962.

Driving wheel diameter 5' 8", 2-cylinder engine (outside)

NBL built 'K3/2' No 61953 is pictured light engine at Bentley in 1961. Outshopped by the NBL in October 1935 this locomotive was withdrawn by BR in March 1952. *Mike Stokes Archive*

NBL built 'K3/2' No 61942 is seen at London King's Cross station with the RCTS 'The Fensman' railtour, on 9 September 1956. Delivered by the NBL in August 1935 this locomotive was withdrawn by BR in September 1962. *Hugh Ballantyne/Rail Photoprints Collection*

LMS Stanier 2-6-4T '2-Cylinder' 4MT

This class was Stanier's 1935 development of the earlier Fowler 2-6-4T type engines. They were fitted with the Stanier style tapered boilers and had slightly larger cylinders than the Fowler engines and incorporated sloping tops to the side water tanks. There were 208 of the class taken into BR stock and allocated numbers in the BR series 42425–42494 and 42537–42672, the majority of which were built at Derby Works.

During 1936/37 the NBL built approximately a third of that total producing 73 engines to order number L896 at the Hyde Park Works (LMS 2545–2617 BR 42545–42617). This order was the last NBL order from the LMS and in fact the last for any home based steam locomotive prior to the onset of the Second World War. So successful was the design that it later formed the basis of the Riddles BR Standard design of 2-6-4T. None of the class survived beyond the end of 1967 and the last two NBL built examples No 42574 and No 42616 were withdrawn by BR in October 1967.

Driving wheel diameter 5' 9", 2-cylinder engine (outside)

NBL built Stanier 4P 2-6-4T No 42591 is seen during a visit to Crewe Works in September 1950. Although sporting its BR number the LMS lettering can still be identified on the side tank. Outshopped from Hyde Park Works in October 1936 this locomotive was withdrawn by BR in October 1962. ***Hugh Ballantyne/Rail Photoprints Collection***

NBL built Stanier 4P 2-6-4T No 42616 is seen at Bradford Exchange with the 07.45 train of through coaches to Yarmouth Vauxhall in July 1967. This locomotive entered service with the LMS in February 1937 and was withdrawn by BR in October 1967. ***Ian Turnbull/Rail Photoprints Collection***

LMS and 'War Department' 2-8-0 8F

Between 1935 and 1944 the 2-8-0 freight locomotive design of William Stanier was built in large numbers for UK railways and the War Department. The class was rightly referred to as the freight engine which helped to win the Second World War. Large numbers of the class saw service overseas during and just after the war years. The build total of 849 Stanier '8F' 2-8-0 engines necessitated the need to utilise several production centres. The locomotive works at Ashford, Crewe, Brighton, Darlington, Doncaster, Eastleigh, Horwich and Swindon together with contractors Beyer, Peacock, Vulcan Foundry and North British all played their part. However, the NBL built the largest total by any contractor constructing 208 of the type to orders L932, L936, L937 and L938 between 1940 and 1942. In 1948/49 BR listed a final total 663 of the type and the number was increased to 666 engines by the end of 1957 (BR numbers in the series 48000–48775), as some War Department allocated locomotive were returned to BR. A total of 92 NBL built Stanier '8F' engines eventually came into BR stock and they carried numbers in the series 48176–48285 and 48773–48774, one NBL engine No 48773 survived into preservation. Withdrawals began in 1962 and steadily gathered pace in 1965 when 543 remained in use. Interestingly 150 of the class remained in traffic during the final year of UK steam. There were 5 NBL built Stanier '8F' locomotives still in traffic as steam haulage on the national network came to an end in August 1968 and they were No 48191, No 48247, No 48253, No 48271 and No 48278.

Driving wheel diameter 4' 8½", 2-cylinder engine (outside)

NBL built Stanier '8F' 2-8-0 No 48276 is seen heading a long mixed freight train through Sandbach station in this 1959 image. Despite the overhead wires, which had arrived in 1959, the signalman's Ford Popular car adds to the period setting. This Stanier '8F' was outshopped by the NBL in July 1942 and withdrawn by BR in November 1967. *Mike Stokes Archive*

Preserved NBL built Stanier '8F' BR No 48773 is seen with a train ex Bridgnorth for Bewdley whilst in LMS livery as No 8233 (the engine's first number). The location is the historic Victoria Bridge over the River Severn on the Severn Valley Railway; the 200 foot span cast iron bridge was completed in 1861. *Keith Langston*

The NBL built preserved Stanier '8F' No 48773 is seen climbing towards Waterworks Crossing on the Severn Valley Railway (SVR) with a Bridgnorth–Kidderminster service. *Keith Langston*

The history of SVR based No 48773 serves well to illustrate the complex nature of this locomotive type's distribution and use. NBL 1940 works number 24607 became LMS No 8233. In 1941 it was transferred to the War Department (WD) becoming No WD 307, sent overseas it then became Iran State Railways No 401-109. In 1952 it was repatriated to the UK becoming No WD 70307 and after being overhauled at BR Derby Works it was transferred to the Longmoor Military Railway becoming No WD 500. In 1957 the locomotive returned to BR stock as No 90733, that number was quickly changed to No 48773 to avoid confusion with the WD 'Austerity' number series.

LNER/BR 'B1' 4-6-0 5MT

The final LNER total of 'B1' class 5MT 4-6-0 Thompson engines in service with BR was 409 engines and by far the biggest majority of those were ordered from the NBL between 1946 and 1952. In addition to the NBL 'B1' class engines others were built at Darlington Works, Gorton Works and by the contractors Vulcan Foundry Ltd. Order numbers L958, L963 and L997 dating from 1946 to 1952 covered the building of 290 'B1' class 2-cylinder engines at Queen's Park Works. The 'B1' locomotives were allocated numbers in the BR series 61000–61409, the NBL built engines being numbered 61040–61139, 61190–61339 and 61360–61399. The 5MT engines represented the last class of steam locomotive built by the NBL exclusively for service in the UK. Good steel was in short supply during this post Second World War period but even so NBL delivered the orders on time with the last engine (BR 61399) being completed in April 1952. The 'B1' locomotives were extremely successful in traffic and were well received by footplate crews and running shed maintenance teams alike. With the exception of 8 engines which retired from traffic and then employed as service locomotives (i.e. stationary boilers etc) all of the class were withdrawn before the end of 1967. Two NBL built 'B1' class engines have been preserved, they are Nos 61264 and 61306.

Driving wheel diameter 6' 2", 2-cylinder engine (outside)

On the 1 in 70 gradient between Inverkeithing and North Queensferry class 'B1' 4-6-0 No 61397 powers through Hookhills Cutting towards the Forth Bridge crossing with an Up freight working. This locomotive was one of the last NBL built steam engines for use in the UK when outshopped in March 1952. The 4-6-0 was withdrawn by BR in 1965. Although fitted with electric lighting equipment traditional oil lamps can also be seen to be fitted displaying the appropriate headcode. *David Anderson*

Seen in LNER livery style at the Great Central railway is preserved NBL built 'B1' class 4-6-0 No 1264 (BR 61264). This locomotive was delivered in December 1947 just one month before the formation of BR and so was more commonly seen in BR black livery during its working life, which ended in December 1965. *Keith Langston*

Preserved NBL built ‘B1’ class 4-6-0 No 1306 (BR 61306) is seen in LNER livery during the 2009 ‘Steel Steam and Stars’ event at the Llangollen Railway. This locomotive has carried the name MAYFLOWER in preservation but never actually ran in LNER livery as it was delivered directly to British Railways (BR) in May 1948. *Keith Langston*

LNER/BR 'L1' 2-6-4T 4MT

The LNER introduced the Thompson designed 'L1' class 2-6-4T in 1945 and building continued under BR, bringing the class total up to 100 engines. The class was eventually allocated numbers 67701–67800 however, locomotives 67701–67716 were originally numbered 69000–69016 (re-numbered between April and July 1948). The class was built at Doncaster Works, Darlington Works and by the contractors Robert Stephenson & Hawthorns Ltd and the North British Locomotive Co Ltd.

The NBL built 35 of that total for British Railways (numbers 67731–67765) between October 1948 and February 1949. The order was placed in 1947 by the LNER but deliveries to NBL works order number L981 from Queen's Park Works were completed after the creation of BR. These powerful tank engines were designed with suburban passenger work in mind but were classified as 'Mixed Traffic' (MT) locomotives. The later built engines (including NBL examples) were distinguishable by virtue of the fact that a section of the running plate in front of the piston valves was cut away. Due to a loud clanking noise made by the locomotives those based on the ex-Great Northern Section of the Eastern Region were nicknamed 'Cement Mixers'!

They were the most powerful 2-6-4T configuration engines to run under BR. NBL built examples carried the numbers 67731–67765 and none of the class survived into preservation and all were withdrawn before the end of 1962. The last NBL built examples in traffic were Nos 67741, 67742, 67744, 67745, 67749 and 67759, all withdrawn by BR in December 1962.

Driving wheel diameter 5' 2", 2-cylinder engine (outside)

Built by North British, Thompson designed 'L1' class 2-6-4T No 67741 is seen whilst between duties standing at GCR signals under the roof at Nottingham Victoria station, in October 1961. This locomotive was delivered in November 1948 and withdrawn by BR in December 1962. Note the profile of the running plate. *Hugh Ballantyne/ Rail Photoprints Collection*

NBL built 'L1' class 2-6-4T No 67760 is seen at East Kilbride with a local service (possibly a 'running in' turn) during January 1949. Locomotive No 67760 was delivered to BR in December 1948 and withdrawn from service in December 1961. *Rail Photoprints Collection*

BR 'K1' 2-6-0 6MT

In 1949/50 the NBL received an order from British Railways (BR) for a further class of LNER type 2-cylinder Mogul (2-6-0) engines. The Arthur Henry Peppercorn designed 6MT class was then put to work as mixed traffic engines in the East and North East of England and also in Scotland. All 70 engines of the class were built by the NBL to order number L982 at Queen's Park Works between 1949 and 1950, the locomotives carried BR numbers 62001–62070.

The order was actually placed by the LNER in 1947 but the engines were delivered after 1948 to the newly formed British Railways (BR). None of the class survived in traffic beyond the end of 1967. One locomotive from the class is preserved, it being No 62005 delivered to BR in June 1949 and being the last to be withdrawn in December 1967.

Driving wheel diameter 5' 2", 2-cylinder engine (outside)

NBL built Peppercorn 'K1' class 2-6-0 engines on shed at York (50A) circa 1965. Above, locomotive No 62042 which entered service in October 1949 and was withdrawn in July 1967. Below, locomotive No 62065 which entered service in January 1950 and was withdrawn in March 1967. ***Both images Mike Stokes Archive***

Preserved NBL built Peppercorn 'K1' class 2-6-0 No 62005 is seen masquerading as sister engine No 62034 whilst passing through the stunning vista of Rannoch Moor during a West Highland Line rail charter in October 2009. The West Highland Line is one of the most scenic railway lines in Britain, linking the ports of Mallaig on the west coast of Scotland via Fort William to Glasgow. *David Gibson*

NBL built Locomotive classes which came into British Railways (BR) ownership

Class/Wheel Arrangement	Designer	Customer (Number to BR stock)	Build dates	BR number series*
'B17' 4-6-0	Gresley	LNER 10 locomotives	1928	61600–61609
'Jubilee' 4-6-0	Stanier	LMS 50 locomotives	1934	45557–45606
'K3' 2-6-0	Gresley	LNER 20 locomotives	1935	61939–61958
'4MT Stanier' (2cyl) 2-6-4T	Stanier	LMS 73 locomotives	1936/37	42545–42617
'8F Stanier' 2-8-0	Stanier	LMS/WD 92 locomotives	1942 1940	48176–48285 48773–48774
'B1' 4-6-0	Thompson	LNER 290 locomotives	1946 1947 1950	61040–61139 61190–61339 61360–61399
'L1' 2-6-4T	Thompson	LNER 35 locomotives	1948/49	67731–67765
'K1' 2-6-0	Peppercorn	(LNER)BR 70 locomotives	1949	62001–62070

* The BR numbers are given for identification in BR listings and do not take into account missing numbers due to scrapping or locomotives of the same class built by other companies but do include locomotives with allocated numbers not carried.

GNR 'N2' 0-6-2T 3MT - 'N2/2'

The Great Northern Railway (GNR) first introduced their Gresley designed 2-cylinder 'N2' tank locomotive class in 1920 and construction of the 0-6-2T engines was continued by the LNER after grouping. The 'N2' was Gresley's enlarged version of the GNR's earlier 'N1' type, basically the new design incorporated larger superheated boilers and the use of piston valves. The class was built at Doncaster Works and by the contractors Beyer, Peacock & Co Ltd, Hawthorn, Leslie & Co, the Yorkshire Engine Co and the NBL.

The first 60 locomotives built were fitted with condensing apparatus to allow working over the 'Metropolitan Lines' to London's Moorgate station. BR took into stock 107 of the class (numbers 69490–69596) of which 50 were built by the NBL, BR numbers 69500–69549. The class had four variants. All of the NBL built members of the class were built at Hyde Park Works to order number L734. Delivered to the GNR between December 1920 and April 1921 the batch were at first designated 'N2', later changed to 'N2/1' and then 'N2/2' by the LNER. None of the class survived in service beyond the end of 1962 and the last NBL built examples in traffic were Nos 69504, 69520, 69529, 69535, 69538 and 69546 which were all withdrawn by BR in September 1962. One NBL built example survived into preservation, that locomotive is GNR No 1744, LNER 4744, 9523 and BR 69523 which is an 'N2/2' variant (delivered in February 1921 and withdrawn by BR in July 1962).

Driving wheel diameter 5' 8", 2-cylinder engine (inside)

Preserved NBL built 'N2/2' resplendent in GNR livery as No 1744 pictured during a 2011 visit to the Severn Valley Railway. The condensing apparatus can be clearly seen. The apparatus takes the exhaust steam that would normally be lost up the chimney and alternatively routes it through a heat exchanger, into the side water tanks. *Keith Langston*

Displaced from London suburban duties NBL built 'N2/2' 0-6-2T No 69523 finds itself stored at New England, Peterborough, in September 1962, the locomotive was delivered to the GNR in February 1921. The 0-6-2T was sold out of service into preservation and in 2013 it was based at the Great Central Railway. *John Chalcraft/Rail Photoprints Collection*

War Department (MOS) 'Austerity' 2-8-0 8F

During the early years of the Second World War period locomotive engineer Robert A. Riddles was transferred from the LMS to the Ministry of Supply (MOS) and charged with designing a 'Class 8' freight locomotive similar in specification to the Stanier '8F' but one which could be built simply and quickly. To help with the design work members of the LMS Derby Locomotive Drawing Office were moved to the North British Locomotive Co Ltd (NBL) at Glasgow where they worked on the new 'Austerity' 2-8-0 and also the follow up 'Austerity' 2-10-0 design. In the summer of 1942 the MOS placed an order for 545 of the new 2-8-0 engines with the NBL. The order number L943 covered the work which was divided between Hyde Park Works and Queen's Park Works.

The accuracy of the word 'Austerity' as applied to the WD engines is easily explained by the examination of a few facts. The Stanier 2-8-0 '8F's used approximately 22 tons of steel castings per engine whilst the WD 2-8-0 '8F's were constructed using only 2½ tons of steel castings. For example cast iron was used for the cylinders, blast pipe, smoke box saddle, chimney and front end cylinder covers. Parallel boilers and round topped fireboxes were a far cheaper option than the Stanier tapered boiler and Belpaire firebox design.

North British Locomotive Co Ltd assembled the first WD 2-8-0 in only 10 working days, thus creating a record for the firm when the first WD 8F was out-shopped on 16 January 1943. Records show that the 'Austerities' were built at almost twice the rate at which it had been possible to build the Stanier '8F' 2-8-0 locomotive. Between 1943 and 1946 a combined total of 934 WD 2-8-0 MOD (WD) 'Austerity' locomotives were built by the NBL and Vulcan Foundry Ltd. Many examples of the class saw service in overseas theatres of war.

A total of 733 of the class came into BR ownership in 1948 (numbers 90000–90732) and the North British Locomotive Co Ltd built examples carried numbers 90000–90421, in the BR series. Unusually locomotives No 90773 and No 90774 both carried the name NORTH BRITISH, the nameplates were removed from both engines early in their BR ownership. None of the class survived beyond the end of 1967 but the last 13 NBL built examples were amongst those withdrawn in September of that year.

Driving wheel diameter 4' 8½", 2-cylinder engine (outside)

NBL built WD 2-8-0 No 90017 is seen at Dundee depot (62B) in March 1966. This locomotive entered service as No 63017 in August 1943 (number changed June 1951) and was withdrawn in September 1963. ***Mike Jefferies/Rail Photoprints Collection***

NBL built WD 2-8-0 No 90376 crosses from the slow lines to take the Midland Line at Chinley North Junction, circa 1960. This engine was delivered in October 1944 as WD 78572 (number changed September 1949) and withdrawn by BR in December 1962. ***Alan H. Bryant ARPS/Rail Photoprints Collection***

NBL built WD 2-8-0 No 90163 seen at Weaver Junction on the West Coast main line, seemingly running 'wrong line' with what looks like an infrastructure train, circa 1949. This locomotive was delivered by the NBL in June 1943 as WD No 77179 (number changed May 1949) and withdrawn by BR in December 1962. ***R. A. Whitfield/Rail Photoprints Collection***

NBL built WD 'Austerity' 2-8-0 No 90137 passes West Ruislip with a Neasden - Woodford Halse freight working in September 1956. This locomotive was delivered in April 1943 as WD No 77042 (number changed May 1951) and withdrawn by BR in December 1962. *Dave Cobbe Collection/ C. R. L. Coles/Rail Photoprints Collection*

War Department (MOS) 'Austerity' 2-10-0 9F

This class of locomotive was built as an enlarged version of the 'Austerity' 2-8-0. The MOS ordered 150 of the 2-10-0 class from the NBL; they were built Hyde Park Works to order numbers L945 and L948 during 1944/45. Both of the Riddles inspired 'Austerity' type freight locomotives were extremely successful locomotive designs which not only fulfilled their wartime roles but a great number of the engines remained in service almost to the end of the UK steam era.

The classe's extra set of wheels reduced their axle loading to 13½ tons (2-8-0 15¾ tons), thus allowing them to work over lighter laid track. One of the MOD WD 'Austerity' 2-10-0's (WD number 73755) had the distinction of being the 1000th WD locomotive built in the UK and shipped to Europe since D-Day, accordingly it was named LONGMOOR by the military. In 1944 a batch of 20 of the 2-10-0s were shipped to the Middle East, a complement of 43 were sent to Belgium and 60 engines to Holland, by June of 1946 those 103 locomotive were all to be found working in the Netherlands. That left 20 in the Middle East plus 7 examples in military use and 20 on the LNER pre-BR stock list. British Railways purchased the 25 UK based WD 8F 2-10-0 engines in 1948. They were given BR numbers in the series 90750–90774; under BR all of the class were based at Scottish sheds. None of the class remained in service beyond 1962 with the last examples being withdrawn in December of that year.

No ex-BR examples were preserved, but locomotive No 600 GORDON from the Longmoor Military Railway was saved and is loaned by the military to the Severn Valley Railway, that loco was built at Hyde Park Works in 1943 and delivered to the military, when retired for preservation No 600 had the distinction of being the last steam locomotive to be owned by the British Army. Named after General Charles Gordon (Gordon of Khartoum) locomotive No 600 also proudly carries the coat of arms of the Royal Engineers.

The nameplates of 2-10-0 No 600 also carry the coat of arms of the Royal Engineers. ***Keith Langston***

Two more WD 2-10-0 engines have been repatriated from Greece. One has been numbered 90775 (one higher than the last BR engine) and has occasionally carried the name STURDEE (as did No 601 before being numbered 90775) and that locomotive home base is the North Norfolk Railway NNR).The other is WD 2-10-0 is No 3672 which has been named DAME VERA LYNN.

The locomotive's home base is at Grosmont on the North Yorkshire Moors Railway (NYMR). Locomotive WD No 73755 (NS 5085) survives in the Dutch Railway Museum (Nederlands Spoorwegmuseum). It carried the nameplate LONGMOOR, after the Royal Engineer's base of that name, also the coat of arms of the Royal Engineers is displayed above the name. Three more examples of the class were in 2012 still listed as being stored out of use in Greece, with 2 of those locomotive classified as operational.

Driving wheel diameter 4' 8½", 2-cylinder engine (outside)

NBL built WD 2-10-0 No 90762 is seen hard at work on Beattock Bank. This locomotive was delivered in July 1945 as WD No 73786 (number changed June 1950) and withdrawn by BR in December 1962. ***David Anderson***

NBL built Austerity 2-10-0 No 90756 is seen at Eastfield (65A) circa 1958. This locomotive entered service in June 1945 and formerly carried the No 73780 (number changed June 1950) and was withdrawn by BR in December 1962. ***Rail Photoprints Collection***

NBL built Locomotive classes which came into British Railways ownership

Class/Wheel Arrangement	Designer	Customer (Number to BR stock)	Build dates	BR number series*
'N2' 0-6-2T	Gresley	GNR 50 locomotive	1920/21	69500–69549
'WD' 2-8-0	Riddles	MOS (WD) 545 locomotive	1943/45	90000–90421** (1949 number allocation)
'WD' 2-10-0	Riddles	MOS (WD) 25 locomotive	1945	90750–90774

* The BR numbers are given for identification in BR listings and do not take into account missing numbers due to scrapping, or locomotives of the same class built by other companies, but do include locomotives with allocated numbers not carried.
** Locomotives 90000–90100 originally allocated numbers 63000–63100, locomotives 90422–90499 originally allocated numbers 63101–63178, and locomotives 90500–90520 originally allocated numbers 63179–63199.

Railway Company abbreviations used in this chapter.

CR – Caledonian Railway, **FR** – Furness Railway, **GCR** – Great Central Railway, **GNR** – Great Northern Railway, **GNoSR** – Great North of Scotland Railway, **GSWR** – Glasgow & South Western Railway, **GWR** – Great Western Railway, **LMS** – London Midland & Scottish Railway, **LNER** – London & North Eastern Railway, **LTSR** – London, Tilbury & Southend Railway, **MOD** – Ministry of Defence, **MOS(WD)** – Ministry of Supply (War Department), **MR** – Midland Railway, **NBR** – North British Railway, **NER** – North Eastern Railway, **ROD** – Railway Operating Division, **S&DJR** – Somerset & Dorset Joint Railway, **SR** – Southern Railway, **TVR** – Taff Vale Railway.

Preserved WD 2-10-0 loco No 600 GORDON, (ex WD 73651) seen hard a work with a demonstration freight train was based at the former operational Longmore Military Railway and is now loaned by the military authorities to the Severn Valley Railway. *Keith Langston*

NBL built WD 2-8-0 8F No 90733 is seen under test at LNWR Heritage Ltd, Crewe following a 2007 restoration to working condition. This loco was originally WD 79257, and it worked for the Dutch Railways as No 4464 and then for the Swedish Railways as No 1931. The BR number it carries in preservation is a fictitious one as the BR number series ended at 90732. *Keith Langston*

Ex-Glasgow & South Western Railway (G&SWR) Manson designed '381' class 4-6-0 No 14662 with an 8-wheeled tender is seen in LMS livery, possibly at Kilmarnock in the mid-1920s. These engines were regularly used on express services between Glasgow St Enoch station and destinations to Kilmarnock, Dumfries and Carlisle. This locomotive was one of 10 actually ordered from Sharp Stewart & Co (Atlas Works order E1202) but delivered by the NBL in June 1903, after the formation of the combine. LMS No 14662 was formerly G&SWR No 387 and the locomotive was withdrawn in 1930. *Mike Morant Collection*

This is one of a class of 8 Drummond designed 0-6-4T engines built by the NBL at Queen's Park works between 1909 and 1912 to order numbers L336 and L366 for the Highland Railway (HR). The locomotives were primarily intended for use as banking engines. LMS No 15305, then resplendent in 'Crimson Lake' livery is seen on shed at Blair Atholl circa 1925, the locomotive was originally HR No 31. The LMS withdrew this locomotive in November 1934. *Mike Morant Collection*

The impressive 4-6-4T engine seen outside the running shed at Ardrossan in June 1936 as LMS No 15404 is a former G&SWR Whitelegg designed 'Baltic Tank'. The NBL Hyde Park Works built 6 of the class to works order number L762 in 1920. The 4-6-4Ts were designated as the '540' class by the G&SWR. These powerful engines were intended for use on the Glasgow to Ayrshire coast express services and were originally painted in an eye-catching green livery style; under LMS ownership the locomotive carried a simple un-lined black livery. LMS No 15404, which was originally G&SWR No 544, was withdrawn from service in September 1936. *Mike Morant Collection*

NBL Queen's Park Works built 11 Drummond designed 2-6-0 engines '403' class engines for the G&SWR in 1915, to works order number L649. G&SWR No 408 is seen as LMS 17827 hauling a Carlisle to Glasgow and Greenock freight service circa 1930. All of locomotive in this class were allocated to Carlisle for use on such services and locomotive No 17827 was withdrawn by the LMS in April 1938. *Mike Morant Collection*

A rambler's excursion titled 'The William Penn Special' had originated at London's Waterloo station on the morning of 15 May 1955 and took the participants to Great Missenden on the former Metropolitan and Great Central Railway. On both the outward and return journeys motive power was provided by Drummond 'T9' class Greyhound 4-4-0 No 30719. Prior to the evening's departure from Great Missenden 30719 an interesting and unlikely event took place when former LNER Thompson designed 'L1' class 2-6-4T No 67749 departed southwards thereby capturing on film two locomotives poles apart in terms of age and lineage, but both built in Scotland! Loco No 67749 was one of 35 engines built by the NBL to order number L981 in December 1948 and withdrawn by BR in November 1961, whilst No 30719 was a Dübs & Co product delivered to the London & South Western Railway (LSWR) as part of a 31 loco batch in September 1899 and withdrawn by BR in March 1961. *Mike Morant Collection*

NBL 4-4-0+0-4-4 Steam Turbine Locomotive 'Reid-Ramsay-McLeod'

The Reid–Ramsay–McLeod steam turbine locomotive is seen in the yard at Hyde Park Works on 12 June 1925. From the wisp of steam emitting from the safety valves the locomotive would appear to have been in steam at the time. The engine is being viewed from the trailing end (back) where the boiler, smoke box and chimney were located, note also the side mounted coal bunkers. The leading end of the machine housed the turbines (forward and reverse) steam turbine driven fan and condenser, the drive cab is located in the centre. The plaques visible on the side tanks commemorate the engine's appearance at the 1924 Empire Exhibition at Wembley. *Mike Morant Collection*

NBL Steam Turbine Locomotive

A brief account of the NBL's experimental work with turbine locomotive is included as the locomotive are very much a part of the 'Built in Scotland' story even though the engines did not survive long enough to be taken into British Railways (BR) stock. The Reid-Ramsay-McLeod turbine locomotive of 1924 was in fact the second experimental steam turbine engine built by the company.

The 1910 Experimental Locomotive

The first was a steam turbine electric locomotive produced in 1910.

Simply put, the basis of the first Sir Hugh Reid inspired design could be described as a steam turbine driven electrical power station constructed on a set of locomotive frames. The 4-4-0+0-4-4 locomotive carried a conventional locomotive-type boiler/chimney with superheating at the trailing end. In turn a turbine powered a dynamo which produced a variable output between 200 and 600 volts DC. The generated electrical power was fed to 275 hp series wound traction motors incorporated in each of the 4 drive axles.

The engine carried an NBL crest and was emblazoned with the words 'ELECTRO-TURBO-LOCOMOTIVE' on the sides of the leading end. Little is recorded about this vehicle's success or otherwise however, after a short trial period in the works and on the main line (hauling a saloon coach) it was laid aside and apparently did not run again. It was the first turbine locomotive to be built in the UK. The engine was listed as being 'NBL Stock' with works number 19266 and built to order number L406 at Hyde Park Works.

The 1924 Experimental Locomotive

The frames, bogies and boiler unit from the 1910 experimental locomotive were reused during the construction of the NBL's second experimental steam turbine engine. That locomotive was constructed at Hyde Park Works during 1924 and was also referred to as 'NBL Stock', the works number was 23140 and order number L791 applied. The experimental engine was described as being Britain's first true Steam Turbine Locomotive.

Although similar in appearance to the NBL's first turbo locomotive the second machine was configured differently and is perhaps best described as a steam turbine locomotive with mechanical (geared) transmission.

As with the first experimental locomotive and in order to maximise airflow, a condenser was mounted at the leading end (front) of the locomotive. That air-cooled evaporative type unit was assisted by an additional steam-turbine driven fan. As stated earlier the boiler, smokebox and chimney were located at the trailing end (back).

Due to the absence of a blast pipe, a supplementary fan was located in the large chimney to provide a firebox draught.

Each bogie on the 4-4-0+0-4-4 configured locomotive carried turbine equipment. However, existing records are unclear on the nature of the exact drive arrangement. The differing accounts were, one which describes two turbines per bogie i.e. one per direction of travel. Another which describes a turbine consisting of three blade rings for high pressure steam forward, low pressure steam forward, and reverse. The turbine(s) were then connected to the wheels using a two stage gear box.

The locomotive was exhibited at the 1924 Empire Exhibition at Wembley, but possibly not in its completed form as testing did not take place until the period March 1926 to April 1927. Reportedly the trials operated on the main Glasgow-Edinburgh route. Problems in the condenser pumps brought an early end to the first trials, but undaunted railway officials commented that there was an 'almost entire absence of vibration, oscillation, and rail pounding' during travel. The second trials were even less satisfactory as the locomotive suffered with axle box problems followed by a turbine failure. There is some doubt as to whether the NBL Turbine Locomotive ever ran again after that. The experimental engine stood for some years rusting away at the back of Hyde Park Works until it was finally scrapped circa 1940.

Chapter 10

ADDITIONAL SCOTTISH LOCOMOTIVE BUILDERS

This chapter does not constitute a complete listing of 'other' Scottish engineering companies who built varying numbers of locomotives or operated on the periphery of that industry. It is however, a selected listing of engineering firms involved with steam locomotive construction in addition to the more prominent companies and locomotive works, which have been detailed individually.

The development of the coal mining, iron ore, iron and steel making, ship building and heavy engineering industries north of the border created a vibrant home grown market for smaller shunting type industrial locomotives. Many Scottish engineering companies responded in order to fulfil those requirements. In addition, some of those lesser known locomotive builders also recognised the export potential of their products, not just to industrialists south of the border but also to companies outside Britain.

Locomotive designs from un-associated firms were often similar in general specification and a great many followed what has since been described as the Kilmarnock type, i.e. as built in that town by Andrew Barclay & Sons (and others) and being of a basic 0-4-0 saddle tank (ST) form. It is thought likely that some engineering and industrial organisations built steam locomotives as copies of a bought in machine already in their possession, whilst others worked from drawings obtained from another locomotive maker or even assembled engines from a supplied kit of parts. The companies are listed chronologically.

A typical Andrew Barclay Sons & Co 0-4-0 industrial saddle tank (ST) built at Caledonia Works, Kilmarnock. ***Mike Morant Collection***

1790 *Dick & Stevenson Airdrie Engine Works, Bell Street, Airdrie*
This engineering firm was founded circa 1790. In the early 1860s the firm was run by Alexander and John Dick together with partner Graham Stevenson. Steam locomotive construction began in 1864, after the retirement from the firm of John Dick. Their first customer for locomotives was the Langloan Iron Co. to whom they supplied a total of 6 locomotives. Thereafter several locomotives were exported to Singapore, Holland and Spain the majority being of 0-4-0ST configuration. The works closed in 1890. See also Martyn Bros, Airdrie.

1795 *William Dixon, Calder and Govan, Glasgow*
In the 1770s William Dixon became lessee of the Govan coalfield and in 1795 he formed a company which became known as the Calder Iron Works as he continued to acquire sites with coal and ironstone deposits. Dixon became both a coal and iron 'master'. He died circa 1822 and left the company to his sons John and William Dixon Jnr, John sold his share in the Calder works to his younger brother. It was William Dixon Jnr who instigated the opening of another works in 1830 and that facility was known as the Govan Iron Works. The production of steam locomotives began after William Dixon Jnr was succeeded by his son William Smith Dixon in 1859. Reportedly 4 locomotives were constructed at the Govan works, in 1860 No 2, in 1866 No 4, in 1874 No 9 and 1901 No 1. An additional locomotive was built at the Calder factory in 1892 and listed as the firm's No 8.

The business was incorporated as a limited liability company in April 1873 as William Dixon Ltd. William Smith Dixon was sole proprietor of the Pollok & Govan Railway and he was also the largest shareholder in the Clydesdale Junction Railway (opened 1845) and that railway was absorbed by the Caledonian Railway in 1846.

In 1951 the company was nationalised under the Iron and Steel Act and became part of the Iron and Steel Corporation of Great Britain. Colvilles Ltd acquired the company in 1953, trading until 1958 when the works closed and the company ceased to trade and went into liquidation in 1960.

1810 *J & C Carmichael, Ward Foundry, Dundee*
James and Charles Carmichael founded a firm in 1810 which manufactured general marine equipment, weighbridges and turbines. The company produced their first steam locomotives in 1833 for the originally 4 foot 6 inch gauge Dundee & Newtyle Railway opened in 1831 which claimed to be the first railway in the north of Scotland (converted to standard gauge in 1849). Delivered first was No1 EARL OF AIRLIE and second No 2 LORD WHARNCLIFFE; both engines were configured as 0-2-4s, the engines were reportedly withdrawn from service in 1854. A third loco of the design was built for the railway in 1834 by James Stirling of the Dundee Foundry, and that loco was named TROTTER.

The firm continued in business becoming a limited company headed by the founder's sons, James Carmichael & Co Ltd circa 1894. Marine engineering continued but no further steam locomotive building took place and the company ceased to operate in 1929.

1818, *James A.B. McKinnell, Palmerston Foundry, Dumfries*
The firm built two locomotives to a vertical boiler design one was supplied to Marcus Bain, for use at Gatelawbridge Quarry, near Thornhill. The second loco thought to be built as a 2ft 6in gauge vertical-boiler 0-4-0 engine was supplied to the Kelhead Lime & Coal Co. of Annan.

1829 *Timothy Burstall, Leith*
Timothy Burstall built the locomotive PERSEVERANCE which he took to the famous Rainhill trials of 1829. However, the locomotive was damaged during transit to Rainhill causing Burstall to spend the first five days of the event trying to repair the locomotive.

With repairs completed PERSEVERANCE ran with some success on the final day of the trials. The engine achieved a speed of 6 mph for which Burstall was awarded a consolation prize of £25, a huge amount of money at that time. Burstall also built a steam powered coach circa 1825 (road locomotive) for which he jointly held a patent with a Mr J. Hill of Greenwich, London.

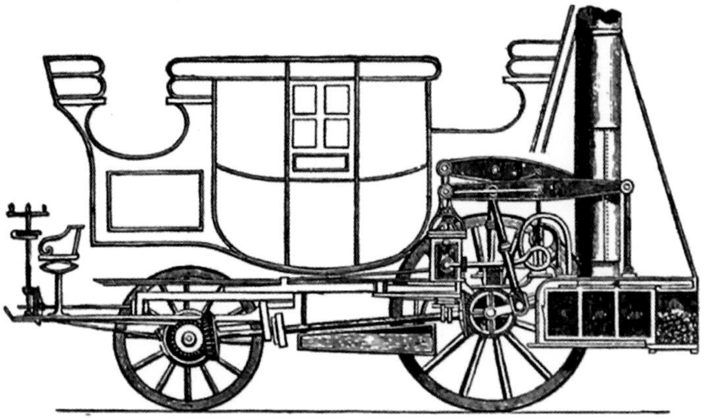

Burstall and Hill steam coach which was similar in design to the Rainhill Trial loco PERSEVERANCE.

1830 c, *McHendrick & Ball, Glasgow*
This company built a vertical boiler 0-4-0T which was supplied to William Lee, Son & Co, lime and cement merchants of Kent, the engine was configured for an unusual 4ft 3in gauge industrial line at Halling.

1831 *Murdoch, Aitken & Co, Hill Street Foundry, Glasgow*
This company built two 0-4-0 configured locomotives for the Monkland & Kirkintilloch Railway in 1831. Between 1833 and 1836 they built three locomotives for the Garnkirk & Glasgow Railway. In 1836 the firm built an 0-4-0 for London & Southampton Railway, named VULTURE , followed in 1837 by two 2-2-2 configured locomotives one for the London & Southampton Railway and the other for the Paisley & Renfrew Railway. Reportedly the firm also built another 0-4-0 type for the Slamannan Railway in 1841.

1834 *James Stirling & Co, East Foundry/Victoria Foundry, Dundee*
The Dundee Foundry was primarily occupied with the manufacture of iron castings and general engineering but later developed interests in steam engines, locomotives and ships' machinery. In 1834 the locomotive TROTTER was constructed for the Dundee & Newtyle Railway and it is thought to have been of similar design to the locomotives constructed by J. & C. Carmichael for the same railway at about that time. Between 1838 and 1839 the firm built a batch of 3 locomotives for the 5 foot 6 inch gauge Arbroath & Forfar Railway. The engines were of the 2-2-2 configuration and were named respectively PRINCESS, VICTORIA and BRITANNIA. The completion of that contract apparently led to a further order for 2 similar locomotives. Circa 1843 the firm was taken over by Gourlay Mudie & Co who then supplied the Dundee, Perth & Aberdeen Railway with 2 locomotives of a 0-4-0 design named CALEDONIA and GOWRIE, in 1847/8. An order from Dundee & Arbroath Railway for 2 similar locomotives followed and those locomotives were reportedly named CRAIGIE and CARLOGIE.

1839 *Jas M Rowan & Co, Atlas Works, Springburn, Glasgow*
In 1839 two 'single' type locomotives were built for the Slamannan Railway, and the two were named respectively BOANERGES and BOREALIS. In 1840 the works built 3 inside cylindered 0-4-0s for the Wishaw & Coltness Railway. Those engines were to a design by George Dodds who was at that time the locomotive superintendent of the Monkland & Kirkintilloch Railway. A 'Bury' outside bar framed loco of 0-4-0 configuration named METEOR was later supplied to the same railway company.

In 1842 a batch of 3 outside frame/inside cylinder type 0-4-0 configured engines were built for the Polloc & Govan Railway. It is possible, but not definitively documented, that a further batch of 2 similar locomotives was built for the Monkland Railway in 1851. Reportedly 'Rail Motor Cars' were built and exported to the Gribscov & Pontiloff Railway (Russia) in the 1880s.

The works were situated on part of the site also occupied by the Clyde Locomotive Works (in 1886) which were then purchased by Messrs. Sharp, Stewart & Co. in 1888 when that company moved to Glasgow.

1838 *Kinmond, Hutton & Steel, Wallace Foundry, Dundee*
This firm supplied the Dundee & Arbroath railway with locomotives of a 2-2-2 configuration between 1838 and 1841; probably 4 engines named respectively WALLACE, RAPID, DART and QUEEN and later possibly 2 other engines GRIFFEN and FURY. A batch of 6 similar engines was supplied to the Kilmarnock & Ayr Railway and after building they were partly dismantled in order that they could be shipped by sea to Ayr, where they were then re-assembled. A batch of 9 locomotives of the 2-2-2 configuration was also supplied to the Glasgow, Dumfries & Carlisle Railway.

The firm also exported locomotives to Canadian railway companies, the Montreal & Lachine Railroad (two 2-2-2 locomotives) the Champlain & St Lawrence Railroad (one 2-2-2 locomotive). In 1853 a branch of the company was established in Montreal and 11 locomotives were constructed there for the Grand Trunk Railway of Canada, but that facility was closed down in 1857. The total Kinmond, Hutton & Steel Company steam locomotive output was in the region of 50 locos. The Wallace Foundry was sold as a going concern in 1861 but apparently no further locomotive building took place.

1839 *Stark & Fulton, Glasgow*
This firm reportedly built several locomotives for Glasgow, Paisley, Kilmarnock & Ayr Railway and a batch of 3 locomotives for the Midland Counties Railway. All were of the 'Bury' type. In 1849 two locomotives (2-2-2) were supplied to the contractors for the Caledonian & Dumbarton Railway (also known as the Dumbarton & Balloch Joint Railway).

1840 *Caird & Co, Greenock.*
The firm were primarily shipbuilders and marine engineers but they did construct four locomotives for Scottish railways, all of the 2-2-2 configuration. To the Glasgow, Paisley & Greenock Railway they supplied locomotives Nos 11 and 12 of 1840 (which eventually became CR No 68 and No 69 respectively).To the Glasgow, Paisley, Kilmarnock & Ayr Railway they

supplied locomotive No 30 WASP and to the Edinburgh & Glasgow Railway the locomotive TREVITHICK of 1841. The company traded in its own right until 1922.

1840, *Thomas Edington & Sons, Phoenix Iron Works, Glasgow*
This firm was thought to have built at least 4 locomotives which they supplied to the Glasgow, Paisley, Kilmarnock & Ayr Railway (G&SWR). The locos were all of a 2-2-2 configuration designed by the firm's engineer Mr J. Miller. They were numbered and named thus, No 7 PHOENIX, No 8 PRINCE ALBERT, No 10 GARNOCK and No 15 KYLE.

1840, *Barr & McNab, Paisley (1840–54).*
Built two 'Bury'* type 0-4-0s were built in 1840 for the Ardrossan Railway. The engines were called FIREFLY (perhaps later named EGLINTON) and KING COLE (perhaps later named BLAIR) respectively. In addition the firm reportedly supplied a 2-2-2 locomotive to the Glasgow, Paisley & Greenock Railway, which was that railway's No 8 HAWK.

1841 c, *Peter Borrie & Co, Tay Foundry, Dundee*
This company is thought to have built 6 locomotives, offering to sell a batch of 5 locomotives to the Edinburgh & Glasgow Railway in 1841. However, only one of those is thought to have been purchased that loco being named EUCLID. The firm also built a 2-2-2 locomotive named CORYNDON which was used by one John Chanter supposedly to demonstrate a patent coal burning firebox. Apparently Peter Borrie's firm became insolvent in 1842 and as a consequence he was made bankrupt.

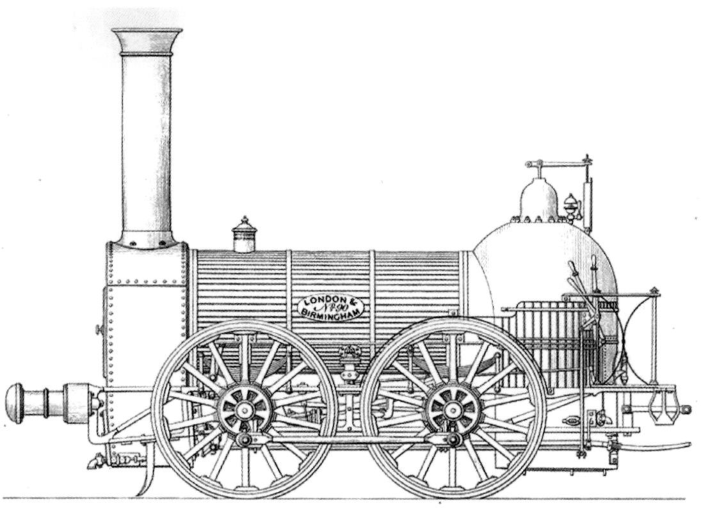

A 'Bury' type 0-4-0 locomotive built by Edward Bury & Co for the London & Birmingham Railway.

1845 *William Simpson & Co, Aberdeen (1845-93)*
This company are said to have built in the region of 6 locomotives of 0-4-2 configuration for the Aberdeen Railway and later a further 2 for the Stirling & Dunfermline Railway. This company may possibly have had a connection with Blackie & Co of Aberdeen.

1846 *Hawthorns & Company Leith Engine Works Great Junction Street, Leith*
The Leith Engine Works was opened by Newcastle-on-Tyne based engineers R. & W. Hawthorn, initially to assemble steam engines ordered by customers in Scotland from parts manufactured in Newcastle. In 1850 the Leith Engine Works was sold to another company, also named Hawthorns & Co, which reportedly produced in excess of 450 locomotives on its own account up until 1872, when the works closed.

Their customers included the York, Newcastle & Berwick Railway and the East Kent Railway. In 1858 they also built a 0-4-2WT for contractors E. & J. Pickering who built the Cape Town – Wellington Railway in South Africa. That locomotive later became the railway's No 9 and was by all accounts known as BLACKIE. It was withdrawn in 1936 and having been described as the first steam railway locomotive to run in that country No 9 was declared a 'national monument' and later placed on a plinth on the concourse of Cape Town station.

Cape Town – Wellington Railway loco No 9 seen on the concourse at Cape Town station in 2007. ***Danie van der Merwe***

* 'Bury Bar Frame' locomotives were originally developed at the works of Edward Bury & Company Liverpool. 'Bury' engines incorporated inside horizontal (or near horizontal) cylinders, inside wrought iron bar frames and a round firebox with a large domed topped boiler incorporating a safety valve.

1847 *Scott, Sinclair & Co, Greenock*
A company of established shipbuilders who are known to have built a total of seventeen locomotives between 1847 and 1849: the last 5 were 0-4-2s, the remainder were 'Allan' type 2-2-2s, their main customer being the Scottish Central Railway. In addition 3 engines were supplied to the Caledonian Railway. Robert Sinclair (Locomotive Superintendent of both aforementioned railway companies) was the nephew of one of the Sinclair partners.

1848 *Blackie & Co, Aberdeen*
This company is credited with building two locomotives for the Aberdeen Railway.

1849 *Alexander Chaplin & Co, Cranstonhill Engine Works, Port Street, Glasgow*
The firm were makers of railway locomotives, cranes, road engines, boilers and stationary engines. They are also recorded as being suppliers of patented vertical boilered locomotives between the 1860s and early 1900s. In addition to supplying Scottish railway operators the firm also built some engines for export which included 4 shunting locomotives sold to the Danish State Railway (1869–1872). The company also built steam cranes and supplied amongst others the Caledonian Railway (2 cranes) and also a 20 ton breakdown crane to the Taff Vale Railway. In 1890 the company moved to new premises in Helen Street, Govan.

1860 *The Airdrie Iron Co of Standard Works, Airdrie*
The company was a general engineering firm. They manufactured various items of colliery plant and equipment, pumps, air compressors, tube making machinery and in addition to being a general ironfoundry they built steam locomotives. The firm was incorporated as a limited company in 1905. They built their first railway locomotive in 1869 and before the works closed down in 1913 they had reportedly produced between 20 and 30 steam locomotives. One of their prominent customers was the locally based Drumgray Coal Company. The firm also supplied Glasgow Corporation Gas Works with a 0-6-0ST shunting engine which was that organisation's locomotive No 5.

1860c *McCulloch, Sons & Kennedy, Kilmarnock*
Mainly manufacturers of colliery machinery, but also constructed a few 0-4-0STs of the Kilmarnock type which were supplied to Wemyss Coal Co and other local collieries. The firm also exported a small number of engines to New Zealand. The firm closed in 1890 and their patterns and drawings passed to Gibb & Hogg of Airdrie.

1863c *John & Thomas Young, Vulcan Foundry, Ayr*
Primarily manufacturer of ship's auxiliary engines and assorted types of colliery and agricultural machinery this company were perhaps also involved with locomotive construction. In March 1863 the 'Ayr Advertiser' newspaper carried a story reporting that they built a small colliery type locomotive for a local coalmine.

1866 *Gibb & Hogg, Victoria Engine Works, Airdrie*
Established as founders and engineers in 1866. However, locomotives were not built until they acquired the drawings etc of McCulloch Sons & Kennedy in 1890. Built 20 Kilmarnock type 0-4-0STs, and reportedly one 0-6-0ST which was supplied to the Eden Colliery, they also supplied one locomotive to Meyer & Co of Widnes in 1903. The company closed down in 1912.

1867 *Miller & Co, Vulcan Foundry, Coatbridge*
This engineering company probably only operated as agents for the supply of other builder's locomotives. One such 3ft gauge 0-4-0ST was supplied to Tudhoe Ironworks in County Durham.

1869 *J & A Taylor, Smith Street, Ayr*
The firm were established builders of mining equipment who additionally constructed a 0-4-0ST locomotive for the Dalmellington Iron Co, circa 1870. That loco became Dalmellington No 8 which worked on that site until it was scrapped in 1912.

Gibb & Hogg built 0-4-0ST seen in the 1970s when on public display at Pittencrieff Park, Dunfermline. The loco originally worked for the Fife Coal Co and later became NCB No 11 at the Glasgow Stepps Cardowan Colliery and in 2013 it was on display at the Summerlee Museum of Industrial Life, Coatbridge. ***David Anderson***

1870 *A. F. Craig & Co, Caledonia Engineering Works, Paisley*
In the 1870s the company constructed a steam locomotive for their own use. Designed by Robert Craig it was built to the unusual 3ft 1½inch gauge and it was still in service in the early 1960s albeit with a replacement boiler.

1870 *Leonard J. Todd, Leith*
This gentleman's company reportedly constructed a locomotive for the Tramvia de Santander in Spain, circa 1871. The engine had a locomotive type boiler but unusually the cylinders were placed above the firebox with the drive being achieved by way of a crankshaft. In 1872 Mr Todd built a steam powered omnibus to run between Leith and Edinburgh and in 1875 he is credited with designing a 'fireless' steam car.

A tram locomotive is seen at the Tramvia de Santander circa 1881. It is uncertain whether this locomotive is the Leonard J. Todd export or a similar vehicle. ***Authors Collection***

1870 *A & W Smith & Co, Eglinton Engine Works, Glasgow*
Advertisements in the journal 'Engineering' during January 1866 showed this firm as being 'manufacturers of a wide range of equipment including locomotives'.

1872 *Alexander Shanks & Sons, Dens Iron Works, Arbroath*
This company was established in 1840 and it is known to have originally produced portable steam engines. The firm reportedly built in the region of 11 shunting locomotives after the 'Kilmarnock' style of 0-4-0ST between 1872 and 1877. The operators of Southampton Docks bought 3 locomotives, London & South Western Railway (LSWR) also bought 3, the London & St Katherine Dock Co. took delivery of 2 and the Millwall Dock Co. operated one of the engines.

Alexander Shanks exported 2 locomotives of a similar style to New Zealand's Otago Railways in the 1870s. They were given the names MOUSE and KANGAROO and were designated as the railway's 'A' class; they were initially based at Invercargill between mid-1876 and mid-1877 and withdrawn from service in the early 1930s.

1873 *G. & J Weir, Cathcart, Glasgow*
Although not locomotive manufacturers this firm is worthy of mention because it occupies a prominent place in the historic development and production of pumps capable of supplying feed water to high temperature boilers. The firm was originally formed by brothers James and George Weir who began their manufacturing enterprise in a small machine shop and smithy in the Cathcart area of Glasgow.

These premises expanded to become the Holm Foundry, accordingly the business of G. and J. Weir was formed into a limited liability company in 1895. Amongst the steam locomotive engineers who specified Weir feed pumps on some of their locomotives were Nigel Gresley (later Sir) of the GNR/LNER and Lawson Billinton (later C.B.E.) of the LBSCR.

Lawson Billinton designed 'K' class 2-6-0 (Mogul) No 337 (became BR 32337) built at Brighton in 1913 for the London Brighton & South Coast Railway, seen when newly delivered. As built this class incorporated Weir feed water pumps. ***Keith Langston Collection***

1874 *Allan Andrews & Co, Britannia Engineering Works, Kilmarnock*
This company became Andrews, Barr & Co circa 1878 and then Barr, Morrison & Co in 1882. In total the firm reportedly built between 30 and 40 locomotives. In 1883 the company was taken over by Dick, Kerr & Co. (see separate chapter).

1880c *Murray & Paterson, Coatbridge*
This firm primarily constructed mining machinery and static steam engines however, in the early 1880s they reportedly built two steam railway locomotives of the 'Kilmarnock' type, one was exported to South America, (possibly Brazil) the other was shipped to Australia in 1885. The company was perhaps better known as rebuilders and repairers of locomotives. The firm traded until 1971.

1880 *Hurst Nelson & Company Ltd, Motherwell*
Major manufacturer of railway rolling stock, including for overseas, equipment for mines and quarries, and tramcars, including some supplied to the London County Council. In addition to their Scottish base the company had premises in Chesterfield, Derbyshire. The firm were not primarily locomotive builders but there is evidence of narrow gauge locomotive(s) of the light rail type often used on plantations having been built by them.

In 1906 R. & W. Hawthorn & Co supplied a steam railcar to the Port Talbot Railway in South Wales, a project in which Hurst Nelson participated by building the actual carriage portion. Circa 1908 the Great Western Railway (GWR) embarked upon a programme of 'Railmotor' building and their principal contractor for a batch of 12 units was Kerr, Stuart & Co Ltd of Stoke on Trent, who sub-contracted the body manufacture to Hurst, Nelson & Co Ltd. In 1918 Wagon Repairs Ltd was founded and that firm acquired the business of various firms including Hurst, Nelson & Co Ltd.

1882 *Lennox Lange, Glasgow*
According to the available records it is not possible to establish whether this firm did or did not manufacture locomotives, but perhaps only factored the products of other builders. Lennox Lange works plates are known to exist, and they were reportedly fixed to a 0-4-2ST dated 1882.

1883 *W B Dick & Co, Britannia Engineering Works, Kilmarnock*
Firm's title changed to Dick Kerr & Co Ltd. in 1883. Company manufactured tramway equipment. Locomotives were manufactured from 1818 to 1919 after which the Britannia Engineering Works became Kilmarnock Engineering Co. In 1886 tramway type 0-4-0 'Well Tank' (WT) locomotives were supplied to the 3-foot gauge Schull & Skibbereen Light Railway in Ireland (the formal name of the operating company being the West Carberry Tramways & Light Railways). Those 3 locomotives were named MARION (scrapped 1906) IDA (scrapped 1926) and ILEN (scrapped 1914). Additionally the Alford & Sutton Tramway in Lincolnshire, and the North London Tramways who placed an order for 10 locomotives. Reportedly traditional industrial locomotives were also manufactured including for several Government agencies during the First World War.

1884 *Clyde Locomotive Co, Springburn, Glasgow*
The Clyde Locomotive Company (CLC) was founded by Walter Montgomery Neilson who was previously the owner of locomotive manufacturers Neilson & Co and a partner of the later established firm Neilson, Reid & Company. In 1886 the CLC built their first locomotives which were a batch of 8 engines for the Highland Railway (HR) and designed by David Jones. Configured as 4-4-0s, those handsome looking HR 'E' class engines famously became known as 'Clyde Bogies'. The CLC later built locomotives ordered by the Girvan & Portpatrick Junction Railway which were actually delivered to that company's successor the Ayrshire & Wigtownshire Railway. Reportedly the Clyde Locomotive Company built 14 locomotives at their Glasgow premises. In 1888, the long established Manchester based engineering firm of Sharp, Stewart & Company decided to move to Glasgow and to facilitate that move they bought the Clyde Locomotive Co. and renamed the newly aquired premises Atlas Works. (See also Sharp, Stewart & Co).

The 'Clyde Bogie' 4-4-0 (HR 'E' class) locomotives built by the Clyde Locomotive Co in 1886 were a development of the Highland Railway 'Duke Class' 4-4-0s. Loco No 79 ATHOLL is seen at Aviemore in full HR livery. The loco was withdrawn from service in 1923 and stored at Aviemore shed until broken up at Kilmarnock Works in 1925. ***Mick Morant Collection***

1886 *Sanquhar & Kirkconnel Collieries Ltd, Fauldhead Colliery, Kirkconnel*
Built two vertical boilered locomotives constructed one in 1886 (when the firm's name was in fact James, Irving, McConnell) and the other in 1903.

1890 *Martyn Bros, Chapelside Works, Airdrie*
Acquired from Dick & Stevenson steam locomotive patterns and drawings as that firm closed down in 1890 and over the next ten years built at least two and possibly six locomotives from these designs. See also Dick & Stevenson.

1891 *D Drummond & Son, Helen Street, Govan, Glasgow*
This company was founded in 1891 by the famous locomotive engineer Dugald Drummond, and was later known as the Glasgow Railway Engineering Co. They built a batch of 7 narrow gauge well tank (WT) 0-4-0 locomotives for

the Glasgow Corporation Gas Works in 1894; in addition two railcars were constructed for the Alexandra Dock & Railway and additionally a 2ft gauge 0-4-0ST LITTLE TICH was built for the Premier Cement Co at Irthlingborough, Northamptonshire.

1896 *Marshall, Fleming & Jack, Motherwell*
This engineering company was known to have manufactured rail mounted steam cranes at their works in Motherwell from around 1900. The rail cranes incorporated vertical cross-tube boilers, mounted at the back of the vehicle so that the weight of the boiler counterbalanced the weight of the jib and load. The remains of a rescued Marshall, Fleming & Jack rail crane were in 2013 on display at the Summerlee Museum of Industrial Life, Coatbridge.

The remains of a Motherwell built Marshall, Fleming & Jack, rail crane on display at the Summerlee Museum of Industrial Life, Coatbridge. *Mike Stokes Collection*

1900c *Alexander Anderson & Sons, Carfin Boiler Works, Motherwell*
This company was known to have built locomotive boilers for other makers including Gibb & Hogg of Airdrie.

1900c *George Inglis & Co, Albert Works, Airdrie*
Firm is known to have built 0-4-0ST locomotives between early 1900s and 1928. One of the first built was supplied to the Lanarkshire Steel Company in 1900 and last, named PINDALE supplied to quarry owners G. & T. Earle at Hope, Derbyshire.

1900 *R Y Pickering & Co, Wishaw (c1900)*
This firm's records were apparently lost in 1980; however, it is possible that they supplied a four-wheel steam railcar to the Kent & East Sussex Railway.

1900 *Shotts Iron Co, Shotts*
One outside cylinder 0-4-0ST was constructed in 1900. The locomotive was claimed to be stored out of use at Monktonhall Colliery in 1968.

1905 *Stewarts & Lloyds Ltd, Mossend, Lanarkshire*
Reportedly this steelworks built one 3ft gauge 0-4-0T for use in its plate mill, circa 1905. The loco was said to be of the same design as Andrew Barclay loco works number 750 of 1894, which at that time worked at the location.

1913 *Glengarnock Iron & Steel Works*
Reportedly built a 0-4-0ST of Grant Ritchie type, but in all probability the engine was actually constructed from bought in parts.

1917 *Kilmarnock Engineering Co Ltd*
In 1917 the Kilmarnock Engineering Co (KE) acquired the former works premises of Dick, Kerr & Co where in addition to other activities they built various non-standard gauge steam locomotives during the early 1920s. This company also had fiscal ties to the English Electric Company and was listed at that firm's London offices. The locomotive manufacturing activities of KE were cut short as the firm did not survive the post depression period; they appointed a receiver in 1933. The firm continued to exist albeit on paper and eventually went into voluntary liquidation in August 1940. The Glacier Metal Company then acquired the Britannia Works site.

1927 *Newbattle Colliery, Newtongrange, Midlothian*
A single locomotive was apparently built in the colliery workshops during 1927, allegedly to the style of Andrew Barclay Sons & Co and from a set of drawings which may have owed their origins to the later company. The locomotive in question was from all accounts a 'Kilmarnock' type saddle tank of 0-4-0 configuration.

Part II

RAILWAY COMPANY LOCOMOTIVE WORKS

Cowlairs Works built 'J36' 0-6-0 BR No 65282, at the time a Bathgate depot (64F) allocated engine is seen shunting a short rake of wagons at one of the local pits, in August 1964. This locomotive was delivered in November 1896 and withdrawn by BR in January 1966. *Rail Photoprints Collection*

Chapter 11

COWLAIRS WORKS

In 1841 the Edinburgh & Glasgow Railway built their locomotive works on a site at Cowlairs in the Springburn area to the north east of Glasgow. The works was named after a nearby mansion. It was a comprehensive facility and when opened was the first railway engineering works in Britain to build locomotives, carriages and wagons on the same site. It was located on the western side of the Glasgow–Edinburgh main line in the vicinity of Carlisle Street.

The name Cowlairs is a direct reference to the fact that the area was in times past a place where animals were kept, with the old Scottish word for such a place being 'Lair'.

One year later the E&GR opened to traffic and the works came into full use. The first locomotives built at the works were two 0-6-0 'Well Tanks' designed specifically for use on the famous Cowlairs Incline*, and they entered traffic in 1844. The 0-6-0WT locomotives were respectively No 21 HERCULES and No 22 SAMSON.

---

* The 1 in 42 Cowlairs incline starts immediately as trains depart from Glasgow Queen Street station. The incline was originally rope operated and powered by a stationary steam engine located at Cowlairs. The rope engine was later replaced with banking locomotives, the first of which, were two 0-6-0s which were amongst the world's most powerful locomotives at the time. The practice of banking trains up the incline continued into the BR diesel era.

Cowlairs Works built NBR 'Glen' (D34) BR No 62484 GLEN LYON is seen passing the busy yard at Upperby as it approaches Carlisle with a train of passenger stock and vans during April 1959.This locomotive was delivered in April 1919 and withdrawn in March 1960. *Rail Photoprints Collection*

In 1865 the E&GR lost its individual identity when it became part of the North British Railway (NBR). In 1866 the works became the main rolling stock manufacturing and repair facility for the NBR.

On 1 January 1923, Cowlairs Works and the NBR became part of the London & North Eastern Railway (LNER) and up to that time an estimated 850 steam locomotives had been built on the site. Cowlairs continued to build and repair engines under LNER management and built its last class of locomotive during 1924, the Reid designed 'N15' class of 0-6-2Ts.

In 1948 the works became part of the then newly created British Transport Commission under the government's 'Nationalisation Plan'. Locomotive repair work continued to be carried out at the site, as did the scrapping of redundant engines.

In 1962 the works became part of British Railways Workshops Division and continued to be active until 1968 when the works closed and the locomotive repair programme was transferred to St Rollox Works.

In September 1904, a new repair complex known as the 'Eastfield Running Sheds' was built on the opposite side of the Glasgow–Edinburgh main line and located slightly to the north of the old Cowlairs Works. That works was closed in 1994 however; the depot site was redeveloped in 2005 and once again put into use as a maintenance works for some of the modern trains operating in the Scottish Region.

BR Standard '73000' series 4-6-0 is seen whilst under repair at Cowlairs Works in July 1965. *Brian Robbins/Rail Photoprints Collection*

Cowlairs Works in July 1965 where 'Ivatt 2-6-0's', 'Black 5s', 'Standard 5's' and a 'B1' are receiving their final overhauls. *Brian Robbins/ Rail Photoprints Collection*

Cowlairs Works built locomotive classes included in British Railway (BR) listings

NBR 'D31' 4-4-0 2P

The North British Railway (NBR) introduced three classes of Matthew Holmes 4-4-0 passenger locomotive classes '574', '633', and '729' between 1884 and 1889 and collectively the original Cowlairs build totalled 48 engines. All of those locomotives were re-built by the NBR between 1918 and 1924 under the respective reigns of engineers William P. Reid and Walter Chalmers the re-builds were designated as the railways 'M' class. The LNER later designated the class of 4-4-0 engines as 'D31' class.

The first of the class was withdrawn in 1931 but 7 locomotives survived to come into BR stock and were initially allocated numbers in the sequences 62059–62072. However the last 3 surviving engines were re-numbered 62281–62283 in 1949 to make way for the then newly built 'K1' class engines (62059 became 62281, 62060 became 62282 and 62072 became 62283). The first 'D31' locomotives to be withdrawn were 62062, 62064 and 62066 in 1948, and never carried their allocated BR numbers. The last 2 engines of the class in service were BR No 62059 and No 62281, both withdrawn in December 1952.

Driving wheel diameter 6' 6", 2-cylinder engine (inside)

Cowlairs Works built NBR 'D31' 4-4-0 2P seen as LNER 9768 at Eastfield depot during the 1930s. The locomotive later became LNER No 2072 and then BR No 62072 before being re-numbered again in June 1949 to BR No 62283. This locomotive was delivered in November 1899 and withdrawn in February 1951. ***Mike Morant Collection***

Cowlairs Works built NBR 'D31' 4-4-0 2P BR No 62282 seen stored only a week before being scrapped at Inverurie in May 1950. Before being re-numbered in June 1949 this locomotive was BR No 62060, it was delivered in September 1890 and withdrawn from service in February 1950. ***Rail Photoprints Collection***

NBR 'Scott/J' 4-4-0 3P – 'D29'

The 'Scott' class was a famous locomotive type designed especially for hauling passenger trains on the North British Railway (NBR) routes. There were 16 of the class originally built with Cowlairs Works building 6 of the 'Scott' engines which came into BR stock. The engines carried names derived from characters in Sir Walter Scott's novels; the LNER designated the class 'D29'.

British Railways (BR) took into stock 12 of the class in the number series 62400–62406 and 62409–62413. The 6 locomotives in the BR number series 62406–62413 were Cowlairs Works built (NBR 243, 338–340 and 459–360). Locomotives allocated BR numbers 62406 and 62409 were withdrawn in 1949 and 1948 respectively and never carried their BR numbers.

The last Cowlairs Works example to be withdrawn was BR No 62411 LADY OF AVENEL in October 1952, whilst still in LNER Apple Green livery.

See also NBR Reid 'Scott/J' 4-4-0 3P – 'D29' locomotives built by the NBL.

Driving wheel diameter 6' 6", 2-cylinder engine (inside)

NBR 'J' Scott' 4-4-0 3P – 'D30'

The North British Railway introduced a class of William P. Reid designed 4-4-0 passenger locomotives between 1912 and 1920. In total 27 of the engines were built at Cowlairs Works and like the earlier 'D29' class they were all named after characters in Sir Walter Scott's novels.

They were introduced as an improved version of the earlier NBR 'J' class engines and the first 2 were built in 1912 and designated by the LNER as 'D30/1' class, the remainder of the class built between 1914 and 1920, with detailed differences but of a similar overall appearance, were designated 'D30/2' class.

Although 2 engines of the class were scrapped before nationalisation the 'D30' 4-4-0s outlasted the 'D29' engines by several years. BR took into stock 25 of the class allocating to them numbers in the series 62417–62442 (NBR 363 and 409–501). The last 2 locomotives of the class to be withdrawn were BR No 62421 LAIRD O' MONKBARNS and BR No 62426 CUDDIE HEADRIGG both withdrawn in August 1960.

Driving wheel diameter 6' 6", 2-cylinder engine (inside)

Cowlairs Works built 'D30/1' 'Glen' class 4-4-0 LNER No 2417 HAL O' THE WYND is seen at Eastfield depot (65A) in 1947. This locomotive was delivered in October 1912 as NBR No 363 and it was the only 'D30/1' variant to come into BR stock, it was withdrawn in January 1951. The name HAL O' THE WYND was later carried by LNER/ BR 'A1' Pacific No 60116. *Mike Morant Collection*

Cowlairs Works built 'D30/2' 4-4-0 BR No 62419 MEG DODS is seen at Thornton Junction depot (62A) in April 1956. This locomotive was delivered in April 1914 as NBR No 410 and withdrawn by BR in September 1957. *Rail Photoprints Collection*

Cowlairs Works built 'D30/2' 4-4-0 BR No 62427 DUMBIEDYKES is seen on the depot at Dunfermline (62C), circa 1956. This locomotive was delivered as NBR No 418 in July 1914 and withdrawn by BR in April 1959. *Rail Photoprints Collection*

NBR 'K' 4-4-0 3P – 'D32' (Intermediates)

The North British Railway introduced these William P. Reid designed 4-4-0 passenger engines as their 'K' class during 1906. Originally built at Cowlairs Works with saturated boilers the 12 engines of the class were all later rebuilt with superheated boilers. The 'K' class engines were almost identical to the NBR 'K' class engines designated as 'D33' but slightly lighter.

The LNER designated the class 'D32' and although BR allocated the 10 surviving engines numbers in the series 62443–62454. Only one locomotive No 62451 carried its BR allocated number, all the others being withdrawn in 1948/49. That one remaining engine was withdrawn by BR in March 1951. Previous NBR numbers carried 882–893.

Driving wheel diameter 6' 0", 2-cylinder engine (inside)

NBR 'K' 4-4-0 3P – 'D33'

The North British Railway introduced these William P. Reid designed 4-4-0 passenger locomotives as additional members of their 'K' class between December 1909 and February 1910. These 'K' class engines were almost identical to the NBR 'K' class engines designated as 'D32' but were slightly heavier. Originally built at Cowlairs Works with saturated boilers the 12 engines of the class were all later rebuilt with superheated boilers.

The LNER designated the class 'D33' and 10 engines came into BR stock and were allocated numbers in the series 62455–62466 (NBR numbers in the series 864–894, 331–333 and 382–385). Locomotives No 62458 and 62463 were withdrawn in 1948/49 and never carried their BR numbers.

Driving wheel diameter 6' 0", 2-cylinder engine (inside)

Cowlairs Works built NBR 'D33' 4-4-0 BR No 62462 is seen at Eastfield depot (65A) in the summer of 1952. This locomotive was delivered as NBR No 333 in December 1909 and withdrawn by BR in November 1952. *Rail Photoprints Collection*

NBR 'K' 4-4-0 'D34' 'Glen' – 3P

The William P. Reid designed North British Railway 'Glen' class of 32 4-4-0 locomotives was built at Cowlairs Works between 1913 and 1920. They were originally intended to be a mixed traffic version of the superheated 'Scott' 'D30' class.

These engines were designed mainly to work over the steeply graded and sharply curved West Highland Line between Glasgow and Fort William.

BR took into stock 30 of the class allocating to them numbers in the series 62467–62498 (NBR numbers were allocated in a non consecutive sequence between 34 and 505 for LNER 1946 numbers disregard the 6 prefix).

Locomotive BR No 62469 was retired in November 1959 after a short period mainly working freight traffic over the Deeside and Elgin lines and then restored to full working order as NBR No 256 GLEN DOUGLAS. The locomotive worked rail tours for several years before being withdrawn and placed on permanent exhibition in the Glasgow Museum of Transport. The last engine of the 'D34' class in traffic was BR No 62496 GLEN LOY which was withdrawn in December 1961.

Driving wheel diameter 6' 0", 2-cylinder engine (inside)

Cowlairs Works built NBR 'K' 4-4-0 3P (commonly called 'Glen' class) and later designated LNER 'D34' class is seen as LNER No 9496 GLEN MOIDART at Eastfield depot in early LNER livery, note the engine number and LNER lettering was at that time applied to the tender sides. This locomotive later became LNER No 2498, and then BR No 62498. The 4-4-0 was delivered in September 1920 as NBR No 496 and withdrawn by BR in March 1960. ***Mike Morant Collection***

Cowlairs Works built NBR 'K' 4-4-0 3P 'Glen' BR No 62488 GLEN ALADALE is seen whilst shunting at Hawick shed (64G), in August 1960. This loco was delivered in April 1920 and withdrawn in December 1959. ***Hugh Ballantyne/Rail Photoprints Collection***

Cowlairs built locomotive classes which came into British Railways ownership

Class	Wheel arrangement	Designer	Customer/ Number to BR	Build dates	BR number series*
'D31'	4-4-0	Holmes	NBR 7 locomotives	1890/99 1949 3 locos re-numbered	62059–62072 (62281–62283)
'D29'	4-4-0	Reid	NBR 6 locomotives	1911	62406–62413
'D30'	4-4-0	Reid	NBR 25 locomotives	1912/20	62417–62442
'D32'	4-4-0	Reid	NBR 10 locomotives	1906/07	62443–62454
'D33'	4-4-0	Reid	NBR 10 locomotives	1909/10	62455–62466
'D34'	4-4-0	Reid	NBR 30 locomotives	1913/20	62467–62498

* The BR numbers are given for identification in BR listings and do not take into account missing numbers due to scrapping, or locomotives of the same class built by other companies, but do include locomotives with allocated numbers not carried.

NBR 'B' 0-6-0 3F – 'J35'

This class of 3F 0-6-0 engines, designed by William Paton Reid was introduced by the North British Railway (NBR) between 1906 and 1913. In total 76 locomotives were built, 40 by the NBL and an additional 36 at Cowlairs Works.

There were 5 class variants 'J35/1, 'J35/2' and 'J35/3' which were all pre-superheater designations, 'J35/4' were slide valve engines whilst 'J35/5' were piston valve engines.

A total of 70 locomotives came into BR stock and were allocated numbers in the series 64460–64535. Cowlairs Works built engines were BR Nos 64470–64477 (8 engines as 'J35/5'variants built 1906–1908), BR Nos 64478–64483 (5 engines as 'J35/4' variants built 1908–1909) and BR Nos 64514–64535 (22 engines as 'J35/4' variants built 1910–1913).

Although designed for freight work the class was often to be seen working secondary passenger train duties. The majority of the class remained in service until the early 1960s, the last Cowlairs Works built example in BR service was No 64480 withdrawn in September 1962.

See also NBR Reid 'B' 0-6-0 3F – 'J35' locomotives built at the NBL.

Driving wheel diameter 5', 2-cylinder engine (inside)

Cowlairs Works built NBR 'B' (LNER 'J35/5') 0-6-0 BR No 64472 labours through Bishopbriggs with a down freight, in November 1961. This locomotive was delivered in July 1908 and withdrawn by BR in March 1962. *Sid Rickard/Rail Photoprints Collection*

NBR 'S' 0-6-0 4F – 'J37' (BR reclassified as 5F in 1953)

The North British Railway (NBR) introduced the William Paton Reid designed 'S' class 0-6-0 between 1914 and 1921, they were designated 'J37' class by the LNER. These locomotives were reportedly the most powerful 0-6-0 tender engines ever built for use on a Scottish railway. A total of 104 of the class came into BR stock (numbers 64536–64639), Cowlairs Works produced 35 of those engines between 1914 and 1921. The class proved both capable and reliable in service whilst hauling mainline freight trains. The locomotives often worked both passenger and freight services over the West Highland Line and in addition were regularly rostered to work heavily loaded coal trains from the Fife and Lothian collieries.

The Cowlairs Works built locomotive carried numbers in the BR series 64536–64555, 64567, 64569–64570, 64574–64575 and 64630–64639 (NBR numbers were allocated in a non-consecutive sequence from 8–518).

Engines of the class remained in service almost to the end of steam on BR with the last Cowlairs Works built examples being No 64547 and 64569 both withdrawn in December 1966.

See also NBR 'S' 0-6-0 4F – 'J37' locomotives built by the NBL.

Driving wheel diameter 5', 2-cylinder engine (inside)

NBR 'C' 0-6-0 2F – 'J36'

Designed for the North British Railway by Matthew Holmes the 'C' class 0-6-0 locomotives were the most numerous on the NBL, the original build total being 168 engines, the class was designated 'J36' by the LNER. The locomotives were built by the contractors Neilson & Co, Sharp, Stewart & Co and at Cowlairs Works between 1880 and 1900. BR took into stock 123 'J36' class engines allocating to them numbers in the series 65210–65346.

Of that BR total 101 locomotives were Cowlairs Works built and they carried the Nos 65210–65236 (NBR Nos in the series 604–660) , 65246–65248 (NBR Nos 45, 68 and 183), and 65264–65346. NBR numbers were allocated in a non-consecutive sequence from 177–794.

The class achieved a modicum of fame when a batch of 25 engines was selected to be sent overseas during the 1917–1918 period of the First World War. On their return to the UK those locos were given the names of famous military leaders and locations associated with the war. Cowlairs Works examples given names were No 65216 BYNG, 65217 FRENCH, 65222 SOMME, 65224 MONS, 65226 HAIG (this loco did not carry its allocated BR number), 65233 PLUMER, 65235 GOUGH, 65236 HORNE, 65268 ALLENBY and 65311 which carried the name HAIG from May 1954. The names were painted on the centre driving wheel splasher, but at the time of nationalisation and for periods in BR ownership the locomotives often ran un-named.

None of the class remained in service beyond the end of 1967 and the last Cowlairs Works built engines in BR service were No 65288 and No 65345 which were both withdrawn in June 1967.

See also NBR 'C' 0-6-0 2F – 'J36' locomotives built by Sharp, Stewart & Co and by Neilson & Co.

Driving wheel diameter 5', 2-cylinder engine (inside)

Cowlairs Works built NBR'C' class 0-6-0 2F – 'J36' seen as BR No 65268 ALLENBY at Eastfield depot (65A) in 1949. This locomotive was delivered in August 1892 as NBR No 183 and withdrawn by BR in December 1962. ***Rail Photoprints Collection***

Cowlairs Works built NBR'C' class 0-6-0 2F – 'J36' BR No 65313 is seen whilst on station pilot duty at Fort William in August 1960. Note the ex-LNER 'Coronation Beaver Tailed Observation Car'. ***Rail Photoprints Collection***

Cowlairs Works built NBR'C' class 0-6-0 2F – 'J36' BR No 65316 is seen in light steam at Hawick during August 1960. Note the tender cab. This locomotive was delivered in April 1899 and withdrawn in December 1962. ***Rail Photoprints Collection***

Cowlairs Works built NBR'C' class 0-6-0 2F – 'J36' BR No 65333 is seen with a snowplough attached at Dundee Tay Bridge shed (62B) in April 1956, this engine was delivered in May 1900 and withdrawn in October 1959. ***David Anderson***

NBR 'G' 0-4-0ST 0F ('Y9' class Pug)

This class of Matthew Holmes designed saddle tanks was introduced by the North British Railway (NBR) between 1882 and 1899 and designated 'G' class engines (LNER 'Y9'). The type were commonly referred to as 'Pugs' and 38 were built, they were intended for use at dockyards and other railway installations with tightly curved sections of track.

The diminutive engines were built with open backed cabs and no coal bunkers accordingly it was common practice to permanently couple them to small 4-wheeled wooden tenders in order to add coal carrying capacity. BR took into stock 33 of the engines allocating to them numbers in the series 68092–68124 of those 31 were built at Cowlairs Works and allocated the BR numbers 68094–68124.

Locomotives No 68096, 68103 and 68109 never carried their BR allocated numbers. One 'Y9' 0-4-0ST allocated BR No 68095 is preserved and that engine was the last Cowlairs Works built example in traffic, being withdrawn in December 1962.

See also NBR 'G' 0-4-0ST 0F ('Y9' class Pug) locomotives built by Neilson & Co.

Driving wheel diameter 3' 8", 2-cylinder engine (outside)

Cowlairs Works built NBR 'G' 0-4-0ST 0F ('Y9' class Pug) is seen as LNER No 10090 at Edinburgh St Margaret's depot circa 1936. Note the attached 'coal wagon tender'. ***Rail Photoprints Collection***

Cowlairs Works built NBR 'G' 0-4-0ST 0F ('Y9' class Pug) BR No 68116, attached to a wooden coal tender, is seen at Kipps depot (65E) in May 1956. This locomotive was delivered in 1897 and withdrawn by BR in February 1958. ***David Anderson***

Cowlairs Works built NBR 'G' 0-4-0ST 0F ('Y9' class Pug) BR No 68124 was the last of the class to be built at Cowlairs Works and is seen at Kipps depot (65E). Note the 'G' class square brass identification plate located on the cab side between the 8 and 1 figures of the BR number. This locomotive was delivered in September 1899 and withdrawn in September 1959, aged 60 years old. Note the stovepipe style chimney. ***David Anderson***

Cowlairs Works built NBR 'G' 0-4-0ST 0F ('Y9' class Pug) BR No 68100 which was delivered in 1889 and withdrawn in May 1960 is seen shunting at Dundee Tay Bridge depot in April 1956. Note the wire basket external spark arrestor stored out of use on the top lamp bracket. ***David Anderson***

NBR 'F' 0-6-0T 0F – 'J88'

The North British Railway introduced 35 William Paton Reid designed light freight 0-6-0T engines between 1904 and 1919. All of the class was built at Cowlairs Works and they were originally designated 'F' class engines by the NBR and later designated 'J88' class by the LNER.

The wheelbase of the small engines was only 11 feet and with wooden block buffers they were ideal for shunting sharply curved sidings (dockyards) as those two features prevented buffer locking.

BR took into stock all 35 of the class and they were allocated numbers in the series 68320–68354.

Some of the engines were later re-built with Drummond boilers and one locomotive No 68345 was fitted with a stovepipe chimney after its original chimney was damaged in an accident. None of the class survived in traffic beyond December 1962 with No 68345 being the last to be withdrawn.

Driving wheel diameter 3' 9", 2-cylinder engine (outside)

Cowlairs Works built NBR 'F' 0-6-0T 0F (LNER 'J88') BR No 68345 was the only member of the Cowlairs built class to be fitted with a non-standard tall straight stovepipe chimney. The locomotive is seen at Eastfield depot (65A) in June 1956. This engine was delivered in 1912 and withdrawn in December 1962. *David Anderson*

Cowlairs Works built NBR 'F' 0-6-0T 0F (LNER 'J88') BR No 68339 is seen in 1955 at Haymarket depot (64B) which was its home shed for many years. Note that this engine is one of several fitted with a Drummond boiler design which incorporated safety valves on the top of the dome. This locomotive was delivered in April 1912 and withdrawn in October 1958. *David Anderson*

Cowlairs Works built NBR 'F' 0-6-0T 0F (LNER 'J88') BR No 68329 is seen at Kipps depot (65E) whilst shunting the yard during April 1956. Note that this locomotive is representative of the original design. *David Anderson*

NBR 'A' 0-6-2T 4MT – 'N15' (BR reclassified as 3MT in 1953)

This class of mixed traffic tank engines was designed by Reid for the NBR as a development of that railway company's earlier 'A' class 0-6-2T engines. The LNER designated the class 'N15'. There were a total of 99 of the class built between 1910 and 1924 and 20 of the locomotives which came into BR stock were Cowlairs Works built between 1923 and 1924, allocated BR Nos 69178 and 69202–69224.

Withdrawals commenced in 1957 and the last Cowlairs Works built example in traffic was No 69178 withdrawn in December 1962.

Driving wheel diameter 4' 6", 2-cylinder engine (inside)

See also NBR Reid 'A' 0-6-2T 4MT – 'N15' locomotives built by the NBL

Cowlairs Works built NBR 'A' class 0-6-2T 4MT – 'N15' No 69210 is seen in the company of NBL built 'J37' at Parkhead depot (65C) in 1955. Locomotive No 69210 was delivered in November 1923 and withdrawn in October 1957. *Authors Collection*

Cowlairs built locomotive classes which came into British Railways ownership

Class	Wheel arrangement	Designer	Customer/ Number to BR	Build dates	BR number series*
'J35'	0-6-0	Reid	NBR 35 locomotives	1906/08 1910/13	64470–64483 64514–64535
'J37'	0-6-0	Reid	NBR 35 locomotives	1914/18 1918 1918 1918 1921	64536–64555 64567 64569–64570 64574–64575 64630–64639
'J36'	0-6-0	Holmes	NBR 101 locomotives	1888/91 1892–1900	65210–65236 65246–65248 65264–65346
'Y9'	0-4-0ST	Holmes	NBR 31 locomotives	1887/1899	68094–68124
'J88'	0-6-0T	Reid	NBR 35 locomotives	1904/19	68320–68354
'N15'	0-6-2T	Reid	NBR	1923 1923/24	69178 69206-69224

* The BR numbers are given for identification in BR listings and do not take into account missing numbers due to scrapping, or locomotives of the same class built by other companies, but do include locomotives with allocated numbers not carried.

Cowlairs Works built 'Y9'class 0-4-0ST is seen at Edinburgh St Margaret's depot still as LNER No 8099, despite the date of this image being May 1950. Note the upper decks of the trams which can be seen on the road above. This locomotive which was delivered in 1887 was withdrawn as BR 68099 in November 1956. ***Mike Morant Collection***

Cowlairs Works built NBR 'J88' class 0-6-0T LNER No 9841 is seen circa 1935 whilst shunting at St Margaret's depot. This locomotive later became LNER No 8325 and then BR 68325. Delivered in January 1905 the engine was withdrawn in May 1961. ***Mike Morant Collection***

Cowlairs Works built NBR 'Glen' 'D34' class 4-4-0 is seen as LNER No 9493 GLEN LUSS, at Edinburgh Waverley station heading a Fife Coast passenger working in 1935. This locomotive later became LNER No 2495 and then BR No 62495. Delivered in July 1920 the locomotive was withdrawn in April 1961. ***Mike Morant Collection***

Cowlairs Works built Drummond 'R' class 4-4-0T No NBR 98 which originally carried the name ABERFOYLE is seen posed in an unknown location circa 1920. Note the solid bogie wheels and dome fitted safety valves. The class of 30 engines was later designated 'D51'and none survived in service beyond 1933. ***Mike Morant Collection***

Railway Company abbreviations used in this chapter.

NBR – North British Railway

Chapter 12

ST ROLLOX WORKS

In 1853 the Caledonian Railway (CR) chose a 15-acre site in the Springburn area of Glasgow on which to construct a locomotive, carriage and wagon works to serve that developing railway's needs. The new works was built on the site of the station of the Garnkirk & Glasgow Railway which the CR had absorbed (1865), the new development was named in recognition of the nearby parish church of St Roche.

The works officially opened in 1854 and in that year reportedly built its first locomotive a 2-4-0. The CR continued to grow and by 1870 a first extension to the works was needed and that was followed by a second expansion of the facilities in 1884.

In 1886 the CR works engineer Dugald Drummond had a hand in designing the locomotive which is in all probability the most famous Scottish built steam locomotive ever, however the building of the 4-2-2 'Single Wheeler' CR No 123 was contracted out to Neilson & Co, Hyde Park Works against CR order No 600. Amongst the better known locomotive classes built at St Rollox Works were the 'Cardean' 4-6-0s and the 'Dunalastair' 4-4-0s.

St Rollox Works built Drummond '294' class 'Jumbo' 0-6-0 BR No 57375, is entrusted with the 'Scottish Rambler 2 Railtour' and is seen at Whithorn on 15 April 1963. Note that the engineman is about to use the 'token' in order to activate the ground frame. This locomotive was delivered in February 1894 and withdrawn November 1963. This Lambie built example was one of several fitted with Westinghouse brakes for working passenger trains. *Rail Photoprints Collection*

In January 1923 the works became part of the London, Midland & Scottish Railway (LMSR) and in 1928 the policies of the new owners heralded the end of locomotive manufacturing at the works, the last engine built at St Rollox being 0-6-0 '4F' LMS No 4476 (BR 44476) which was one of a final batch of 10 of the class built there between May and August of that year.

The works continued to be heavily involved in the repair of steam locomotives and carriages however, wagon repairs were transferred to Barassie Works at about that time. The works was a major employer in the area and the 1947 records show that there were then some 3,382 members of staff. In January 1948 St Rollox Works became part of the British Transport Commission at the time of Nationalisation.

In 1962 the works became part of the British Railways Workshops Division. As the result of a 1968 reorganisation scheme St Rollox became the main BR works in Scotland following the closure at that time of Cowlairs Works. In January 1970 the works became part of British Rail Engineering Ltd (BREL) and in 1972 the site was re-titled Glasgow Works. In 1987 the works became part of British Rail Maintenance Ltd (BRML) operating as Springburn 'Level 5' Depot.

In 1995 BRML was privatised.

St Rollox built locomotive classes included in British Railway (BR) listings

LMS/SDJR Fowler 0-6-0 '4F'

The combined total of Fowler 0-6-0 '4F' freight engines introduced to the Somerset & Dorset Joint Railway (SDJR) in 1922 and the LMS between 1924 and 1940 and then taken into BR stock was 580 engines in the number series 44027-44606. The large number built is testament to the success of the uncomplicated design and although the 0-6-0s were primarily designed as freight locomotives they were often to be seen on local passenger services and double heading duties. The class was built at St Rollox Works, Derby Works, Crewe Works, Horwich Works and additionally by contractors Kerr, Stuart & Co Ltd, Andrew Barclay Sons & Co Ltd and North British Locomotive Co Ltd.

St Rollox Works built 60 of the class for the LMS which were later allocated BR numbers 44177–44206 (30 engines 1924/25) 44312–44331 (20 engines 1927/28) and 44467–44476 (10 engines 1928).

None of the class remained in traffic beyond the end of 1966 and the last St Rollox Works built example was BR No 44188 which was withdrawn in November 1965.

See also LMS/SDJR Fowler 0-6-0 4F locomotives built at the NBL and also by Andrew Barclay Sons & Co Ltd.

Driving wheel diameter 5' 3", 2-cylinder engine (inside)

St Rollox Works built LMS/SDJR Fowler 0-6-0 4F BR No 44189 is seen at the west side bay platform of Dumfries station waiting to depart with the morning branch line service to Kirkcudbright via Castle Douglas in the summer of 1956 (that branch was closed to all traffic in June 1965). The locomotive was delivered in April 1925 and withdrawn in December 1962. ***David Anderson***

CR 'Dunalastair' 4-4-0 2P

In 1895 John F. McIntosh became the Locomotive Superintendent of the Caledonian Railway (CR) and almost immediately he inaugurated a locomotive building plan which became known as his 'Big Engine' policy. Included in that plan was his 'Dunalastair' class of engines of which there were four variants.

The engines were designed to work all the main line passenger services on the 'Caley'. They were considered at the time to be amongst the most advanced steam locomotives in the country. Furthermore the 'Dunalastair' class superheated re-built locomotives were the first Scottish engines to be superheated.

The 'Dunalastair I' class was introduced in 1896 and they were the first inside cylinder 4-4-0s built by McIntosh. In total 15 engines were built and the LMS re-numbered them 14311–14325 and gave them a 2P power rating, all of the 'Dunalastair 1' class engines were withdrawn between 1930 and 1935.

The 'Dunalastair II' class was introduced in 1897 and they were effectively enlarged versions of the 'Dunalastair I' class engines. In total 15 engines were built and the LMS re-numbered them 14326–14336, and gave them a 2P power rating. Those engines were all withdrawn between 1936 and 1947. However, 4 engines were re-built with superheaters in 1914 (LMS Nos 14330–14333) and those engines were rated at 3P and were withdrawn between 1935 and 1937.

CR 'Dunalastair III' 4-4-0 (Superheated) 3P

Between 1899 and 1900 the railway introduced the 'Dunalastair III' class which were effectively enlarged versions of the 'Dunalastair II' class engines. In total 16 engines were built and the LMS re-numbered them 14337–14348, and gave them a 2P power rating. All of those engines were withdrawn between 1932 and 1947.

However, 4 engines were re-built with superheaters between 1914 and 1918 and those engines were re-numbered by the LMS 14434–14437 and rated at 3P.

They were withdrawn from 1928 onwards but one locomotive survived to come into BR stock and was allocated the BR number 54434, but was withdrawn in April 1948 and never carried that number.

Driving wheel diameter 6' 6", 2-cylinder engine (inside)

The Memorial to those who died in the Quintinshill rail disaster which stands in Rosebank Cemetery, Leith. *David Anderson*

CR 'Dunalastair IV' 4-4-0 2P

The 'Dunalastair IV' class was introduced between 1904 and 1910 and it was the final development of the class with initially 19 saturated boiler engines being built. Those engines were allocated the LMS numbers 14349–14365 and classified 2P, they were withdrawn between 1937 and 1948. Between 1915 and 1917 LMS locomotives Nos 14438 and 14439 were re-built with superheated boilers and given a 3P power classification. The last saturated boiler member of the class came into BR stock and was allocated the number 54363, but was withdrawn in October 1948 and never carried that number.

Driving wheel diameter 6' 6", 2-cylinder engine (inside)

CR 'Dunalastair IV' 4-4-0 (Superheated) 3P

Between 1910 and 1914 the railway introduced batches of 2 and then 22 CR 'Dunalastair IV' class engines which were fitted with superheated boilers. Those locomotives carried the LMS numbers 14438, 14439 and 14440–14460.

Locomotive CR No 121 from the class was destroyed in the 1915 Quintinshill* accident and locomotive LMS No 14442 was withdrawn in 1946, the remaining 22 engines all came into BR stock and were allocated the BR numbers 54438–54460.

None of the class remained in traffic beyond August 1958 when the last of the class BR No 54439 was withdrawn.

Driving wheel diameter 6' 6", 2-cylinder engine (inside)

---

* The Quintinshill rail disaster occurred on 22 May 1915 near to Gretna Green at Quintinshill, an intermediate signal box (now demolished) with loops on each side, which was located on the Caledonian Railway Main Line linking Glasgow and Carlisle (now part of the West Coast Main Line).

The crash, which involved five trains remains the worst ever rail crash in the UK. In the disaster a 213 yard long troop train was telescoped down to 67 yards, a third of its original length.

The vast majority of soldiers involved were from the 1/7th Battalion of the Royal Scots, based at Dalmeny Street in Leith. Most of these men came from Leith, Musselburgh or Edinburgh, with a small number from West Lothian. There was also a detachment of men from the Highland Light Infantry travelling on the train, and some of the casualties were therefore from the south west of Scotland rather than from the Edinburgh area.

An annual remembrance service is held at Rosebank Cemetery, Leith where there is a memorial to the dead.

See also www.pen-and-sword.co.uk/the-quintinshill-conspiracy/p/4088/

Caledonian Railway 'Dunalastair IV' Superheated' class 4-4-0 CR No 122 (LMS No. 14449 and BR No 54449) was built at St Rollox Works, Glasgow and delivered in July 1912 being withdrawn by BR in November 1953. The locomotive is seen leaving Carlisle Citadel with a Down express circa 1922. Note the CR route indicator on the top lamp bracket showing the 'Main line to and from Carlisle, Carstairs and Glasgow' aspect, also the cabside mounted lamp. *Steve Armitage Archive/ Rail Photoprints Collection*

St Rollox Works built Caledonian Railway 'Dunalastair IV' Superheated' class 4-4-0 BR No 54446 is seen at Carstairs Junction whilst performing station pilot duties during April 1955. This locomotive was delivered in May 1912 as CR No 118 and withdrawn in August 1955. *David Anderson*

CR '113', '918', and '72' 4-4-0 3P

Between 1916 and 1922 William Pickersgill introduced his own version of the 'Dunalastairs' which were the last express passenger engines built for the Caledonian Railway, and were commonly referred to as 'Caley Bogies' (BR numbers 54461–54508).

The express passenger 4 cylinder 4-4-0 locomotives were identified by three class designations, all in the '3P' classification. In 1948 BR took into stock 48 of the type of which 22 were NBL built engines. In addition St Rollox Works (16 engines) and Sir W. G. Armstrong Whitworth & Co Ltd (10 engines) also built locomotives of this class(s). The '72' class locomotives which were introduced from 1920 onwards were fitted with slightly larger cylinders than the other two variants.

In total 16 of the St Rollox Works built '113', '918' and '72' class engines came into BR stock and were allocated numbers in the series 54461–54466 (CR numbers in the series 113–124) and 54477–54486 (CR numbers in the series 72–81) the latter batch being '72' class engines. None of the class saw service beyond the end of 1962 and the last St Rollox Works built example to be withdrawn was No 54463 in December 1962.

See also Caledonian Railway '113', '918', and '72' 4-4-0 3P built by the NBL.

Driving wheel diameter 6' 6", 2-cylinder engine (inside) Cylinder size variants 20" dia x 26" stroke BR 54467–54476, 20½" dia x 26" stroke BR 54497–54508.

St Rollox Works built CR '113' class 4-4-0 3P BR No 54465 is seen with the two restored Caledonian Railway coaches, whilst in charge of the Branch Line Society, 'Scottish Central Tour' at Bonnybridge, Falkirk, on 7 May 1960. This 'Caley Bogie' locomotive was delivered in February 1916 as CR No 121 and withdrawn in October 1962. *Steve Armitage Archive/Rail Photoprints Collection*

St Rollox Works built CR '113' class 'Caley Bogie' 4-4-0 3P BR No 54461 is seen marshalling an engineer's train at Strawfrank Junction, Carstairs on a Sunday during May 1957 before heading up the WCML for track repairs at Symington. Above the engine the Carstairs coaling plant and the sharply curving line which allowed traffic to and from Edinburgh Princes Street to bypass the station can be seen. This locomotive was delivered in February 1916 and withdrawn in May 1958. *David Anderson*

St Rollox Works built locomotive classes which came into British Railways ownership

Class	Wheel arrangement	Designer	Customer/ Number to BR	Build dates	BR number series*
LMS & SDJR 4F	0-6-0	Fowler	LMS/SDJR 60 locomotives	1925 1927/28 1928	44177–44206 44312–44331 44467–44476
CR 'Dunalastair III' Superheated	4-4-0	McIntosh	CR 1 locomotive	1900	54434
CR 'Dunalastair IV'	4-4-0	McIntosh	CR 1 locomotive	1910	54363
CR 'Dunalastair IV' Superheated	4-4-0	McIntosh	CR 22 locomotives	1907/14	54438–54460
CR '113' '918' '72'	4-4-0	Pickersgill	CR 16 locomotives	1916 1920	54461–54466 54477–54486

* The BR numbers are given for identification in BR listings and do not take into account missing numbers due to scrapping, or locomotives of the same class built by other companies, but do include locomotives with allocated numbers not carried.

CR '60' 4-6-0 4P (re-classified 3MT in 1948)

Between 1902 and 1922 engineers John F. McIntosh and William Pickersgill respectively built a total of nine individually different 4-6-0 engines The survivors of those builds were 9 engines which the CR designated 'Class 60' and those were the later built Pickersgill designed locomotives.

The first 6 of those engines, allocated BR Nos 54650–54654 and LMS No 14655 were built by the CR at St Rollox between 1916 and 1917 whilst the remainder were built by the LMS between 1925 and 1926. Three of the class were withdrawn before Nationalisation and the remaining 23 engines came into BR stock being allocated numbers in the series 54630–54654.

However, only 14 locomotives actually carried their BR numbers 54630, 54634–54636, 54638–54640, 54642, 54647–54651 and 54654 the others all being withdrawn between 1948 and 1950. The last CR '60' class 4-6-0 in traffic was BR No 54639 which was withdrawn in December 1953.

Driving wheel diameter 6' 1", 2-cylinder engine (outside) Cylinder size variants 20½" dia x 26" stroke BR 54650–54654 all LMS built engines and 20" dia x 26" stroke BR 54630–54650 all CR built engines.

St Rollox built CR '60' class 4-6-0 No 14642 is seen at Motherwell as an LMS engine circa 1947. This locomotive was delivered in September 1926 and withdrawn as BR No 54642 in October 1959, having been re-numbered in May 1948. *Mike Morant Collection*

St Rollox built CR '60' class 4-6-0 No 54647 is seen in BR ownership at Motherwell (66B) in February 1949. This locomotive was delivered in November 1926 as LMS No 14647and withdrawn in March 1951. *Mike Morant Collection*

CR '19' and '92' 0-4-4T 2P

These 0-4-4T locomotives were introduced between 1895 and 1900 to a John F. McIntosh design and were regarded as the original Caledonian Railway suburban and branch line tank engines. They were a very successful introduction from which other CR classes of 0-4-4T locomotives were developed.

The original St Rollox Works build total was 32 engines and the first members of the class were withdrawn in 1946. All of the class was originally fitted with condensing apparatus for working over the Glasgow Central Low Level lines but that apparatus was later removed from most of the engines. A number of the class were later fitted with a stovepipe style of chimney. The first 10 engines built were fitted with smaller side tanks and those engines were designated '19' class, the remainder, which had larger side tanks and high sided coal bunkers were designated '92' class.

In total 26 engines came into BR stock and they were allocated numbers in the series 55116–55124 (CR numbers in the series 20–28), 55125–55130 (CR numbers in the series 13–18), 55132–55136 (CR numbers in the series 99–103), 55138–55144 (CR Numbers in the series 880–886) and 55145–55146 (CR numbers 437–438).

Locomotives allocated BR numbers 55116, 55117, 55127, 55130 and 55133 were withdrawn before ever carrying their allocated BR numbers. The last example of the class in service was BR No 55124 which was withdrawn in October 1961.

Driving wheel diameter 5' 9", 2-cylinder engine (inside)

St Rollox Works built 4-4-0T BR No 55124 is seen at Dalry Road depot (64C) shortly before being towed away for scrap in 1963. This locomotive was a '19' class example with smaller side tanks and coal bunker. Note the Westinghouse brake equipment fixed to the cab side and one of the associated reservoirs suspended below the bunker framing. Note also that this variant has a rounded coal bunker lip, in comparison to the square design of the later '92' class engines. This locomotive was delivered in May 1895 and was the last of the class to be withdrawn in October 1961. ***David Anderson***

St Rollox Works built CR '439' class 0-4-4T 2P BR No 55212 is seen storming away from the Perth to Inverness main line at Ballinluig Junction between Dunkeld and Pitlochry, on the nine mile long former Highland Railway branch line to Aberfeldy. The '439' class appears to be leaking plenty of steam as it heads the 4.55 pm working to Aberfeldy away from the station during June 1957. The locomotive was delivered in June 1911 as CR No 462 and withdrawn in December 1958. ***David Anderson***

CR '439' 0-4-4T 2P

This class of initially John F. McIntosh, but later William Pickersgill designed 0-4-4T locomotives were built at St Rollox Works between 1900 and 1922. The '439' class engines were a development of the earlier '92' class engines, but were not fitted with condensing apparatus. They were also referred to as the Caledonian Railway 'Standard Passenger' class.

In total 78 engines were built, and a number were later fitted with stovepipe style chimneys. The last 10 engines of the class were the Pickersgill built 1915 to 1922 (LMS Nos 15227–15236) examples.

BR took into stock 76 of the class allocating them numbers in the series 55159–55236 (CR numbers in the non consecutive series 112–473), locomotives BR Nos 55184, 55188, 55190 and 55192 were withdrawn without ever carrying their BR allocated numbers.

The last 3 examples of the class in BR service were Nos 55189, 55204 and 55234 which were all withdrawn in December 1962. Locomotive BR No 55189 (LMS No 15189 and CR No 419) is preserved.

Driving wheel diameter 5' 9", 2-cylinder engine (inside)

St Rollox Works built CR '439' class 0-4-4T 2P BR No 55215 was one of the class fitted with a stovepipe chimney. The engine is seen departing Oban station in July 1957 with an afternoon local branch service to Connel Ferry and Ballachulish. Note the Stanier 'Black Five' waiting to depart with a train to Glasgow Buchanan Street. The '439' class locomotive was delivered as CR No 457 in July 1912 and withdrawn in October 1961. *David Anderson*

St Rollox Works built CR '439' class 0-4-4T 2P BR No 55216 is seen on shed at Kyle of Lochalsh (a sub shed to Inverness 60A) in May 1957. Note the splendid selection of fire irons laid out beside the engine. This locomotive was delivered as CR No 458 in July 1912 and withdrawn in December 1961. *Hugh Ballantyne/Rail Photoprints*

CR '431' 0-4-4T 2P

Introduced in 1922 the William Pickersgill designed '431' class 0-4-4T engines were a variant of the earlier '439' class which were fitted with strengthened cast iron buffer beams, to facilitate banking duties at Beattock. BR took into stock 4 of the engines and allocated them the numbers 55237–55240 (CR Nos 431–434), at some time during its later working life BR No 55237 carried a stove pipe style chimney. All four of the class were withdrawn in 1961 with No 55240 being the last in service when withdrawn in November of that year.

Driving wheel diameter 5' 9", 2-cylinder engine (inside)

St Rollox Works built CR '431' class 0-4-4T BR No 55239 is seen on shed at Polmadie (66A) in June 1956. This locomotive was delivered in September 1922 as CR No 433 and withdrawn in July 1961. ***David Anderson***

CR '944' 4-6-2T 4P

This class of Pacific Tanks is included in some listings as being St Rollox Works built and the class was in fact designed at the works. However, this 12 locomotive class was built for the Caledonian Railway to a Pickersgill CR design by the North British Locomotive Co Ltd (NBL) at their Glasgow Hyde Park Works to order No L672, and the engines were allocated the NBL works numbers 21480-91.

See also CR '944' 4-6-2T 4P built by the NBL.

CR 'Pugs' 0-4-0ST 0F

The Caledonian Railway and the North British Railway in Scotland both used 0-4-0ST engines for dockyard and other shunting duties specifically in goods yards with tightly curved track layouts. The engines of both railways were given the name 'Pug', with the NBR engines later becoming the LNER 'Y9' class.

Dugald Drummond and John F. McIntosh were both involved in the design and building of the CR version, which was in fact developed from an earlier Neilson & Co design.

The 'Caley' introduced 34 of the type between 1885 and 1908 and the diminutive shunting engines had open backed cabs and were built without coal bunkers. Accordingly they were often coupled to four wheel open wooden trucks which carried an extra stock of coal. The CR 'Pugs' could be distinguished from the LNER 'Y9' class engines by their tall flared top tapering chimneys, although some of the class were later fitted with an alternative design of stovepipe chimneys.

BR took into stock 14 of the class and they were allocated numbers in the series 56010–56039 (CR Nos 268, 270, 1510, 1515, 611–614, 621–623, 626, 431 and 463). Three of the class became departmental engines (but were not re-numbered) No 56025 was the St Rollox Works shunter and Nos 56027 and 56032 carried out those duties at Crewe Works. Locomotive BR No 56029 was the last in general traffic to be withdrawn in December 1962.

Driving wheel diameter 3' 8", 2-cylinder engine (outside)

The St Rollox Works shunter CR 'Pug' BR No 56025 is seen at the works in pristine condition resplendent in BR Mixed Traffic livery. Note the added back cab section and a silver CR star on the smokebox door. This locomotive was delivered as CR No 1515 in May 1890 and withdrawn in May 1960 when in its 70th year. Given the way that the staff at St Rollox cherished this little engine it is perhaps surprising that it was not preserved. ***Mike Morant Collection***

St Rollox Works built CR 'Pug' BR No 56031 is seen in a delightful period setting whilst shunting at Greenock Central station in April 1956. The locomotive was delivered in July 1900 as CR No 622 and withdrawn in April 1962. ***David Anderson***

St Rollox Works built locomotive classes which came into British Railways ownership

Class	Wheel arrangement	Designer	Customer/ Number to BR	Build dates	BR number series*
CR '60'	4-6-0	Pickersgill	CR 23 locomotives	1917/26	54630–54654
CR '19' '92'	0-4-4T	McIntosh	CR 26 locomotives	1895–1900	55116–55146
CR '439'	0-4-4T	McIntosh	CR 76 locomotives	1900/22	55159–55236
CR '431'	0-4-4T	Pickersgill	CR 4 locomotives	1922	55237–55240
CR '944'	4-6-2T	Pickersgill	CR 10 locomotives	1917	55350–55361
CR 'Pugs'	0-4-0ST	D Drummond and McIntosh	CR 14 locomotives	1885–1908	56010–56039

* The BR numbers are given for identification in BR listings and do not take into account missing numbers due to scrapping, or locomotives of the same class built by other companies, but do include locomotives with allocated numbers not carried.

CR '498' 0-6-0T 2F

This class of initially John F. McIntosh, but later William Pickersgill designed 0-6-0T engines were also referred to as 'Caledonian Dock Tanks' and they were introduced between 1912 and 1923.These compact and powerful engines had only a 10ft coupled wheelbase which made them ideal for dock shunting work.

McIntosh built 5 engines in 1912 and they were his first and only outside cylinder design. The remainder of the class were Pickersgill engines which were introduced between 1918 and 1921 and those locomotives had larger capacity coal bunkers. Some of the class were later fitted with stovepipe style chimneys.

BR took into stock 23 of the class and they were allocated numbers in the series 56151–56173 (CR Nos 498, 499, 527–538, 502–504 and 510–515).

Numbers 56151 and 56152 were introduced by McIntosh; all the others were of Pickersgill origin. The last example in BR service was No 56159 withdrawn in April 1962.

Driving wheel diameter 4' 0", 2-cylinder engine (outside)

St Rollox Works built CR '498' class 0-6-0T 2F BR No 56168 is seen in the company of 'Y9' class 0-4-0ST BR No 68114 at Dawsholm shed (65D) in August 1958. This Pickersgill '498' class locomotive entered service in December 1920 as CR No 532 and was withdrawn in April 1961. *David Anderson*

CR '782' '29' 0-6-0T 3F

The Caledonian Railway engines known as the '782' and '29' classes respectively were built under the supervision of John F. McIntosh from a design by John Lambie which he completed just before his death in service. These locomotives were the most numerous goods tank locomotives built for freight and general shunting work by the CR. A good many of the class were later fitted with stovepipe style chimneys.

A total of 147 of the class were built and they all came into BR stock in the number series 56230–56376 (CR numbers in the non consecutive series 29–781 and 5001). Locomotive No 56250 was sold out of service to the Wemyss Private Railway and that engine was scrapped in 1959.

St Rollox Works built CR '782'class 0-6-0T 3F BR No 56253 with a stovepipe chimney is seen in 1955 with the daily freight working at Murrayfield between Leith North and Edinburgh Lothian Road on the ex CR branch line which was originally part of the Edinburgh, Leith & Granton Railway. This locomotive was delivered in January 1899 and withdrawn in November 1958. *David Anderson*

St Rollox Works built CR '782' class 0-6-0T 3F BR No 56375 is seen at Grangemouth shed (65F) in April 1955. This locomotive is fitted with a shorter chimney than normal and it was delivered in June 1922 and was withdrawn in August 1958. *David Anderson*

Locomotives BR numbers 56231–56239 were the original '29' class and all the others were designated '782' class. Some engines were fitted with condensing apparatus for use on the Glasgow Underground but that gear was removed between 1920 and 1922. Three batches of engines were fitted with Westinghouse brakes and they were BR Nos 56231–56239, 56290–56303 and 56347–56351.

Locomotives No 56270 and No 56351 although allocated BR numbers never carried them and were scrapped in 1948. The last three examples of the class in BR service were No 56302, No 56325 and No 56336 which were all withdrawn in December 1962.

Driving wheel diameter 4' 6", 2-cylinder engine (inside)

CR '294' 'Jumbo' 0-6-0 2F

Designed by Dugald Drummond this class of 0-6-0 locomotives became known as the Caledonian Railway (CR) 'Standard Goods' nicknamed 'Jumbo' class and they were introduced between 1883 and 1897. They were the forerunner of Drummond's '700' class of 0-6-0 engines introduced by the London & South Western Railway (LSWR) in 1897.

A total of 244 engines of the class were built under Drummond, John Lambie and John F. McIntosh in the aforementioned period making them the most numerous Caledonian Railway class. In addition to St Rollox Works they were built by the contractor Neilson & Co.

British Railways (BR) took into stock 238 of the class allocating to them numbers in the series 57230–57473 (CR numbers in the non consecutive series 201–760, 1259, 1260, 1310–1365, 1517, 1548–1588, 1680, 1704–1708, 1910, 1924). Lambie built engines were BR numbers 57352–57392, McIntosh built engines were BR numbers 57387, 57388, 57473–57493 and Drummond built engines were BR numbers 57230–57351, and 57357. Of that total 203 were St Rollox Works built BR numbers 57237–57240, 57250, 57251 and 57272–57473.

Amendments to the design of various locomotives included the fitting of condensing equipment for working on the Glasgow Underground, stovepipe style chimneys and Westinghouse brake equipment. Some of the engines were later re-built with LMS boilers.

A batch of 25 engines saw First World War service with the ROD the St Rollox Works built examples in that batch being BR numbers 57290–57294.

None of the class survived in service beyond 1963 and the last St Rollox Works built 'Jumbo' class locomotives in service for BR were No 57296 and No 57355, both withdrawn in November 1963. Surprisingly no member of this large class survived into preservation.

See also CR '294', 'Jumbo' 0-6-0 2F locomotives built by Neilson & Co.

Driving wheel diameter 5' 0", 2-cylinder engine (inside)

St Rollox Works built CR '294' Drummond 'Jumbo' BR No 57345 is seen on shed at Perth (63A) during June 1956. Note the stovepipe chimney and Westinghouse brake equipment. This locomotive was delivered in April 1892 and withdrawn in February 1962. *David Anderson*

828
C R

Preserved St Rollox Works built CR '812' class 0-6-0 3F is seen as CR 828 whilst leaving Hampton Loade with a train for Kidderminster during the locomotive's 2012 visit to the Severn Valley Railway. *Keith Langston*

CR '812' 0-6-0 3F

The Caledonian Railway (CR) introduced this John Farquharson McIntosh designed class of 0-6-0 freight locomotives between 1899 and 1900. The 79 engines were built at St Rollox Works and by contractors Sharp, Stewart & Co, Dübs & Co. and Neilson, Reid & Co and they were an enlarged version of the CR 'Jumbo' class engines. As originally built they were fitted with 'Dunalastair I' type boilers and 'Dunalastair II' type cabs, most of the engines were later re-built with LMS boilers. BR took into stock 76 of these engines and allocated to them numbers in the series 57550–57628.

The class was originally referred to as 'Mixed Traffic' engines however, only 17 locomotives were fitted with Westinghouse brakes and 5 with vacuum for passenger train working. Of the BR total 29 were St Rollox Works built locomotives, numbered 57550–57566 and 57617–57638 which were delivered in 1899 as CR Nos 812–828 (LMS numbers 17550–17566) and 282–293 (LMS numbers 17617–17628). None of the class remained in traffic after 1963 and the last surviving St Rollox Works built engine was BR No 57627 which was withdrawn in November 1963. One locomotive of the class BR No 57566 (LMS No 17566 and CR No 828) is preserved; the engine was delivered in August 1899 and withdrawn in August 1963.

See also CR '812' 0-6-0 3F locomotives built by Neilson, Reid & Co, Sharp, Stewart & Co and Dübs & Co.

Driving wheel diameter 5' 0", 2-cylinder engine (inside)

The now preserved St Rollox Works built CR 3F '812' 0-6-0 BR No 57566 is seen on shed at Glasgow Corkerhill (67A) in 1955. *David Anderson*

CR '652' 0-6-0 3F

This John Farquharson McIntosh design of 0-6-0 for the Caledonian Railway was almost identical to the '812' class except for the fact they were fitted with 'Dunalastair III' type cabs and deeper mainframes behind the wheel splashers. The engines were introduced between 1908 and 1909 and BR later took into stock 17 of the class.

The '652' locomotives were allocated BR numbers in the series 57629–57645 (LMS numbers 17629–17645 and CR numbers 652–665, 325–328 and 460).

Locomotives BR Nos 57629, 57636, 57639 and 57641 were scrapped without ever receiving their allocated BR numbers. The last of the class in service was BR No 57630 which was withdrawn in November 1963.

Driving wheel diameter 5' 0", 2-cylinder engine (inside)

St Rollox Works built CR'652' 0-6-0 3F BR No 57632 is seen between duties at Polmadie depot (66A) in June 1956. This locomotive was delivered in July 1909 and withdrawn in November 1961. *David Anderson*

CR '294' '670' 0-6-0 3F

This class of engines was introduced between 1918 and 1920 and built to a design by William Pickersgill. The 0-6-0 locomotive design was arrived at by combining several features of the earlier McIntosh CR '30' and '812' 0-6-0 class locomotives.

The 43 engines were originally built with saturated boilers which were later superheated by the LMS. BR took into stock 29 of the class and allocated to them numbers in the series 57650–57691 (LMS numbers 17650–17691 and CR numbers 300–324, 670, 294–323, 280 and 281).

Locomotives BR numbers 57650–57682 were designated '294' class whilst locomotives BR numbers 57684–57691 were designated '670' class.

None of the class remained in service beyond 1963 and the last BR examples were No 57652, No 57679 and No 57688 which were all withdrawn in November 1963.

Driving wheel diameter 5' 0", 2-cylinder engine (inside)

St Rollox Works built CR '294' 0-6-0 3F BR No 57658 gets away from Ayr Harbour with a rake of coal empties bound for the Ayrshire coalfield in July 1962. This locomotive was delivered in March 1918 and withdrawn in December 1962. ***J & J Collection - Sid Rickard/Rail Photoprints Collection***

St Rollox Works built CR '670' 0-6-0 3F BR No 57691 is seen between duties on shed at Grangemouth (65F) during April 1955. This locomotive was delivered in February 1920 and withdrawn in August 1962. ***David Anderson***

St Rollox Works built locomotive classes which came into British Railways ownership

Class	Wheel arrangement	Designer	Customer/ Number to BR	Build dates	BR number series*
CR '498'	0-6-0T	McIntosh and Pickersgill	CR 23 locomotives	1912/21	56151–56173
CR '782' '29'	0-6-0T	McIntosh (Lambie)	CR 147 locomotives	1895–1922	56230–56376
CR '294' Jumbo	0-6-0	D Drummond	CR 203 locomotives	1883/97	57237–57240 57250–57251 57272–57473
CR '812'	0-6-0	McIntosh	CR 30 locomotives	1899	57550–57566 57617–57628
CR '652'	0-6-0	McIntosh	CR 17 locomotives	1908/09	57629–57645
CR '294' '670'	0-6-0	Pickersgill	CR 29 locomotives	1919/20	57650–57691

* The BR numbers are given for identification in BR listings and do not take into account missing numbers due to scrapping, or locomotives of the same class built by other companies, but do include locomotives with allocated numbers not carried.

Former Caledonian Railway '492' Class 0-8-0T is seen as LMS No 16955 at Motherwell in 1929. These McIntosh designed St Rollox Works built inside cylinder 0-8-0s were also known as 'Mineral Tank Engines' and were fitted with Westinghouse brakes for working brake fitted trains of 30 ton mineral wagons. A total of 6 were built and put into traffic at Motherwell, Hamilton and Dundee depots. After grouping the engines were painted black with tank side numbers and LMS insignia on the bunkers. This locomotive was withdrawn in March 1939 and none of the class survived beyond 1940. ***Rail Photoprints Collection***

Former Caledonian Railway Pickersgill inside cylinder 4-4-0 seen as LMS No 14465 circa 1940 at a location thought to be in the Glasgow area. The locomotive was delivered as CR No 121 in February 1916 and withdrawn as No 54465 by BR in October 1962. The CR '113' and '918' 4-4-0 class represents Pickersgill's later designed version of the famous 'Dunalastair' locomotives. ***Mike Morant Collection***

St Rollox built CR McIntosh '652' class 0-6-0 is seen as LMS No 17639 whilst passing Paisley with an empty stock working in July 1939. This locomotive was delivered as CR No 659 in June 1908 and withdrawn without ever carrying its allocated BR No 57636, in December 1948. ***Mike Bentley Collection***

St Rollox built CR Pickersgill '294' class 0-6-0 seen as BR No 57667 whilst awaiting departure from Oban with a local service, in June 1959. This locomotive was delivered as CR No 311 in August 1918 and withdrawn in August 1962. *Rail Photoprints Collection*

St Rollox built Lambie designed CR 'Class 1' 4-4-0T seen as CR No 5 (became LMS No 15024) at Perth circa 1922. These locomotives were originally painted in a 'Caley' blue livery style and the LMS painted them in an un-lined black livery with large style numerals on the side tanks. This locomotive was delivered in 1893 and withdrawn in 1935. *Mike Morant Collection*

St Rollox built McIntosh designed '439' class 0-4-4T seen at Alyth station in 1929 as LMS No 15229 (became BR No 55229). This locomotive was delivered in September 1915 as CR No 162 and withdrawn in September 1961. *Rail Photoprints Collection*

Railway Company abbreviations used in this chapter.

CR – Caledonian Railway, **LMS** – London Midland & Scottish Railway, **S&DJR** – Somerset & Dorset Joint Railway

Chapter 13

KILMARNOCK WORKS

No locomotives built at Kilmarnock Works came into British Railways (BR) stock. However the works occupied an important place in the history of Scottish locomotive manufacturing.

The building of the locomotive works commenced in 1854 by the Glasgow & South Western Railway Company (G&SWR) on a 13 acre site in Kilmarnock and it superseded a previous G&SWR works in Cook Street, Glasgow. The works was partly opened in 1856 under the engineer Patrick Stirling and declared fully open and complete in 1858.

There was a very grand administration building complete with a clock tower, carriage, wagon and locomotive workshops. The first steam locomotive, a 'Class 2' 2-2-2 was completed there in 1857. By the start of the First World War the works had become run down and was in need of investment to bring it up to date, and that investment was not forthcoming. In 1921 the Locomotive Superintendent Robert Harben Whitelegg made the decision to cease locomotive production at the site, but repairs continued. A total of almost 400 steam locomotives were reportedly built at Kilmarnock Works between 1857 and 1921.

A Hugh Smellie designed G&SWR 4-4-0 '119 class' engine referred to by enginemen of the time as a 'Wee Bogie' is seen at Glasgow St Enoch station in 1929, as LMS No 14135. The locomotive was formerly G&SWR No 128. Kilmarnock Works built 24 engines of this class between 1882 and 1885. Note the Westinghouse brake gear. Although undoubtedly handsome looking locomotives their spectacle cab fronts actually afforded the crew little or no protection from the elements. *Mike Morant Collection*

In 1923 the G&SWR became part of the London, Midland & Scottish Railway (LMS) and its locomotives were taken into LMS stock. Most of the locomotive repair work was transferred to St Rollox Works and a section of the Kilmarnock Works was demolished in 1929. Some locomotive repair work continued and in January 1948 the works became part of the British Transport Commission (BTC) on Nationalisation.

Locomotive repairs were discontinued in 1952 but activity at the works continued as redundant locomotives were transported there for scrapping. It was not unusual for withdrawn locomotives to stand out of use at Kilmarnock Works for a great many months before actually being cut up. On 4 July 1959 the works was closed completely.

Kilmarnock Works built G&SWR 4-4-0 No 462 was a Hugh Smellie designed '153 class' engine. A total of 20 such locomotives were built between 1886 and 1889 and they carried the G&SWR numbers 448–466 and thereafter the LMS numbers 14138-56. All of the class were scrapped before 1930. This wonderful old image was discovered with no available data but the location is thought to be the north side of Kilmarnock station, looking approximately to the north east. *Mike Morant Collection*

A Hugh Smellie designed G&SWR 4-4-0 '119 class' engine is seen on the turntable at Muirkirk at the time of 'Grouping' as G&SWR No 712. This locomotive was built at Kilmarnock and delivered in November 1883 and withdrawn as LMS No 14127 in May 1930. *Mike Morant Collection*

R.H. Whitelegg re-build of a Kilmarnock built James Manson designed 4-cylinder 4-4-0 seen as LMS No 14509 LORD GLENARTHUR, at Ayr. This locomotive was the only example of the G&SWR '11 class', it was built in 1897 and delivered as No 394 and withdrawn in 1934. Under the LMS the engine worked Glasgow – Ayr express trains and was fitted with an enlarged tender with 5 ton coal and 3260 gallon water capacity. This engine's re-build was completed only 10 days before the LMS took control of Kilmarnock Works. *Mike Morant Collection*

Kilmarnock Works built, James Manson designed 0-4-0T G&SWR '272' class engine seen at Ardrossan as LMS No 16046, circa 1926. This was one of a class of six 0-4-0T shunting engines built between 1907 and 1909 which were the heaviest locomotives of that wheel arrangement ever to work in Britain (39 tons 12 cwts). The class allocations were 3 engines to Ladyburn depot in order to work at Greenock Docks and 3 engines to Ardrossan and they carried the G&SWR numbers 316–321. LMS No 16046 was delivered in December 1908 as GSWR No 318 and withdrawn in 1930. *Rail Photoprints Collection*

The scrapping of redundant steam locomotives was carried out at Kilmarnock Works throughout the 1950s and in this March 1953 picture ex-Caledonian Railway St Rollox built 'Dunalastair IV' class 4-4-0 BR No 54445 is seen awaiting its date with the cutting torches. *David Anderson*

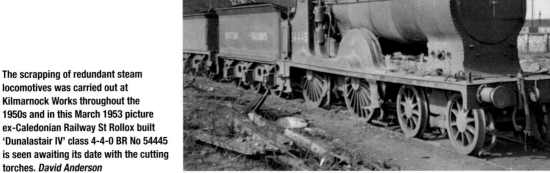

Chapter 14

LOCHGORM WORKS

Lochgorm Locomotive Works was the main workshops and engineering headquarters for the Highland Railway (HR). The works was built and opened between 1864 and 1865 by the Inverness & Nairn Railway and that organisation was later absorbed by the Highland Railway.

The workshops consisted of several different buildings and included machine shops, an erecting shop, a paint shop and a roundhouse which had a large capacity turntable to allow engines to be quickly mobilised. The Lochgorm Locomotive Works produced many steam engines with local names such as CLACHNACUDDIN and STRATHPEFFER and continued to be the principal workshops of the Highland Railway.

Manchester born David Jones (1834–1906) was appointed to the post of Locomotive Superintendent of the Highland Railway in 1855, when he was only 21 years old.

Much of his time was spent re-building existing HR engines in order to simply keep the railway supplied with motive power.

Lochgorm Works built Peter Drummond HR 'W' class 0-4-4T, BR No 55053 is seen at Balornock, formerly St Rollox, (part of the Springburn area of Glasgow) in April 1954. The locomotive is in pristine condition following a visit to the works and the shine on the newly applied paint is made even more pronounced by the pouring rain! This engine was delivered as HR No 25 in March 1905 and withdrawn in July 1956. Note that the loco crew posing for the picture are trying to stay dry. *Rail Photoprints Collection*

However, his great claim to fame was his 4-6-0 goods locomotive design which was the first class of that wheel arrangement to run in Britain. The 15 engines of the class were built by the contractors Sharp, Stewart & Co, Glasgow and not at Lochgorm Works. The last steam locomotives to be built at Lochgorm Works were the 4 HR 'W' class 0-4-4T engines built between 1905 and 1906 specifically for branch line working.

A Lochgorm Works maker's plate dating from 1897.

The Highland Railway was absorbed by the London, Midland & Scottish Railway (LMS) in 1923 and its locomotives were taken into LMS stock. The LMS inherited in the region of 35 Lochgorm Works built steam locomotives and the works continued to repair locomotives for that company. Despite their small numbers, quite a few Highland Railway classes (from various builders) survived well into the LMS era, and two locomotive types were taken into British Railways (BR) stock in January 1948 as the works became part of the British Transport Commission (BTC) on Nationalisation. After the running shed at Inverness (60A) closed (May 1973) what remained of the works became a modern traction heavy repair depot. Interestingly from time to time the coke ovens of the Highland Railway works were used by the Caledonian Bank to burn out of circulation, old and tattered banknotes. Bank directors were always on hand during the burning ceremonies to make sure no notes were misappropriated. Reportedly some of the railway's employees would nevertheless keep an eye on the chimney stack, just in case the odd note made it out that way!

HR 'Small Ben' 4-4-0 2P

In 1896 Peter Drummond (the perhaps not so well known brother of Dugald Drummond) succeeded David Jones at the Highland Railway and he introduced his own design of inside cylinder 4-4-0 locomotives, the two classes were named respectively 'Small Ben' class built between 1898 and 1906 and 'Large Ben' class built between 1908 and 1909, the latter were all withdrawn between 1932 and 1937.

These were the first inside cylinder HR tender engines and observers immediately noted that they were in fact very similar in design to the Dugald Drummond 'T9' class. The 'Small Ben' class total was 20 locomotives (HR Nos 397–416 and LMS Nos 14397–14416) with 10 of those engines coming into BR stock, and being allocated numbers in the series 54397–54416. Dübs & Co and Lochgorm Works and the NBL also participated in the construction of the class. All of the class carried the names of Scottish Bens.

The BR total included 2 engines built at Lochgorm Works which were BR No 54409 BEN ALISKY and No 54410 BEN DEARG. However both of those locomotives were withdrawn in 1949/50 without ever carrying their allocated BR numbers.

See also HR 'Small Ben' 4-4-0 2P locomotives built by Dübs & Co and the NBL.

Driving wheel diameter 6' 0", 2-cylinder engine (inside)

Ex-Highland Railway 'Small Ben' class 4-4-0 is seen as LMS No 14410 BEN DEARG at Inverness depot in March 1948. Note the uniquely ornate water tower and also the vertical row of holes drilled into locomotive's buffer beam to facilitate the fitting of a snow plough. The locomotive was delivered as HR No 14 in August 1900 and withdrawn in December 1949 without ever carrying its BR No 54410. ***Steve Armitage Archive/Rail Photoprints Collection***

HR 'W' class 0-4-4T

The Highland Railway built 4 'W' class engines to a Peter Drummond design between 1905 and 1906 and the small tank locomotives were the last to be built at Lochgorm Works. The first of these engines were withdrawn by the LMS in 1930 but the last 2 engines of the class survived for many years and they were almost exclusively used to work trains over the branch line between The Mound and Dornoch, because of their light axle loading. Locomotive No 55051 carried the name STRATHPEFFER until 1920.

The 0-4-4Ts were allocated the BR numbers 55051 and 55053 and were withdrawn in 1956 and 1957 respectively. Interestingly BR transferred 2 ex-GWR pannier tanks No 1646 and No 1649 to take over their duties on the Dornoch Branch. When withdrawn in January 1957 No 55053 had the distinction of being the last Highland Railway locomotive to remain in service.

Driving wheel diameter 4' 6", 2-cylinder engine (inside)

Ex-Highland Railway Lochgorm Works built 0-4-4T BR No 55053 is seen crossing the causeway over Loch Fleet, as it leaves The Mound with a mixed train for Dornoch during May 1953. This locomotive was delivered as HR No 45 in December 1905 and was withdrawn in January 1957. The photographer's position is now buried under the main A9 trunk road. *Rail Photoprints Collection*

Ex-Highland Railway Lochgorm Works built 0-4-4T BR No 55051 is seen on shed at Helmsdale (60C) in May 1953. *Rail Photoprints Collection*

Lochgorm Works built locomotive classes which came into British Railways ownership

Class	Wheel arrangement	Designer	Customer/ Number to BR	Build dates	BR number series*
'Small Ben'	4-4-0	P Drummond	HR 2 locomotives	1900	54409–54410
'W'	0-4-4T	P Drummond	HR 2 locomotives	1905	55051–55053

* The BR numbers are given for identification in BR listings and do not take into account missing numbers due to scrapping, or locomotives of the same class built by other companies, but do include locomotives with allocated numbers not carried.

Railway Company abbreviations used in this chapter.

HR – Highland Railway

Chapter 15

INVERURIE WORKS

Inverurie Works built Great North of Scotland Railway (GNoSR) 'V' class 4-4-0 seen as BR No 62271 (LNER 'D40' class) is leaking plenty of steam whilst making a spirited departure from Craigellachie station, with a local service to Boat of Garten via Grantown-on-Spey in October 1956. This locomotive was delivered in September 1914 and withdrawn in November 1956; only one month after this picture was taken. *David Anderson Collection*

Inverurie Locomotive Works was built on a 15 acre site by the Great North of Scotland Railway (GNoSR) at a location some sixteen miles north of Aberdeen. The works opened in 1903 and of all the main railway company locomotive works it was the most northerly in Britain.

Inverurie Works did not construct a large number of locomotives but served as an important locomotive repair centre for some 66 years. The first locomotive built at the works was a 'V' class 4-4-0 GNoSR No 27 which was completed in April 1909. The last locomotive to be completed at the works was a GNoSR 'F' class 4-4-0 No 46 BENACHIE, which was the 10th steam locomotive to be built at Inverurie (both became LNER 'D40' class engines).

Following 'Grouping' in 1923 the works became part of the London & North Eastern Railway (LNER) and in January 1948 it became part of the British Transport Commission (BTC i.e. British Railways BR) on 'Nationalisation'. In 1955 the workshops were re-organised in order to allow the servicing and repair of larger locomotives and in 1962 the undertaking became part of BR Workshops Division. Inverurie Works was finally closed on 31 December 1969 following the regional decline in rail traffic.

Inverurie Works built locomotive classes included in British Railway (BR) listings

GNoSR 'V' 4-4-0 2P – 'D40' (BR reclassified as 1P in 1953)
Between 1899 and 1921 the Great North of Scotland Railway (GNoSR) introduced a William Pickersgill designed class of 2-cylinder 4-4-0 locomotives which were designated 'V' class (BR number series 62260–62262, 62264–62265, 62267–62273). In addition to the Inverurie Works 'D40' class variants were built by Neilson, Reid & Co Ltd and the NBL.

In 1920/21 Thomas Heywood introduced a superheated version of the class with piston valves and extended smoke boxes (BR number series 62274–62279) those locomotives were designated GNoSR 'F' class and were the first of the GNoSR 4-4-0 fleet to be officially given names. There were originally 21 engines in the class with the first 3 locomotives being withdrawn in 1947, just prior to the creation of BR. In total BR took into stock 18 locomotives of this class.

Included in that total were two batches of Inverurie Works built 'D40' class engines BR Nos 62265–62272 (5 locomotives 'V' class built with saturated boilers, GNoSR Nos 113–115, 25 and 26) and BR Nos 62273–62274 (2 locomotives 'F' class built with superheated boilers, GNoSR Nos 45 and 46).

None of the class remained in traffic beyond the end of 1958 and the last Inverurie Works built 'D40' 4-4-0 to be withdrawn was BR No 62271 in November 1956.

See also GNoSR Pickersgill 'V' 4-4-0 2P – 'D40' locomotives built by Neilson, Reid & Co Ltd and the NBL.

Driving wheel diameter 6' 1", 2-cylinder engine (inside)

Inverurie Works built ex-GNoSR 'V' class 4-4-0 is seen as BR No 62265 ('D40' class) at Keith circa 1955. Note the cab side running lamps and the Westinghouse brake gear. This locomotive was delivered in April 1909 and withdrawn in December 1956. *David Anderson*

Inverurie Works built locomotive classes which came into British Railways ownership

Class	Wheel arrangement	Designer	Customer/ Number to BR	Build dates	BR number series*
'D40'	4-4-0	Pickersgill	GNoSR 9 locomotives	1909–1921	62265–62274

*The BR numbers are given for identification in BR listings and do not take into account missing numbers due to scrapping, or locomotives of the same class built by other companies, but do include locomotives with allocated numbers not carried.

Railway Company abbreviations used in this chapter.
GNoSR – Great North of Scotland Railway

Chapter 16

SHED CODES

Looking splendid in ex-works condition and in light steam ex-Midland 2P 4-4-0 BR No 40574 awaits railtour duty outside the covered portion of Ayr shed (67C) in May 1958. ***Dave Cobbe Collection/Rail Photoprints Collection***

Shed Codes

This list of BR Scottish Region shed codes primarily covers the years from 1948 to the end of steam. The original railway company names are also included but not the pre-BR codes.

The closure dates are included to indicate the cessation of steam locomotive allocations to the relevant depots. However, new or changed codes applied after the end of the steam era are not included.

The term 'shed' in relation to railway depots is taken to mean the whole of the locomotive stabling and servicing area at a particular location, and not just the running roads within the covered buildings.

During the latter part of the steam era shed code changes did not always result in allocated locomotives being fitted with new cast shed plates, as more often than not the changes were purely of an administrative nature.

Highland Railway 4-6-0 'Jones Goods' LMS No 17919 (was HR 106) is seen on the turntable at Inverness circa 1930. *Keith Langston Collection*

60A Inverness (LMS/BR) – Highland Railway opened 1863, closed June 1962
Sub sheds
Dingwall closed December 1962 – Kyle of Lochalsh closed June 1962- Fortrose closed October 1950

60B Aviemore (LMS/BR) – Highland Railway opened 1863 closed July 1962
Sub shed
Boat of Garten closed November 1958

60C Helmsdale (LMS/BR) – Highland Railway opened 1871 closed July 1961
Sub sheds
Dornoch closed June 1960 – Tain closed June 1962

60D Wick (LMS/BR) – Highland Railway opened 1874 closed July 1962
Sub shed
Thurso closed December 1962

60E Forres (LMS/BR) – Inverness & Perth Junction Railway opened 1863 – Highland Railway 1865 closed May 1959

In 1957 the regular branch engine of the Dornoch Light Railway broke an axle and was declared 'beyond economic repair'. British Railways transferred two ex-Great Western Railway design 16XX locomotives, BR (Western Region) Nos 1646 and 1649, to Scotland (60C) to work the branch. They were both scrapped from Helmsdale in December 1962 when they were not quite twelve years old. *Rail Photoprints Collection*

Highland Railway 'Strath' class 4-4-0 seen as LMS No 14275 GLEN TRUIM, at Forres depot circa 1928. This locomotive was built by Neilson, Reid and Co in 1892, was delivered as HR No 98 and withdrawn by the LMS in 1931. *Rail Photoprints Collection*

LNER 'J72' 0-6-0T BR No 68700 is seen at Aberdeen Kittybrewster depot in 1958. *David Anderson*

61A Kittybrewster (LNER/BR) – Great North of Scotland Railway 1854 closed June 1961
Sub sheds Alford closed January 1950 – Ballater closed April 1958 – Fraserburgh closed June 1961 – Inverurie closed March 1959 – Macduff closed October 1951 – Peterhead closed June 1961

Stanier 'Black Five' 4-6-0 LMS No 44703 and LNER 4-6-2 'A2' BR No 60532 BLUE PETER (a preserved engine) are seen together at Aberdeen Ferryhill in October 1966. Note the depot names stencilled on the buffer beams, 'Dundee' for the 'A2' and 'Ferryhill' for the 'Class 5'. *Brian Robins/Rail Photoprints Collection*

Gresley 'A4' Pacific BR No 60019 BITTERN (a preserved engine) is seen on the turntable at Aberdeen Ferryhill depot with both upper and lower portions of the smokebox 'cods mouth' opened in order to make for easier ash clearing. *Bill Rhind Brown*

Stanier 'Class 5' 4-6-0 No 44703 is seen with LNER preserved engine 'BLUE PETER' and diesel locomotive at Ferryhill in October 1966. ***Brian Robbins/Rail Photoprints Collection***

North British Railway – 1908

61B Aberdeen Ferryhill (LNER/BR) – North British Railway 1908 closed March 1967

61C Keith (LNER/BR) – Great North of Scotland Railway – 1856 closed June 1961
Sub sheds
Banff closed July 1964 – Elgin closed June 1961

62A Thornton Junction (LNER/BR) – North British Railway closed April 1967
Sub sheds
Anstruther closed December 1960 – Burntisland closed December 1958 – Kirkcaldy closed December 1959 – Ladybank closed December 1958 – Methil closed December 1958

LNER 'A2' Pacific BR No 60527 SUN CHARIOT is seen whilst waiting to be serviced at Dundee Tay Bridge depot in April 1956. *David Anderson*

LNER Gresley 'J39' 0-6-0 BR No 64950 is seen at Dundee Tay Bridge in April 1956. *David Anderson*

62B Dundee Tay Bridge (LNER/BR)- North British Railway closed May 1967
Sub sheds
Arbroath closed January 1959 – Dundee West closed December 1958 – Montrose closed May 1966 – St Andrews closed September 1960 – Tayport closed October 1951

62C Dunfermline Upper (LNER/BR) – Edinburgh & Northern Railway 1849 – North British Railway 1862 closed May 1967
Sub sheds
Alloa closed January 1967 – Inverkeithing closed December 1966 – Loch Leven closed April 1951

A general view of Perth depot seen in July 1957, the 4-6-0 locomotives seen left to right are 'Black Five' No 45472, 'Jubilee' No 45673 KEPPEL and 'Black Five' No 44798. *David Anderson*

Former Highland Railway 'Castle' Class 4-6-0 LMS No 14676 BALLINDALLOCH CASTLE is seen at Perth depot in June 1936. The locomotive was built by Dübs & Co and delivered in June 1900. *Rail Photoprints Collection*

North British Locomotive built 'Caley Bogie' 4-4-0 BR No 54469 is seen at 63A in 1957. *David Anderson*

A rural scene at Aberfeldy as the branch line engine ex-CR '439' class 0-4-4T BR No 55212 stands outside the wooden shed building after taking water, in July 1957. Aberfeldy was a sub shed of 63A; note that the building has lost a section of its roof. ***David Anderson***

Gresley 'A4' Pacific BR No 60034 LORD FARINGDON and Stanier 'Class 5' BR No 44720 are seen together on shed at Perth in 1966. ***Brian Robbins/Rail Photoprints***

Inverness allocated Stanier 'Black Five' BR No 45360 is seen on the turntable at (63A) Perth in this 1960 image, note the snow plough and cab side tablet catcher. ***David Anderson***

63A Perth (LNER/BR) – North British Railway 1899 closed May 1967
Sub sheds
Aberfeldy closed December 1962 – Alyth closed December 1951 – Blair Atholl closed December 1962 – Crieff closed June 1964

63B Stirling became **65J** June 1960 (LNER/BR) – Forth & Clyde Junction Railway 1861- North British Railway 1896 closed June 1966
Sub sheds
Stirling Shore Road North closed September 1957 – Stirling Shore Road South closed September 1957

63C Forfar became sub shed of **63A** in November 1959 (LMS/BR) – Caledonian Railway 1899 closed July 1964
Sub shed
Brechin closed April 1952

Two 'J37' class 0-6-0s at Mallaig, BR Nos 64636 and 64592 are seen whilst undergoing turning having worked in on the SRPS 'Jacobite' railtour in June 1963, unfortunately both of the engines were declared failures at Mallaig! *Rail Photoprints Collection*

63D Fort William (LNER/BR) – West Highland Railway 1894 – North British Railway 1908 closed June 1962
Sub shed
Mallaig closed June 1962

63E Oban (LMS/BR) – Callander & Oban Railway 1880 – Caledonian Railway closed March 1962, became **63D** in May 1955 and **63C** in 1959
Sub shed
Ballachulish closed March 1962

Reid designed 'C11' Atlantic LNER No 9875 MIDLOTHIAN built for the North British Railway, after re-instatement to traffic at St Margaret's in 1938. It was hoped that the loco would be preserved but it was withdrawn for repairs in late 1939 and scrapped during the Second World War. *John Chalcraft/Rail Photoprints*

LNER 'V2' 2-6-2 BR No 60919 on shed at Edinburgh St Margaret's in March 1964. *Rail Photoprints Collection*

64A St Margaret's (LNER/BR) – North British Railway 1846 closed May 1967
Sub sheds
Dunbar closed June 1964 – Galashiels closed April 1962 – Granton closed December 1964 – Hardengreen closed December 1962 – Longniddry closed June 1959 – North Berwick closed February 1958 – North Leith closed December 1951 – Peebles closed October 1955 – Penicuik closed September 1951 – Polton closed September 1951 – Seafield closed October 1962 – South Leith closed December 1960

LNER 'A3' 4-6-2 BR No 60035 WINDSOR LAD is seen during August 1958 adjacent to the turntable at its then home depot, Haymarket shed (64B). *David Anderson*

NBR Reid 'Scott' 4-4-0 (D30) BR No 62429 THE ABBOT is seen on the turntable at Haymarket during 1955. ***Rail Photoprints Collection***

Ex-GCR 'D11' class 4-4-0 'Scottish Directors' BR Nos 62692 ALLAN-BANE and 62677 EDIE OCHILTREE are seen at Haymarket shed with full coal tenders whilst waiting their next turns of duty, circa 1955. ***David Anderson***

64B Haymarket (LNER/BR) – Edinburgh & Glasgow Railway 1848 – North British Railway 1865 closed September 1963

Edinburgh Dalry Road shed (64C) is the location in this 1960 image. The two Stanier 4-6-0 'Black Fives' BR Nos 45434 and 44811 are seen being prepared for their next turns of duty. 'Class 5' No 45434 is being coaled by hand prior to working an Edinburgh Princes Street to Birmingham New Street service, locomotive No 44811 was at that time a Leicester (15A) allocated engine which had 'worked in' the previous day with a special. ***David Anderson***

Fowler 'Patriot' 4-6-0 BR No 45503 THE ROYAL LEICESTERSHIRE REGIMENT is pictured over the ash pit at Dalry Road shed in July 1955. The Crewe North allocated locomotive would have worked an express service to Edinburgh from Birmingham New Street and has been coaled and serviced ready for the return journey. *David Anderson*

64C Dalry Road (LMS/BR) – Caledonian Railway 1848 closed October 1965

64D Carstairs became **66E** in June 1960 (LMS/BR) – Caledonian Railway 1848 closed December 1966

A general view of the eastern side of Polmont shed (64E) taken in 1957. Locomotives included 'J69/1' class 0-6-0T No 68524 and '4MT' 2-6-0 No 43140. *David Anderson*

64E Polmont (LNER/BR) became **65K** in June 1960 – North British Railway 1914 closed May 1964
Sub shed
Kinneil closed September 1952

64F Bathgate (LNER/BR) Edinburgh & Bathgate Railway 1849 – LNER closed December 1966

64G Hawick (LNER/BR) Edinburgh & Hawick Railway 1849 – LNER closed January 1966
Sub sheds
Jedburgh closed April 1949 – Kelso closed July 1955 – Riccarton Junction closed October 1958 – St Boswells closed November 1959

64H Leith Central (from 1959 to 1972) previously a sub shed of 64A

Scottish 'Director' ex-GCR/LNER 'D11/2' class 4-4-0 BR No 62687 LORD JAMES OF DOUGLAS is seen at Eastfield depot (65A) in 1951. *Rail Photoprints Collection*

WD 'Austerity' 2-10-0 BR No 90756 is seen adjacent to the water tank at Eastfield depot in 1958. *Rail Photoprints Collection*

65A Eastfield (LNER/BR) North British Railway 1904 closed November 1966
Sub sheds
Aberfoyle closed October 1951 – Kilsyth closed October 1951 – Lennoxtown closed October 1951 – Whiteinch closed December 1961

A fascinating general view of St Rollox shed circa 1965, taken as the Red Road flats were under construction. The locomotives include Stanier 'Class 5' No 45016, BR Standard Caprotti 'Class 5' No 73146 and Gresley 'A4' Pacifics No 60034 LORD FARINGDON and No 60006 SIR RALPH WEDGWOOD. *Bill Rhind Brown*

LMS locomotive No 17804 is seen in 1928 at Balornock Shed, which was the old name for the shed known later as St Rollox. The locomotive is a Caledonian Railway '34' class 2-6-0 built in 1912 at the then nearby St Rollox Works. The class consisted of 5 locomotives which were design conversions from the earlier CR '30' class 0-6-0 engines. ***Keith Langston Collection***

65B St Rollox (LMS/BR) – Caledonian Railway 1856 closed 1916 and re-opened as Balornock but was often still referred to as St Rollox, closed November 1966

A row of rusting withdrawn LNER engines stored out of use in August 1963, at Parkhead depot prior to being scrapped. The locomotives are Gresley 'V3' class 2-6-2Ts Nos 67600, 67680 (both were last allocated to 65A) and the unidentified locomotive furthest from the camera is another of the same class. ***Rail Photoprints Collection***

65C Parkhead (LNER/BR) became sub shed of **65A** in 1962 – North British Railway 1871 closed October 1965

65D Dawsholm (LMS/BR) Caledonian Railway 1896 closed October 1964
Sub sheds
Dumbarton closed October 1964 – Stobcross closed October 1950

NBR 'Y9' Pug BR No 68106 is seen in the company of Gresley 'N2' class 0-6-2T adjacent to the coaling plant at Kipps (65E). It would seem that the fireman of the 'Y9' has got by far and away the better quality load of coal, as there seems to be an awful load of slack in the 'N2' bunker in this 1955 image. ***Keith Langston Collection***

65E Kipps (LNER/BR) became a sub shed of **65A** in 1962 – Monklands & Kirkintilloch Railway 1837 – Edinburgh & Glasgow Railway and thereafter the North British Railway in 1865, closed January 1963

65F Grangemouth (LMS/BR) – Caledonian Railway 1870 closed November 1965

65G Yoker (LMS/BR) – Caledonian Railway 1907 closed December 1964

65H Helensburgh became a sub shed of **65A** in 1960 (LNER/BR) – North British Railway 1894 closed November 1961
Sub shed
Arrochar closed October 1959

65I Balloch (LNER/BR) Caledonian & Dunbartonshire Junction Railway aka the Dumbarton & Balloch Joint Railway 1850 – North British Railway 1865 closed November 1960

LMS Fowler 'Royal Scot' class 4-6-0 LMS No 6134 ATLAS is seen at Glasgow Polmadie depot in April 1928. This locomotive was built by the NBL in 1927 and was re-named THE CHESHIRE REGIMENT in 1930, BR number 46134. ***Keith Langston Collection***

The engine turntable at Glasgow Polmadie depot (66A) is the location for this 1960s detailed image of Stanier 8P 'Duchess' Pacific BR No 46221 QUEEN ELIZABETH. Polmadie was a good place to see express passenger locomotives which were rostered to work on the Anglo-Scottish express trains over the WCML. ***David Anderson***

Crewe allocated Stanier 8P 'Princess Royal' 4-6-2 BR No 46210 LADY PATRICIA is seen at 66A after being serviced before heading another express south. ***David Anderson***

66A Polmadie (LMS/BR) – Caledonian Railway 1875 closed May 1967
Sub shed
Paisley St James closed January 1953

66B Motherwell became sub shed of **66A** in 1963 (LMS/BR) – Caledonian Railway 1866 closed May 1967
Sub shed
Morningside closed November 1954

A Dübs & Co built CR '670' class 0-4-2 is seen as LMS No 17008 at Hamilton shed in 1927. The Caledonian Railway '670' class was designed by George Brittain and introduced in 1878, originally 30 examples were built. The LMS took into stock 21 of the class which were all withdrawn between 1923 and 1932. ***Rail Photoprints Collection***

66C Hamilton (LMS/BR) – Caledonian Railway closed November 1962

66D Greenock Ladyburn (LMS/BR) Caledonian Railway 1884 closed November 1966
Sub shed
Greenock Princes Pier closed May 1959

BR Standard 6P5F 'Clan' class 4-6-2 No 72005 CLAN MACGREGOR, then a 68A allocated engine, is seen after being coaled at Glasgow Corkerhill depot in this early 1960s study. ***David Anderson***

67A Corkerhill (LMS/BR) Glasgow & South Western Railway 1896 – LMS 1923 closed May 1967

67B Hurlford (LMS/BR) Glasgow & South Western Railway 1877- LMS 1923 closed October 1966
Sub sheds
Beith closed November 1962 – Muirkirk closed October 1964

67C Ayr (LMS/BR) – Glasgow, Paisley, Kilmarnock & Ayr Railway 1839 – became Glasgow & South Western Railway 1850 – LMS1923 closed October 1966

67D Ardrossan (LMS/BR) – Glasgow, Paisley, Kilmarnock & Ayr Railway 1840 became Glasgow & South Western Railway 1850 – LMS1923 closed February 1965

68A Carlisle Kingmoor became **12A** in 1966 (LMS/BR) located in the English county of Cumberland – Caledonian Railway 1876 closed January 1968
Sub shed
Carlisle Durran Hill (Midland Railway)

A general view of Dumfries shed in April 1957. Locomotives seen include BR Standard 4MT 2-6-0, Stanier 'Black Five' with snow plough, ex-CR '812' class 0-6-0, a Stanier '8F' 2-8-0 and a ex-CR '782' class 0-6-0T. ***David Anderson***

68B Dumfries (LMS/BR) became **67E** in 1962 – Glasgow, Dumfries & Carlisle Railway 1848 – Glasgow & South Western Railway 1850 – LMS 1923 closed May 1966
Sub shed
Kirkcudbright closed December 1955

68C Stranraer (LMS/BR) – Glasgow & South Western Railway and Caledonian Railway joint shed 1861 – LMS 1923 closed October 1966
Sub shed
Newton Stewart closed December 1959

68D Beattock became **66F** in 1962 (LMS/BR) – Caledonian Railway 1847 closed April 1967
Sub shed
Lockerbie closed February 1951

Carlisle Canal (LNER/BR) Newcastle & Carlisle Railway 1837 – North British Railway 1862, located in the English county of Cumberland – Under BR became **12B** 1950 to 1951 and thereafter **68E** 1951 to February 1958 and then **12D** for a short period before finally becoming **12C** in April 1958 – closed June 1963

Chapter 17

PRE-GROUPING RAILWAY COMPANIES

North British Railway

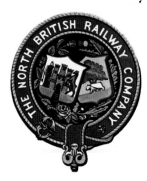

The Edinburgh based North British Railway was first promoted in 1842 following the opening of the Edinburgh & Glasgow Railway. The proposal was to build an east coast railway line south from Edinburgh via Dunbar and Berwick. Although the promoters of the line offered a generous dividend of 8 per cent, raising the necessary finance in Scotland still proved problematic. Funding was only made available after George Hudson persuaded the York & North Midland Railway to invest £50,000 in the scheme. The North British Railway Bill was passed in 1844 and construction of the line which began shortly afterwards, was completed in 1846.

Although the NBR started operations in 1844 it did not reach its final form until 1862 following a long series of amalgamations and takeovers. The NBR became the biggest Scottish railway company and the firm whose original intention was only to link Berwick and Edinburgh, through associations with other railways, actually provided a direct link to London via Rugby, Sheffield and York.

The purchase of a line to Glasgow preceded the connection to Fort William and Mallaig (the West Highland line) and then a further expansion saw the NBR start running services to Dundee, Fife and Perth. The building of the Forth and Tay bridges replaced ferries operated by the company, including one of the very few rail freight ferries to operate in Britain (from Granton to Burntisland).

In its final form the NBR owned approximately 1,389 miles of track which served 21 Scottish and 2 English counties, the railway also operated several large dock complexes (Burntisland, Methil etc).

The NBR operated services between Edinburgh Waverley station and Glasgow Queen Street station and to Carlisle via Galashiels and Hawick (the Waverley Route) and between Newcastle on Tyne and Aberdeen. The company locomotive works was at Cowlairs, Glasgow a facility originally opened by the Edinburgh & Glasgow Railway in 1841 which was taken over by the NBR in 1865.

The NBR's main competitors were the Caledonian Railway (CR) to the west and the North Eastern Railway (NER) to the south.

In 1923 the NBR became part of the London & North Eastern Railway (LNER) and in 1948 that railway became part of the British Transport Commission (BTC on Nationalisation, British Railways Scottish Region) in 1948. Cowlairs Works continued to be active until 1968 when the works closed and the locomotive repair programme was transferred to St Rollox.

For detailed information see www.nbrstudygroup.co.uk

In this delightful branch line scene NBR 'C15'class (LNER) 4-4-2T BR No 67460 is seen making a spirited departure from Arrochar with a local train to Craigendoran, during September 1959. This push-pull fitted Reid designed and Yorkshire Engine Co built locomotive was delivered as 'M' class NBR No 135 in August 1912 and withdrawn in April 1960. *Dave Cobbe Collection/Rail Photoprints Collection*

Preserved North British Railway Reid designed 'Glen' class 4-4-0 No 256 GLEN DOUGLAS which was built at Cowlairs Works in 1913 is seen heading north at Queensferry junction with a 1960 railtour. *David Anderson*

A North British Railway poster of the period. *Keith Langston Collection*

Great North of Scotland Railway

Preserved GNoSR Pickersgill designed North British Locomotive Co built 'D40'class (LNER) 4-4-0 No 49 GORDON HIGHLANDER is seen leaving Dumfries for Glasgow with an 'SLS' special in June 1959. The locomotive was delivered as a Heywood superheated variant designated GNoSR 'Class F' in October 1920. ***David Anderson***

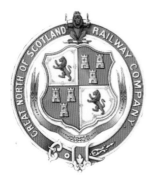

The creation of the Aberdeen based Great North of Scotland Railway (GNoSR) was first proposed in a prospectus published in 1844. The original stated aim of the company was the building of a line between Aberdeen and Inverness. However, that aim was not fulfilled.

The GNoSR had original plans to lay a double track railway on the route which would have cost an estimated £1.5 million, a huge sum in those days and evidently beyond the means of the people of the area to raise. Several branches were also planned at the same time in order that the many perceived advantages of railway travel could be enjoyed by all the residents of the mainly rural area.

What actually happened was that the company eventually built its line only as far as Keith in Banffshire (1853–1856). The rest of the route to Inverness was instead built by a separate company (which later became part of the Highland Railway) and was promoted independently by the people of Inverness and district, who allegedly would have nothing to do with the Aberdeen folk who promoted the GNoSR.

By 1866, branch lines to Fraserburgh and Peterhead, Alford, Macduff, Banff, Portsoy and Dufftown had been built. From Dufftown, a line had also been built in Speyside linking with the Morayshire Railway at Craigellachie and also eventually with the Highland Railway at Boat of Garten. The year also saw a series of amalgamations.

In the early years the company undertook all of its maintenance work and some locomotive construction at Kittybrewster, but the site there was eventually judged to be too congested, so a new locomotive works was opened at Inverurie in 1903, where locomotives and items of rolling stock were constructed until the time of 'railway grouping'.

Throughout its history the GNoSR had to survive on comparatively low levels of traffic as there was little industry apart from whisky distilling in what was predominantly a farming area. In 1923 the railway became the Northern Scottish Area of the London & North Eastern Railway (LNER). At that time the railway operated approximately 334 route miles and owned 122 steam locomotives the majority of which were 4-4-0 tender types.

In 1948 it became part of the British Transport Commission (BTC on Nationalisation–British Railways Scottish Region). Inverurie Works survived until 1969.

For more detailed information see www.gnsra.org.uk

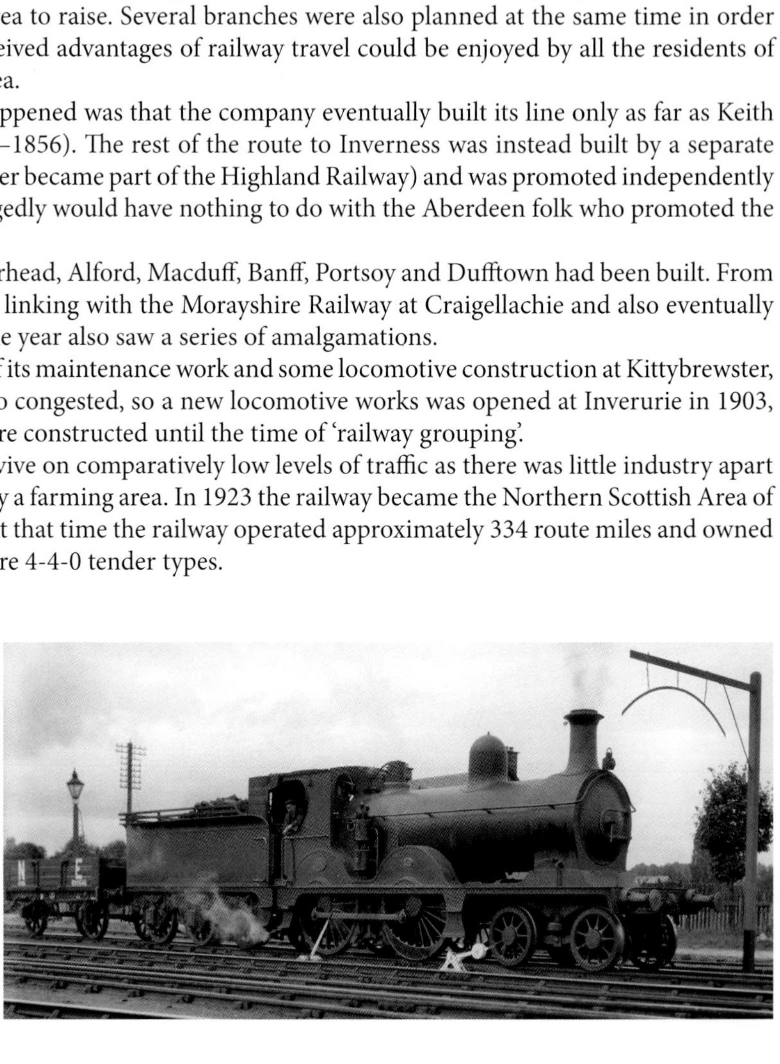

GNoSR Manson designed 4-4-0 No 65 is seen at a location thought to Elgin circa 1919. Kitson & Co built 6 engines of this class in 1884 (Nos 63-68) all of which were withdrawn by the LNER between 1925 and 1932. Note the tender cab, the weather protection properties of which were doubtless appreciated by the engine crews. ***Mike Morant Collection***

Caledonian Railway

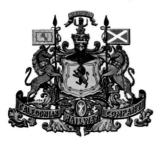

The Caledonian Railway Act was passed by Parliament in 1845. It has been observed that the grand title of this railway company was suitably matched by its adoption of the Royal Arms of Scotland as its crest! The CR was originally envisaged as a northern extension of the West Coast main line which already ran from London to Carlisle.

The promoters of the railway fully expected that it would be the only main line into Scotland from the south and accordingly they laid out the route Carlisle to both Edinburgh and Glasgow in a 'Y' shape, with Carstairs being the all important convergence point of the two lines from the north and the line from the south.

The company expanded through acquisitions and mergers and between 1899 and 1906 Glasgow Central station was re-built with the greatly increased capacity afforded by 17 platforms built on two levels. During the same period in Edinburgh the original CR Lothian Road station was replaced by a newly built facility at Princes Street. The CR territory extended over time to cover the Glasgow, Stirling and Edinburgh triangle and later was additionally extended to serve Oban, Ballachulish, Dundee, Perth and Aberdeen. In lowland Scotland the CR competed for business with Glasgow & South Western Railway (G&SWR) but however, not north of the River Clyde, and also the North British Railway (NBR). The railway hardly competed at all north of Oban, Ballachulish, Dundee, Perth and Aberdeen where the Highland Railway (HR) had established its operations.

The Caledonian Railway was ever mindful of presenting an attractive face to the travelling public with splendid stations, luxury appointed rolling stock and well designed locomotives being most important features of its operation. The CR blue livery as applied to its locomotives was a particularly striking feature. The company also operated hotels to the highest standard with Gleneagles and its adjoining golf course being worthy of special mention.

The all important cross-border services were operated in conjunction with the London & North Western Railway (LNWR), the carriages being jointly owned in an operating pool referred to as West Coast Joint Stock. The CR started its own steamship services from Gourock by the creation of a subsidiary company called the Caledonian Steam Packet Company, in 1889.

In 1923 the CR became part of the London, Midland & Scottish Railway (LMS) but due to legal complication the change did not take place upon the planned 1st January date but instead on the 1st July of that year. According to records the CR controlled a total length of line (including sidings) of approximately 2,827 miles.

The Caledonian Railway's locomotive works were originally at Greenock but moved to St Rollox, Glasgow in 1856. The works was a major employer in the area for many years which in 1923 became part of the London, Midland & Scottish Railway (LMS).

In 1948 it became part of the British Transport Commission (BTC on Nationalisation (British Railways Scottish Region).

For more detailed information see www.crassoc.org.uk

A George Brittain designed Caledonian Railway '670' class is seen as LMS No 17002 at Hamilton in 1927. This class of 30 engines was built by Dübs & Co between 1878 and 1881. A batch of 9 of the class was withdrawn circa 1921 but 21 engines came into LMS ownership, all being withdrawn between 1923 and 1932. *Rail Photoprints Collection*

CR McIntosh designed '139' class 4-4-0 No 135 is seen on a train of 9 coaches at an un-recorded location in 1921. This locomotive was built as part of a 12 engine class at St Rollox Works and delivered in May 1911. The '139' 4-4-0 became LMS No 14444 and subsequently BR No 54444 and was withdrawn in October 1953. *Martin Gemmell/Semaphores & Steam*

The superbly restored CR 0-6-0 No 828 delights the admiring onlookers whilst departing from Hampton Loade with a train for Bridgnorth on the Severn Valley Railway during a September 2011 visit to the railway. Note the CR semaphore route indicator on the buffer beam. *Keith Langston*

Glasgow & South Western Railway

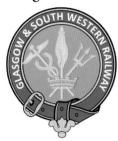

The Glasgow & South Western Railway (G&SWR) had its origins in two earlier railways when the Glasgow, Paisley, Kilmarnock & Ayr Railway, which gained construction powers in 1837, absorbed the Glasgow, Dumfries & Carlisle Railway in 1850 and then took on the new title of the Glasgow & South Western Railway. The amalgamation made the undertaking the third largest railway company in Scotland. The company in the main served the south west of Scotland, after the line from Glasgow and Carlisle was completed.

Initially, competition and access difficulties created by the other London-Glasgow west coast companies restricted the G&SWR's plans for through working to England. However, when the Midland Railway (MR) opened their Settle to Carlisle route in 1876 the two companies commenced running 'through' express trains between Glasgow St Enoch station and London St Pancras station.

The MR route was slower than that of the LNWR/CR but on the credit side it passed through attractive scenery whilst using luxurious carriages. Pullman coaches, after the American style, were used in the early days and the Glasgow & South Western Railway continued using the Pullman name for its Carlisle expresses long after the actual Pullman cars were discontinued in favour of MR built jointly owned stock.

The main line had an outstanding structure in the Ballochmyle Viaduct on which the railway crossed the River Ayr near Mauchline, it being at the time the largest single span stone arch in the world, at 157 feet.

There was a consolidation of routes with various branches and inter-connecting lines being built up to 1906, the last two being the coast line from Ayr to Girvan via Turnberry, complete with a luxurious hotel and associated golf courses, and also the Dumfries to Moniaive branch.

Early G&SWR locomotives were built by contractors. However, in 1854 the company commenced the construction of its own works on a site in Kilmarnock, and that facility was fully open and complete in 1858.

The G&SWR main line ran from Glasgow St Enoch station (the company HQ) along the west coast to Gretna and the railway also served Paisley, Greenock, Ardrossan, Troon and the ports on the west coast. The company also operated a fleet of Clyde steamers from those ports.

In 1921 the G&SWR made the decision to cease locomotive production at its works, but repairs continued. A total of almost 400 steam locomotives were built at Kilmarnock Works between 1857 and 1921, records for 1921 show that the railway operated over some 1,128 route miles.

In 1923 the G&SWR became part of the London, Midland & Scottish Railway (LMS) and in 1948 became part of the British Transport Commission (BTC, British Railways Scottish Region). Kilmarnock Works was closed in 1959.

For more detailed information see www.gswrr.co.uk

Ex-Glasgow & South Western Railway '336' class (LMS 2P) 4-4-0 is seen as LMS No 14220 at Glasgow St Enoch station circa 1926. The locomotive was built by Dübs & Co and delivered as G&SWR No 353 in March 1889 (later re-numbered 367) and withdrawn by the LMS in November 1931. ***Steve Armitage Archive/ Rail Photoprints Collection***

G&SWR Manson designed North British Locomotive Co built '381' class 4-6-0 No 501 is seen in 1921, note the double bogie tender. Although 17 of these impressive looking engines were built they were retired early as the LMS strived for locomotive type standardisation. The class along with '128' class locomotives were the only G&SWR 4-6-0s. *Martin Gemmell/Semaphores & Steam*

The lack of protection from the elements for the engine crew can be clearly seen in this picture of G&SWR '119' class 4-4-0 LMS No 14135 (G&SWR No 128) outside St Enoch station circa 1925, although a canvas sheet can be observed folded on the cab roof. *Keith Langston Collection*

Highland Railway

The Highland Railway (HR) was created in 1865 by the amalgamation of the Inverness & Aberdeen Junction Railway and the Aberdeen & Perth Junction Railway and was one of Britain's smaller railway companies. The railway was extended from Perth to serve the area farthest to the north of Britain.

The railway company had its headquarters in Inverness and developed to serve the towns of Wick and Thurso in the north, and the Kyle of Lochalsh in the west. When fully operational the HR provided rail services in Caithness, Sutherland, Ross and Cromarty, and linked the towns of Inverness, Perth, Nairn with Morayshire and Banffshire.

Acquisitions and mergers took place as the railway became established. To the south of its operating territory the HR connected with the Caledonian Railway (CR) at Stanley Junction to the north of Perth and to the east with the Great North of Scotland Railway (GNoSR) at Boat of Garten, Elgin, Keith and Portessie.

Importantly during the First World War the British naval base at Scapa Flow in the Orkneys was serviced by the HR from a railhead at Scrabster Harbour near Thurso. Of special note

Preserved Highland Railway 'Jones Goods' 4-6-0 No 103 was the first engine in the class of 16 David Jones designed Sharp, Stewart & Co built locomotives, as such it was the first 4-6-0 to run in Britain. The engine is seen at Carstairs in June 1960 prior to working an excursion to Auchinleck. *David Anderson*

is a train of that period referred to as the 'Jellicoe Express' which ran on a daily basis connecting London with Thurso, the journey time for which was approximately 22 hours.

Lochgorm Works was the main workshops and engineering headquarters for the HR and that facility was originally built by the Inverness & Nairn Railway, a company taken over by the HR. In 1923 the HR became part of the London, Midland & Scottish Railway (LMS) and in 1948 became part of the British Transport Commission BTC on Nationalisation (British Railways Scottish Region).

For more information see also www.hrsoc.org.uk

Ex-HR Drummond designed Dübs & Co built 'Castle' class 4-6-0 is seen as LMS No 14677 DUNROBIN CASTLE, note the snow plough and cab mounted tablet catching equipment. This class of engines was introduced in 1900 and they were a development of the 'Jones Goods' class designed for express train working over the steeply graded Highland Line, all were withdrawn circa 1939. ***Mike Morant Collection***

The last class of HR engines to be designed by David Jones was the 4-4-0 'Loch' class comprising of 18 engines which were built for the railway by the North British Locomotive Co Ltd and Dübs & Co between 1896 and 1917. A 'Loch' class locomotive is seen as LMS No 14380 LOCH NESS circa 1930. The class remained at work on express passenger services until withdrawn by the LMS circa 1941. ***Mike Morant Collection***

Highland Railway 'Clan' class 4-6-0 No 54 CLAN CHATTAN is seen emerging from Abronhill Tunnel near Cumbernauld with a Glasgow Buchanan Street to Inverness working circa 1923. The locomotive was built by Hawthorn Leslie & Co circa 1919 and withdrawn by the LMS in 1944. ***Mike Bentley Collection***

G&SWR Smellie built '22' class 0-6-0 No 604 is seen on shed at Carlisle in 1923, this loco was built by G&SWR Kilmarnock Works in 1891 and survived until 1925 when it was withdrawn by the LMS as No 17162. *Martin Gemmell/Semaphores & Steam*

Drummond Highland Railway 'Ben' 4-4-0 as LMS No 14397 BEN -Y-GLOE is seen southbound at Blair Atholl circa 1926. This locomotive came into BR stock but never carried its allocated number (54397) and was withdrawn in February 1949. *Rail Photoprints Collection*

Preserved NBR No 256 and HR No 103 make a fine sight when seen together in the sunshine at Dawsholm in 1957. *Mike Morant Collection*

Chapter 18

THE WEST COAST ROUTE

LMS-BR

The West Coast Main Line is the name given to the railway route between London Euston and Scotland and it comprises the major part of the former London & North Western and Caledonian Railway's main line to Glasgow Central, Edinburgh Princes Street and Aberdeen and it was in direct competition with the East Coast route from London King's Cross to Edinburgh Waverley.

The Edinburgh route diverged at Carstairs Junction and the lines to Glasgow and Aberdeen ran via Law Junction and Motherwell.

When Glasgow Central was opened in 1879, the distance from London was 401 miles and to Aberdeen 540 miles. As far as Preston, the Anglo-Scottish route was mainly four tracks, but further north only double tracks. The severe gradients over Shap and Beattock were a disadvantage to passenger train operation in the days of steam traction, and as a result banking locomotives were often employed.

In Scotland, the main depot which maintained express passenger locomotives for services between Glasgow and Carlisle was at Polmadie (66A) which had an allocation of Stanier Pacifics for such prestige workings as the 'Royal Scot', the 'Mid-Day Scot' and the various West Coast postal trains together with a large variety of locomotives for working the many Anglo-Scottish services.

Glasgow Central station was opened by the Caledonian Railway on 1 August 1879 and then significantly enlarged between 1901–1906.The building's grand entrance features ornate ironwork. Seven pillars support the glazed porte-cochere arcade which now houses the travel centre behind and the stone edifice of the Central Hotel towering above. Over 34 million people use the station each year equating to approximately 104,000 people on every day of the week.

21st century 'Steam Team'.......Driver, fireman and traction inspector all hard at work as preserved Stanier Pacific No 6201 PRINCESS ELIZABETH climbs up Shap during a preservation era commemorative WCML run to Glasgow Central. ***Chris Dixon***

Stanier 'Black Five' 4-6-0 No 45172 fitted with a domeless boiler was one of the Armstrong–Whitworth 1935-built series (Nos 5125-5224) for the LMSR. The Perth shed-based engine is seen here at speed near Symington on the West Coast main line with a southbound 'Creative Tourist Agents Conference – Scottish Tours Express' in June 1960. No fewer than 842 engines of this successful class were built up to 1951. No 45172 was withdrawn from service in May 1964 and was scrapped later in that year. *David Anderson*

At Beattock summit, a dead-end refuge sliding on the 'up' side of the West Coast main line accommodated freight trains to allow express passenger traffic a clear route to the south. Here, Stanier 'Black Five' No 44969, with domed boiler waits on the siding before reversing its parcels train back to Beattock summit signal box after the passage of the 'Mid-Day Scot' to continue its journey to Carlisle in 1958. No 44969 was built at Crewe in April 1946 and was scrapped in 1964. *David Anderson*

6P5F 'Jubilee' 4-6-0 No 45691 ORION, a long time resident of Glasgow Polmadie shed for West Coast main line passenger working was photographed near Harthope on the climb to Beattock summit in July 1960. The train is an unidentified holiday relief from the Midland Region to Glasgow Central. No 45691 was built at Crewe Works in March 1936 and survived in Scottish Region service until withdrawn in December 1962. *David Anderson*

Stanier 6P5F 'Jubilee' 4-6-0 No 45702 COLOSSUS darkens the sky over Elvanfoot on the northern approaches to Beattock summit on the West Coast main line with the 4.30 p.m. Glasgow Central to Liverpool and Manchester express on an April evening in 1960, often a regular working for a Manchester Newton Heath shed locomotive (26A at that time). The 4-6-0 was built at Crewe Works in May 1936 and withdrawn for scrap in August 1963. *David Anderson*

Built at Crewe Works in 1936, Class 6P5F 'Jubilee' 4-6-0 No 45727 INFLEXIBLE was photographed heading a Glasgow Central to Liverpool and Manchester express between Carstairs Junction and Symington on the Scottish West Coast main line on 14 June 1958. No 45727 was scrapped in 1963. *David Anderson*

Under Summer skies, one of Glasgow Polmadie shed's mid-1950s allocation of five Class 7P rebuilt 'Royal Scot' class 4-6-0s No 46121 *HIGHLAND LIGHT INFANTRY THE CITY OF GLASGOW REGIMENT attacks the final mile of Beattock bank with a Liverpool and Manchester to Glasgow Central express with through coaches for Edinburgh Princes Street in July 1959. Fifty engines of this famous class were ordered straight off the drawing board from the North British Locomotive Company Works in Glasgow in 1927 with a further twenty following from Derby Works in 1930. No 46121 was scrapped in May 1964. *David Anderson*

Class 8P 'Princes Royal' 4-6-2 No 46212 DUCHESS OF KENT is pictured in Glasgow Polmadie shed yard ready to back down to Glasgow Central station to work a late afternoon West Coast main line express to London Euston in April 1956. No 46212 was built at Crewe Works in October 1935, the last member of a series of thirteen engines designed by William Stanier (later Sir William Stanier) for express main line haulage. The engine was scrapped at Crewe Works in April 1962. *David Anderson*

* Shortest to the longest. When built No 46121 was the LMS loco with the shortest name, the abbreviation H.L.I. On 22 January 1949 it became the loco with the longest name in the 'Royal Scot' class when it was given the 8 word full name of the regiment, in a ceremony at Glasgow Central Station (no comma was included but a regimental crest was added). Five words, THE CITY OF GLASGOW REGIMENT were shown in smaller sized letters under the bolder 3 word title, HIGHLAND LIGHT INFANTRY.

Class 8P 'Duchess' Pacific No 46232 DUCHESS OF MONTROSE makes short work of the climb to Beattock summit on 8th July 1960. The loco is seen passing Harthope with the Glasgow Central portion of the summer timetabled 10.10am from London Euston. The Crewe Works built engine entered service in July 1938 and was withdrawn in December 1962. *David Anderson*

Polmadie shed-based Stanier 'Duchess' Pacific No 46231 DUCHESS OF ATHOLL is pictured on the West Coast main line a short distance to the south of Crawford with the morning Glasgow Central to Birmingham New Street express in July 1959. No 46231 was built at Crewe Works in June 1938 at a cost of £10,659 and was withdrawn from service to be scrapped in December 1962. *David Anderson*

The late afternoon sun illuminates the down *'Royal Scot' as the Stanier-designed 'Duchess' Pacific No 46253 CITY OF ST ALBANS tackles the gradient from Beattock station to the summit of the climb near Harthorpe, note that there is a banking engine assisting at the rear. The locomotive, which on this occasion carries the standard style train nameboard nameboard, was built at Crewe Works in September 1946 and was withdrawn from Crewe North shed for scrapping in January 1963. The protective tunnel carrying the steam operated coal pusher is visible at the rear of the tender. *David Anderson*

* The Royal Scot. The inaugural run of this service took place on 11 July 1927; the title was withdrawn in 1939 and reintroduced on 16 February 1948. This train made its last titled run (modern traction) on 1 June 2002.

The allocation of the ten 1951/52 Derby-designed and Crewe Works built Riddles 'Clan' Pacifics No's 72000-9 was shared between Glasgow Polmadie and Carlisle Kingmoor depots. Here, No 72003 CLAN FRASER waits to leave Polmadie depot to take charge of a Glasgow Central to Liverpool and Manchester express during April 1956, a regular duty for these locomotives. No 72003 was scrapped in March 1964. *David Anderson*

Class 8P 'Duchess' Pacific No 46246 CITY OF MANCHESTER coupled to 8P 'Princess Royal' Pacific No 46203 PRINCESS MARGARET ROSE take water at Polmadie shed before backing down to Glasgow Central station to head the southbound *'Mid-Day Scot' on 22 April 1956. No 46246 was built at Crewe Works in streamlined form in August 1943 and in 1960 it was the last member of the class to lose its sloping smokebox. The 'Duchess' Pacific was withdrawn from service in January 1963.

Streamlined LMS 'Princess Coronation/ Duchess' class Pacific LMS No 6226 DUCHESS OF NORFOLK is seen on the outskirts of London whilst heading north with a 1938 'Mid-Day Scot' working. *CRL Coles/Rail Photoprints Collection*

London, Midland & Scottish Railway (LMS) logo style

LMS crest. *Keith Langston Collection*

Variations of the so called cycling lion emblem (Lion on a Bike) were used on steam locomotives between 1950 and early 1956. *Keith Langston*

Variations of the logo often referred to as the 'ferret and dartboard' crest, was used on steam locomotives from 1956 onwards. *Keith Langston*

* The Mid-Day Scot. This named train made its first run between London Euston and Glasgow Central on 26 September 1927 the title was withdrawn during WWII, and reinstated in September 1949 with the last titled run of this train of taking place on 13 June 1965.

In this atmospheric Highland landscape image Stanier 'Class 5' 4-6-0 BR No 45468 leaves Strathyre with the 7.50am Glasgow to Oban, sister locomotive BR No 45359 will follow on with the Stirling to Oban daily goods, August 1960. *Hugh Ballantyne/Rail Photoprints*

45468

The Forth Bridge as seen from North Queensferry. *David Anderson*

Chapter 19

THE EAST COAST ROUTE

LNER-BR

The 1.5 mile long Forth Railway Bridge was the world's first major steel bridge when built, and as such it ranks as one of the greatest ever feats of engineering. Building work started in 1883 and was formally completed on 4 March 1890 when HRH Edward Prince of Wales tapped into place a 'golden' rivet.

Following lessons learned in the aftermath of the Tay Bridge disaster, civil engineers Sir John Fowler and Benjamin Baker opted to use a construction method called the 'balanced cantilever' principle.

Over 4,000 men were employed during the main construction period and approximately 55,000 tons of steel and some 6,500,000 rivets were used. Rescue boats were stationed under each of the cantilevers as work progressed but even so 57 workers lost their lives.

Tay Bridge

The aforementioned Tay Bridge disaster occurred on the night of 28 December 1879. At 7.15 pm the structure collapsed after its central spans gave way during a fierce winter gale. A train with six carriages carrying 75 passengers and crew plunged into the icy storm-tossed waters of the River Tay. There were no survivors.

A replacement bridge was built close to the site of the original; that structure was opened on 13 July 1887 and it survives into modern times.

The East Coast Route LNER-BR

The East Coast Main Line from London King's Cross to Scotland comprises the lines formerly operated by the Great Northern, North Eastern and North British Railways. In Scotland, the northernmost 38 miles from Kinnaber Junction to Aberdeen (which became well known during the 'Races to the North') was shared operationally by the otherwise rival Caledonian and North British railway companies.

The route was only fully completed when the Royal Border Bridge spanning the River Tweed at Berwick-upon-Tweed was opened and then later in 1890, the Forth Bridge which allowed the East Coast companies to extend their main line through to Dundee and Aberdeen.

The majority of the East Coast Main Line locomotives for the route to the north of Newcastle were operated by the Gresley and Thompson-designed Pacifics based at Edinburgh Haymarket (64B) and Aberdeen Ferryhill (61B) depots, the Edinburgh allocation of steam locomotives regularly worked the prestigious Anglo-Scottish express trains.

The famous 'Flying Scotsman' made its first London King's Cross to Edinburgh run on 11July 1927 and the 'title' survived into the modern era. The 'Heart of Midlothian' last travelled the same route on 4 May 1968.The 'North Briton' service between Leeds City and Glasgow Queen Street was also discontinued on that day. The 'Queen of Scots Pullman' service between London Kings Cross and Glasgow Queen Street last ran in June 1964. The 'Talisman' ran between King's Cross and Edinburgh Waverley until May 1968 and the 'Night Scotsman' sleeper train, between London and Edinburgh made its last run in May 1968.

Gresley 'A4' Pacific BR No 60019 BITTERN is seen at Perth station in July 1966, this locomotive is preserved. *Rail Photoprints Collection*

One of Haymarket shed's 'top-link' Gresley Pacifics for East Coast main line express train working was class 'A4' Pacific No 60012 COMMONWEALTH OF AUSTRALIA which in its usual pristine condition, is seen leaving Haymarket shed for the short journey 'light engine' to Edinburgh Waverley from where it will head the southbound 'Elizabethan' to London King's Cross. Built at Doncaster Works in June 1937, No 60012 was sent for scrap in May 1965 after spending most of its working life at Haymarket, before being transferred to Aberdeen in order to haul the three-hour express passenger services between Glasgow Buchanan Street and that city. *David Anderson*

Gresley 'A4' Pacific No 60024 KINGFISHER is seen on familiar territory, the locomotive is taking water at Forfar whilst in charge of an Aberdeen – Glasgow service in July 1965. *Brian Robbins/Rail Photoprints*

Another of Edinburgh Haymarket shed's famous Class 'A4' Pacifics was No 60031 GOLDEN PLOVER which is seen here at the west end of its home shed on 8 May 1955 with its 'cod's mouth' in the open position to gain access to the smokebox. In early British Railways days between 1949 and 1952, No 60031 was painted in light blue livery. The 'A4' was fitted with a double chimney in March 1958 and was withdrawn from service in November 1965. *David Anderson*

Leaving Haymarket shed en route to Edinburgh Waverley station class 'A3' Pacific No 60077 THE WHITE KNIGHT was photographed whilst passing Haymarket Central Junction signal box in September 1957. Built by the North British Locomotive Company Glasgow as LNER No 2576 in October 1924 and named after the 1907 and 1908 Ascot Gold Cup winner, the Pacific was withdrawn from British Railways service in November 1964. *David Anderson*

Edinburgh Haymarket shed invariably turned out their engines for the East Coast route in immaculate condition and here Gresley Class 'A3' No 60090 GRAND PARADE crosses Jamestown viaduct between Inverkeithing and North Queensferry with an Aberdeen and Dundee Tay Bridge express in April 1957. Built at Doncaster Works as No 2744 in August 1928, the engine was named after the 1919 Derby Winner. After being involved in a collision at Castlecary* between Edinburgh and Glasgow Queen Street in December 1937, the badly damaged engine was rebuilt and it survived in service until withdrawn for scrap in October 1963. *David Anderson*

Making light work of the 1 in 70 gradient from Inverkeithing towards the Forth Bridge crossing, Edinburgh Haymarket shed-based No 60097 HUMORIST heads over Jamestown viaduct with an Aberdeen to London King's Cross express in May 1956. Built at Doncaster Works in March 1929 and named after the 1921 Derby winner, the engine was the subject of various chimney and smoke deflector experiments during its lifetime and is seen here fitted with large smoke deflectors which were carried by the 'A3' until its withdrawal from service in September 1963. *David Anderson*

'A3' Pacific No 60099 CALL BOY was built at Doncaster Works in April 1930 and was in main line service until withdrawal in October 1963. The Edinburgh Haymarket shed-based engine was photographed heading an Aberdeen and Dundee Tay Bridge express at Dalmeny station during a halt to allow Glasgow Queen Street bound passengers to change trains. No 60099 was named after the 1927 Derby winner and is seen here in more or less its original 'as built' condition. *David Anderson*

* The accident occurred on the evening of 10 December 1937 in snowy weather conditions. Two trains were involved in a collision on the Edinburgh to Glasgow main line of the LNER, killing 35 people. LNER Class A3 No. 2744 GRAND PARADE, hit the rear of the standing local service in Castlecary station at an estimated 70mph causing the rear four coaches of the local train to disintegrate completely. The engine of the local train, an LNER Class 'D29', was pushed forward 100 yards with the brakes on. This was Britain's worst snow-related rail crash.

Peppercorn class 'A1' Pacific No 60152 HOLYROOD emerged from Darlington Works in July 1949 and received her name in June 1951, which commemorated the North British Railway class 'C11' Atlantic No 9904. For periods between 1951 and 1953, the engine was sent to Polmadie shed and worked passenger trains out of Glasgow Central. Here, No 60152 is pictured standing under the bridge which carried the former Caledonian Railway Leith North and Granton lines over the Edinburgh Waverley to Glasgow Queen Street main line as she waited to back down to Waverley station to work an Aberdeen express in September 1957. The Pacific was scrapped in December 1965. *David Anderson*

Allocated to Edinburgh Haymarket shed for the depot's 'No2' link workings and always perfectly turned out for East Coast main line passenger workings which regularly included the 'Queen of Scots Pullman' as far as Newcastle, Peppercorn 'A1' Pacific No 60161 SAINTJOHNSTOUN, the last engine of the class to be built at Doncaster Works in December 1949, speeds past its home shed (to the left in this picture) with an Edinburgh Waverley to Dundee Tay Bridge and Aberdeen express. No 60162 was withdrawn in 1963 and scrapped during the following year. *David Anderson*

The class of Thompson-designed Class 'B1' 4-6-0s were turned out by Darlington Works, Gorton Works, the Vulcan Foundry and the North British Locomotive Company between April 1946 and April 1952. The engines allocated to the Scottish Region of British Railways were used on passenger work to Glasgow, Perth and Dundee and certain fast goods trains between Edinburgh and Carlisle as well as over the East Coast main line to Newcastle. No 61007 KLIPSPRINGER was built at Darlington Works in April 1944 and its seen here at Haymarket depot in May 1955. The locomotive was withdrawn for scrap in March 1963. D*avid Anderson*

Normally confined to overnight freight workings over the East Coast main line from the Newcastle and York areas, former North Eastern Railway Raven-designed Class 'B16' 4-6-0s were rarely seen or photographed in Scotland during the daylight hours. Here, No 61414, a Leeds Neville Hill (50B) shed-based engine is pictured at the west end of Haymarket shed in September 1955. A total of seventy of this 3-cylinder type were built at Darlington Works in September 1920, No 61414 ended its working days in late 1961. *David Anderson*

The LNER 'P2' class 2-8-2 (Mikado)

Sir Nigel Gresley introduced the LNER 'P2' class engines in 1934 and the Doncaster built class was specifically designed for working heavy express passenger trains over the difficult Edinburgh to Aberdeen route. As they were to serve only on Scottish expresses, they were given famous names from Scottish folklore.

The first locomotive of the class, LNER No 2001 COCK O' THE NORTH was built with Lentz rotary-cam poppet valve gear and was tested in France where a modern locomotive-testing facility was available, no such facility existing within the UK at that time.

The class (with the exception of No 2005) featured a Kylchap-type blastpipe/chimney system to aid efficiency. The second engine of the class No 2002 EARL MARISCHAL was completed with the usual Walschaerts valve gear and proved to be the more efficient engine of the two, the only major deficiency being a softer exhaust that led to a second pair of smoke deflectors being utilised to clear the smoke away from the driver's view forward.

The production series of a further four engines was completed in 1936 and were all based mechanically upon No 2002. They were all later given a wedge-shaped streamlined front end, akin to that on the 'A4' class locomotives, which successfully solved the smoke deflection problem.

Some observers at the time questioned the successfulness or otherwise of the 'P2' engines claiming that their eight-wheel chassis was reportedly too rigid for the many sharp curves on the route. In the event Gresley's successor, Edward Thompson, oversaw the re-building of the entire class into LNER 'A2/2' class Pacifics.

Gresley 'P2' 2-8-2 LNER No 2002 EARL MARISCHAL is seen on shed at Aberdeen Ferryhill depot, circa 1937, the loco was rebuilt in 1944 as a 4-6-2 and reclassified 'A2/2' class. ***Rail Photoprints Collection***

Gresley 'P2' 2-8-2 LNER No 2002 EARL MARISCHAL is seen at Aberdeen Ferryhill depot circa 1936. ***Mike Morant Collection***

Gresley 'P2' class build details

LNER No.	Build Date	Date of streamlining	Date of rebuild to A2/2	Name
2001	May 1934	April 1938	September 1944	COCK O' THE NORTH
2002	October 1934	October 1936	June 1944	EARL MARISCHAL
2003	June 1936	As built	December 1944	LORD PRESIDENT
2004	July 1936	As built	November 1944	MONS MEG
2005	August 1936	As built	January 1944	THANE OF FIFE
2006	September 1936	As built	May 1944	WOLF OF BADENOCH

London & North Eastern Railway (LNER) Logo style

LNER crest. ***Keith Langston Collection***

British Railways Logo styles

Variations of the so called cycling lion emblem (Lion on a Bike) were used on steam locomotives between 1950 and early 1956. ***Keith Langston***

Variations of the logo often referred to as the 'ferret and dartboard' crest, was used on steam locomotives from 1956 onwards. ***Keith Langston***